D0475624

The
HEART
of
Heart of the Matter
A Memoir

The HEART of Heart of the Matter

A Memoir

JOAN BAKEWELL

BBC BOOKS

This book is published to accompany the 1996 television series of *Heart of the Matter*

Published by BBC Books,
an imprint of BBC Worldwide Publishing,
BBC Worldwide Limited, Woodlands,
80 Wood Lane, London W12 0TT
First published 1996

ISBN 0 563 37167 6

Designed and set by BBC Books and Graham Dudley Associates
Cover Photograph © BBC by Stuart Wood
Printed in Great Britain by Martins the Printers Ltd, Berwick upon Tweed
Bound in Great Britain by Hunters & Foulis Ltd, Edinburgh
Jacket printed by Lawrence Allen Ltd, Weston-super-Mare

For Jack

Acknowledgements

The world knows that television is a team effort and a programme presenter merely the tip of a human iceberg. But it is occasionally the good fortune of a broadcaster to work with people who are not merely good at their job but who are, beyond the call of duty, intelligent, dedicated and fun. Such has been my happy experience throughout my years on Heart of the Matter.

My thanks to its three successive editors: Olga Edridge for whose invitation to work on the programme I am continually grateful; Michael Waterhouse who presided throughout the independent years at Roger Bolton Productions; and Ann Reevell, currently the series' guiding hand. More particularly, the stories referred to in this book would not have been told without their thoroughly-committed camera crews and the stamina and talents of the following people: Roger Bolton, Carrie Britton, Emma Brook, Jayne Egerton, Pat Gross, Claire Hobday, Tim Holmes, Liz McIntyre, Mike Mitchell, Christine Morgan, Selina O'Grady, Candida Pryce-Jones, Nick Stuart-Jones, Ann Tobin, Alison Turner, Karen Whitfield, Emma Willis.

For the book itself, I am grateful for the editing skills of Kelly Davis and Charlotte Lochhead and the research of Harriet Batten-Foster.

Contents

Introduction

For more than seven years on BBC 1's *Heart of the Matter* I have been charting the moral state of the nation. In telling over 130 stories I have observed at first hand the shift in the country's values. At the heart of each programme has been an immediate human dilemma and someone willing to share it. I have come close to individuals as they made difficult decisions and arrived at brave choices. I have watched developments in medicine alter how we view birth and death. I have seen the churches grapple with the shifting social attitudes of the secular world. I have seen the triumph of moral relativism and the collapse of old values. This book tells of the people whose lives and dilemmas I have found most poignant or most troubling and who each, in some way, have helped shape my own conscience.

Can We Forgive Myra Hindley?

Heart of the Matter deals in moral dilemmas. With the backing of the BBC's Religious Department, it deals courageously with the big words: truth, justice, loyalty, forgiveness, integrity, responsibility, duty, honour. While much is currently made of how these concepts have fallen from grace or popular use, we find they are instantly recognized and understood wherever we go. People may not always act on them, but the broad public certainly believes it knows what they mean: and many people also feel such ideals have some relevance in their own lives. This may amount to no more than telling the tale of your own errors and mischief in such a way as to excuse your falling short. But that, too, endorses the broad consensus.

Indeed, such concepts may command more immediate understanding and approval than ideas like pragmatism, feasibility, accountability, which are the common currency of our daily political discourse. What's more, it is widely acknowledged – though perhaps not expressed in these terms – that such values are rooted in the Judaeo-Christian tradition which underpins our constitution and legal system. Those of other faiths by and large recognize the values all faiths hold in common and thus find themselves able to live comfortably within British society.

Heart of the Matter is therefore able to tackle, head on, moral issues – forgiveness, loyalty – which might not sit easily within the constraints of News and Current Affairs, or would simply remain unfocused within the looser context of human interest documentaries. Never was this more the case than on 10 July 1994 when we posed the question: 'Can we forgive Myra Hindley?'

The question was timely for many reasons. A House of Lords ruling in 1992 had insisted that all prisoners, including lifers, had a right to know their 'tariff date' – roughly how many more years they could expect to serve in prison. In July 1993 the Home Secretary, Michael Howard, countered by setting out a new criteria for the release of such prisoners. He claimed the right to detain prisoners who had completed their tariff – that is their legal punishment – and who were no longer a danger to the public, on the basis that the public might not find their release acceptable. This move was seen by some as being deliberately aimed at Myra Hindley. Her supporters clearly felt so: they let it be known that she would appeal to the European Court of Human Rights.

There were a multitude of issues here: this new stage in a prisoner's sentence – public acceptability – not only challenged the entire parole system, but raised the issue of how far public opinion should be a determining factor in the administration of justice. And behind the phrase 'public opinion' lay a mass of tangled emotions – rage, distress, pain – and complex questions: Could a person as wicked as Myra Hindley reform? Does redemption have any meaning? And do Christians have a duty to forgive a repentant sinner? It seemed a good time to set out these issues in the programme and let people decide for themselves.

It was thirty years before, in 1964, that the 23-year-old Myra Hindley and Ian Brady had committed the crimes for which she had served twenty-eight years: the torture and murder of three children. After serving twenty-one years she had admitted her part along with Ian Brady in the murder of Keith Bennett, Pauline Reade and John Kilbride.

She had been given a life sentence and might well have done her time in quiet anonymity, and possibly by now have been allowed out on licence. But from the start the case of Myra Hindley has been high-profile. Two powerful protagonists have spoken out: Lord Longford has vouched for her Catholic piety; Ann West has affirmed her eternal wickedness. The tabloid press, sensing the ancient battle of good and evil, have played the conflict to the hilt, mocking the piety of a sincere and devout man, and playing on the bitterness and grief of a distraught woman. To add colour to such a clash, one is the grandee head of a distinguished family, the other an ill and broken working-class woman. The casting is perfect for a story that will run and run. At this point it has little to do with justice, forgiveness, healing or even retribution. It is just one of the hottest news stories of the century. And the person who has come to know that best is Myra Hindley.

Lord Longford, a tireless crusader for prisoners and ex-prisoners since the 1930s, befriended Myra Hindley early on in her sentence and made that friendship public, clearly in what he hoped would be her best interest. With the passion of the convert to Catholicism, he proclaimed Hindley's return to her Catholic faith, her utter remorse and repentance for what she had done. Throughout the 1970s he did what, as a good Christian, he believed it was his duty to do: told the good news of a sinner brought back into the fold, told it on television and in numerous articles. It was a mistake. It earned him the mockery of headline writers who, one suspects, can't hold a candle to him for moral integrity. That mockery has done much to swing public opinion – the very public opinion the Home Secretary will now consult – against the view that very wicked people do repent and subsequently lead good lives.

But by the 1980s there had been a change. It is likely that others concerned with Myra Hindley's case persuaded Lord Longford to take a lower profile in the belief that Hindley's cause would, from then on, be better served by quieter methods.

It was against this background that on 1 June, the *Heart of the Matter* producer, Alison Turner, telephoned Myra Hindley's solicitor, Andrew McCooey, and followed up the call with a letter. She also wrote directly to Myra Hindley.

Having explained the intent of the programme, 'to examine the issue of open-ended sentences, asking whether they are legally and, more importantly, *morally* justified', she went on:

'I would be very pleased to get some input from you into this programme, which I believe will be the first time the issue has been examined in a cool and considered way. If you decide, in principle, that you would like your views represented in some way, would it be possible to call me, so that we could discuss how that might be achieved? I am, of course, happy to talk in complete confidence at this stage and to answer any queries you may have.'

Myra Hindley did not make such a call, though she has access to a phone and is allowed to use it. Instead she let it be known that her solicitor and her priest could speak. (There was briefly talk of my visiting Hindley in prison myself, but mindful of how everything concerning her becomes public, it was considered impractical.)

At that point it looked as though we might have a programme. It is always our policy to interview people from both sides of any story. Without such a careful balance of opinions, the point of a dilemma – that it is a problem without a solution – is lost. So from that first week in June we began to talk to others who might contribute.

We had, for reasons already clear, decided not to interview Lord Longford. But slowly, and against our initial inclination, we found ourselves drawn towards interviewing Ann West, the mother of Lesley Ann Downey, the ten-year-old victim of Hindley and Brady.

Ann West has a high profile in the media. Out of her grief and bitterness she has created a life centred around Hindley. She is always available with comments for the press. She is alerted by anonymous phone calls to every move related to Hindley and in response phones the tabloids. She writes to both the Home Secretary and Prime Minister at the merest hint of parole. She also makes more dramatic gestures, usually with a photographer in attendance. She turned up when Myra Hindley was allowed to attend her sister's funeral, hurled abuse and tore Hindley's wreath to shreds. We felt that her case was already familiar to the public, and in seeking to take a fresh and balanced look at the issues, we would do better to have other contributors. And yet... And yet.

It soon became obvious to the entire production team – editor Michael Waterhouse, producer Alison Turner, researcher Selina O'Grady, and executive producer, Roger Bolton – that it is simply not possible to make a programme about forgiveness, punishment and retribution, without hearing the voice of one of those most directly injured. We were already intending to hear a strong legal case for Hindley put by her lawyer, and a strong religious case put by her priest. The even-handedness that is the essence of the BBC ethic, as well as the particular balance that is characteristic of *Heart of the Matter* required such a presence. We decided to interview Ann West. It was a decision that was to have important consequences for the programme. But we would only discover that later.

In the meantime we had also approached the Reverend Peter Timms. He is an ex-governor of Maidstone Prison, a counsellor and Methodist minister. It was to the Reverend Timms that Myra Hindley had first made a confession of her crimes. That was in 1986: he had been visiting her at Cookham Prison and she specifically asked the Home Office for permission to talk to him. 'I'm twenty years too late, and know that' she had said to him.

Subsequently she made her statement to Detective Chief Superintendent Peter Topping, and was then taken back to Saddleworth Moor, where she was able to indicate where a further body might be found. And, indeed, the body of Pauline Reade was exhumed, and given decent Christian burial. The body of Keith Bennett remains at some unknown place on the moors. Topping has written of Hindley's account of the murder of Lesley Ann Downey : 'She showed a lot of emotion all the time that she was talking about the death of the little girl.'

Now, on the telephone to Alison Turner, the Reverend Timms was quite clear in his opinion: 'You can't be a prison governor for thirty years, and a trained counsellor for almost as long, and not spot people who are manipulative. I know Myra Hindley better than most people and she is genuinely repentant.'

This was valuable testimony and we agree to interview him. Here, too, we would have problems later.

On 8 June we took the train to Manchester to interview Ann West. *Heart of the Matter* is made under exacting pressures of time: five days' filming, plus a single week in which to edit, write, revise and dub the commentary. That day I was to spend some four hours with Ann West. Those hours were enough to convince me of the view I now hold, that the fulcrum of debate about Myra Hindley is not the rational exchange of opinion between experts, but the passionate intensity of feeling between these two women: Hindley, the criminal, the evildoer; and Ann West, her scourge and pursuer who, like some enraged Valkyrie, will hunt her down relentlessly to the end of her days. And whereas Hindley, in having Lord Longford as her champion, has antagonized many newspapers and their readers, Ann West has scarcely put a foot wrong. Ann West is Myra Hindley's destiny.

No one looks less like an avenging angel than the portly, untidy woman who welcomes us somewhat resignedly into her home. We are the media. She knows us, if not personally, then as the instrument of her life's work. It is at once apparent that she is far from well: her husband, Alan, ever hovering in support, explains that she is on a whole variety of pills; she suffers from angina and has only recently had further operative treatment for cancer. Nonetheless, steadfastly and with an obsessiveness that has consumed her life and health, she has kept the story of her daughter's murder always present in the public consciousness.

I am aware throughout the interview of how tenaciously she grips the story that has shaped her life. She is needful of comfort, from minute to minute. She grasps my hand in hers, creating an immediate intimacy, woman to woman. She says my name often – 'You see, Joan, it was like this... and, Joan, you'll understand.' Somehow the aura of her pain embraces me, and I, the interviewer, am thoughtful suddenly of my children and grandchildren. But this apparent dependency masks a steely will and a set of attitudes unyielding to discussion, inaccessible to other ideas than her own. Slowly, and with a sigh from the depths of her being, she begins again the oft-told tale.

It was Boxing Day 1964 – teatime and snowing. Lesley Ann wanted to go to the funfair making its seasonal visit to a site some ten minutes away. Her elder brother, Terence, had flu; Tommy, the eight-year-old, had already gone down there. Lesley went to call for a friend, and when she couldn't come, went to the fair alone; something strictly forbidden by her mother. She never returned. Tommy had the last sight of her, whirling around on one of the fairground rides. Ironically it was called the Wall of Death.

Ann West, thirty-five at the time, and two years divorced, had met Alan some eight months earlier and they were planning to marry. For ten months they waited to find out what had happened to Lesley. They scarcely slept. Hoping some childless couple might have kidnapped Lesley and, feeling remorse, bring her home, they left a light on in the window, a touchingly dramatic expression of the hope that still lingered. In vain. Eventually the police found shreds of clothing. Lesley's.

What follows defies belief for its insensitivity. Although Lesley's body had been in the ground ten months, the police insisted Ann, and no other, should do the identifying. Half the frail body was covered with a cloth. What Ann saw then burned its image onto her mind's eye and into her heart. 'It's what I see when I fall asleep,' she told me. Worse, she reached out to touch her child, and was held back. She must not have contact. At that point she fainted with the strain.

Yet more torture lay ahead. As Ian Brady and Myra Hindley were committing their atrocities, some crazed impulse made them tape-record what went on. At the trial, extracts of this tape were played for all to hear. Ann West had to listen to her own child pleading – 'Please let me go home to my Mummy.' The cruelty of the judicial system has much to answer for. I believe the actions – of the police and the court, at that time in the mid-sixties – so severely damaged Ann West, so insistently and unremittingly went on aggravating her grief by forcing her to face sights and sounds intolerable to a mother, that they left no space for recovery, grieving or healing. I believe Ann West is still in shock, thirty years after her daughter's death.

It is in that condition of protracted psychosis that she has acted as she has. She has focused her hatred – and in so doing, that of the broader public – on Myra Hindley. She agrees it is because Hindley is a woman and thus her crime in killing children is greater than Brady's. 'Don't get me wrong. I hate him. But I detest her.' She constantly declares that if Hindley is allowed out she will kill her. Such threats to Hindley's safety must surely influence official decisions made about her future.

Ann West's distress has hindered her growing away from these terrible events in any way at all. For twenty-nine years her views have simply become more entrenched. They run as follows: first Myra Hindley should have been hanged. The law abolishing capital punishment had just reached the statute book: she missed it by a matter of months. 'If they'd hanged her that would have been it. I might have been able to start a little bit of life.' If not hanging, then the sentence life imprisonment must mean life. 'I want her to die in prison. I think she should die in prison, for the things she's done. She's helping to keep me alive 'cos I don't intend dying until she's dead. I really don't.' She constantly refers to Hindley's fate as being intimately linked to her own. 'I'm serving a life sentence; why shouldn't she?'

When I put it to her as gently as I can – for I feel awed by the naked suffering that surrounds us – 'Do you not think it's possible for someone to change?', she is adamant: 'No, I think it's born in them, evil. I really and truly do... You're human, Joan. I'm human. She could not be human to stand there and let a little girl... an innocent ten-year-old...' The well of grief is being plumbed again. Ann West is remorseless with herself. It puts her beyond logic, for it is logical to argue that if Myra Hindley was born evil, then she was helpless to do anything about it. She would not logically be responsible for her actions and thus for what happened. That is not a view I share: neither in reality does Ann West. But her condition, her self-perpetuating suffering, puts her beyond reasonable argument or the tranquil consideration of such an idea as forgiveness.

By now I am completely absorbed in this woman and her condition. It sounds bizarre to suggest that, surrounded as we are by the paraphernalia of television, this can happen. But her distress is so compelling, I am concerned only to find a way to alleviate it. I set out as tenderly as I can to help:

Q: 'One of the things Christians believe is that to forgive someone is to bring peace of mind to yourself. Do you think you could do that?'

A: 'Never. Never. I could never forgive what they did to my child. Never. Never. Till the day I die. I can never forgive.'

Q: 'But Ann, the forgiveness might bring you some rest; make you feel better in your spirit.'

A: 'I don't think so. People write to me and say they will never forgive her. And they're strangers.'

Q:'You don't feel that forgiveness would heal all the injuries you've had?'

A: 'It's too far gone, Joan, too far gone.'

Q: 'You don't feel that the hatred is making you ill?'

A: 'Well, I don't think I could be any iller.'

Q: 'Everyone who knows this story wants nothing more than that you should find some peace of mind.'

A: 'When she dies, when she dies. When she dies I'll find some peace of mind.'

Ann has offered up her life to her grief for her child. It makes her a formidable opponent to those who wish Hindley's case to be heard calmly and coolly.

Ann West takes comfort from any judgement passed on Hindley. It brings her into contact with some odd people: 'The man who hanged Ruth Ellis said to me, "I would come out of retirement to hang her now"... Two separate people who have been in prison with her say she runs the prison. They're all afraid of her ... I spoke to Brady's mother and she said he couldn't drive, and without a car they couldn't have taken the children to the moor... We had Myra's handwriting analyzed and the analyst said, "This person is evil, and always will be evil; and whatever this person's done, they will re-do if they get the chance."'

In refusing the role of passive victim, she continues to display an unerring instinct for the dramatic and newsworthy. She has taken initiative after initiative designed to feed the media's perception of this as a war between two women, between good and evil. When in the 1980s Ann West decided she wanted to make contact with Lesley's spirit through the medium Doris Stokes, it was *The People* who arranged it. In 1986 when Ann West began a correspondence with

Ian Brady, the *Daily Mail* arranged a visit with Brady's mother. If an intelligent but uneducated woman can achieve so much, one wonders what she might have become in other circumstances. But it is her tragedy to have found purpose and drive in her life, only through her loss. It is hatred and revenge that fuel her unremitting energy.

As we leave Ann West's home, the production team express their concern about her role in the programme. Some feel that any prolonged exposure of her bitterness and grief could overwhelm the audience's ability to weigh the arguments in a balanced way. Others feel that Ann West's behaviour – as she has told the story so often – has an over-dramatic, even synthetic quality that could antagonize viewers. It becomes imperative that we include a strong expression of the case for Hindley. This proves not to be easy. The problem is Hindley herself.

It has become clear that Hindley strongly opposes our interviewing the Reverend Timms. We get the impression, from the way this message is relayed, that if we go ahead with the Timms interview then she might instruct her solicitor and her priest to refuse. This is a crisis for the programme – and it is meant to be. Without the collaboration of Hindley's supporters there can be no *Heart of the Matter*. We know that their policy is to maintain a low profile and that their agreeing to help us has been, for them, a delicately balanced decision. We wanted to speak to the Reverend Timms because he was the first to hear Hindley's confession. But the Reverend Bert White is currently her priest at Cookham Wood Prison. He is also aware of Hindley's spiritual condition. We agree that White will be interviewed, rather than Timms.

But first, the legal case. Andrew McCooey, Hindley's solicitor, is a brisk capable lawyer in early middle age. He puts the case for her being given parole in terms that are logical, consistent and fluent:

'It is for the trial judge, initially, to set the time to be served. He should take into account the punishment for the crime, retribution to be made for having committed it, and deterrence. He must mark the seriousness of the crime by saying to the world at large, if you commit this kind of crime you will expect to serve this many years in gaol.

'Although the crime of murder brings with it a mandatory life sentence, the courts have, since 1967 when the parole system was introduced, made it possible for a prisoner serving life to have some hope of release. So that, given they serve the sentence designated long enough for punishment and deterrence, and have committed no further offences in prison, they can expect parole, unless that person is thought to be still dangerous.'

McCooey believes that Hindley meets such criteria. And indeed a Prison Review Committee recommended her release nine years ago. In 1985 Leon Brittan announced that the Parole Board had determined to postpone a decision for at least five years.

So has Hindley served her punishment?

'She was sentenced in 1966, she was imprisoned in 1965 waiting for trial. She's now been nearly thirty years in gaol, which is equivalent to a judge giving a 45-year sentence. Understandably, society expects punishment of considerable severity for taking the life of children. And she certainly has served a very long time.'

But is she reformed? Or could she still be dangerous?

'The people responsible for assessing that – prison governors, probation people, psychiatrists, chaplains – have unanimously, I believe, come to the conclusion that Myra Hindley has reformed.'

The final decision on parole has always rested with the Home Secretary who has regularly weighed up the established criteria. But Michael Howard's statement introducing the new criteria of public opinion is what worries Andrew McCooey:

'The parole system is there for all prisoners: if you're now saying there are exceptions, then Parliament must enact that. The parole system has been legislated in Parliament to give hope to everyone, including people like Myra Hindley. Now, along comes Michael Howard making a speech in the Commons, saying there's an additional factor – the view of the public about the release of this prisoner. And that can rapidly degenerate into a vote-catching, knee-jerk response to what I see in the tabloid press.'

This is logical enough. After all, there are some 3000 other lifers currently averaging some eleven or twelve years in gaol before release on licence. There is another woman, Mary Bell, guilty of child murder who has completed her time and is now living out in society without any fuss being made, or anyone knowing. It can certainly be argued that it is the notoriety of Myra Hindley that keeps her from parole.

McCooey grows passionate:

'Michael Howard is moving the goal posts and for the first time suggesting that certain categories of prisoners are beyond the parole system. This is bad for the legal system and our sense of justice: what is happening here is what happened in Russia in Communist times. People would serve twenty years and just at the end they'd say, no, another ten years. A political decision.'

This is an inappropriate comparison: in Russia it was often people innocent of any crimes who were treated so arbitrarily. It is nonetheless important to establish whether politics – the politics of a populist right-wing Home Secretary – is interfering with established legal procedures.

Sir Louis Blom Cooper QC sat on the Lane Committee examining life imprisonment. He foresees a time when the Home Secretary will no longer be the final arbiter on parole:

'The whole trend in the penal systems of Europe is towards judicializing the whole process. That's a good thing because it means the balance between the interest of the prisoner and the public interest will be struck by those who are objective, independent and uninfluenced by the political situation.'

It's a view with which David Mellor, formerly a Minister at the Home Office, profoundly disagrees:

'All these folk of whom you talk are place men, appointees, people with no bond with the public. They have their role and, of course, the separation of the judiciary from the executive is fundamental. But the judicial part of these proceedings is taken care of at the trial. Parliament has determined that the mandatory sentence for murder is life imprisonment. It then becomes not a judicial matter but for the executive to determine how long that life imprisonment should be. I actually see it as one of the strengths of the process that the Home

Secretary takes account of public feeling. It would be very foolish in a democracy to have within our own nation a body of people who, without any kind of democratic mandate, can determine when it is safe or whether it is right to release a murderer on to the streets.

'I think the injustice in the Hindley case, if there is one, is not that she and Brady are going to be made to pay, but how many other almost equally dreadful offenders there are. I think the public would be shocked if they knew that some child sex murderers are actually released in less than fifteen years.'

I find myself sympathetic to these points of view. But then the opposite case is equally persuasive. This is not at all unusual in a true dilemma. Indeed, we know we're making a good programme when members of the production team find themselves swayed by opposing arguments. It is exactly the sense that dilemmas are difficult, rather than black and white, that we seek to stir in our viewers. With some success.

The Hindley case raises the question: Where does justice reside? With the judicial system of courts, judges and parole boards? Or with the people and their elected MPs, one of whom is the Home Secretary? And how are the two to be held in balance?

Brady and Hindley were the first killers to escape hanging after capital punishment was abolished in late 1965. Ever since, public opinion has been overwhelmingly in favour of bringing it back – a view consistently rejected by Parliament. David Mellor points to the fine balance this establishes between the public and its elected representatives:

'I'm one of those politicians who has voted consistently against capital punishment which the public overwhelmingly support. I would say the only fair basis on which I could go back to my constituents and say, "I reject your advice on capital punishment. I think I know better", is that I'm not also saying, "I think the likes of Brady and Hindley should be walking the streets within a few years".'

Stripped of its rhetoric, there is an important point here: that while public opinion will tolerate – just – being flouted in the matter of capital punishment itself, it will be extremely wary of any further liberalizing of the treatment of those it feels should be dead.

On the other hand, the penal system must take account of the handling of prisoners. As Louis Blom Cooper points out:

'If prisoners are told their sentence is literally life, they can turn round and say, well, I'm here for ever, why should I behave? It's important you shouldn't deprive them of the ultimate hope...

'What's more, had Hindley gone into court and pleaded madness, she'd have had a greater chance of being released into the community and might even be free already. When it comes to those who have committed perhaps just as horrific crimes, but are hospitalized, and have a restriction order on them, the process of their release is the Mental Health Review Tribunal – an independent body which can ultimately discharge them.'

This is extraordinary indeed, and the direct opposite of what the public might reasonably suppose, that those who are knowingly wicked should be apprehended, punished, and in time released; whereas those who are mad need to be detained for ever.

It is widely rumoured that Ian Brady is now mad; it is one of those facts in wide circulation but without verification. It thus becomes part of the folk wisdom surrounding the case. If Ian Brady has now gone mad, the thinking goes, then it is somehow right that he has done so. He committed crimes of abhorrent violence and brutality and subsequently, and as a consequence, lost his reason. This somehow satisfies our feeling towards him.

Hindley, on the other hand, has done something far worse, and far more challenging for each of us. She has stayed sane. She has become or remained normal. She has revealed herself to be logical, polite, persistent, capable of reasoned argument in the letters she writes. I am aware of how a page of her neat, ordered script compares with the jerky, irregular scrawl of Ian Brady – much crossed-out, frantically underlined. Hindley, in her behaviour, reminds us that in so many ways she is like ourselves. And this knowledge is intolerable.

I talk to Joan Smith, the writer and feminist, about the public perception of Hindley:

'There is a fascination with women who kill, and it's very clear that women who kill are treated much more harshly than men who commit murders. In a curious way violence is seen as not exactly excusable, but more natural for men, ... that men are prone to explosions of violence they can't control. Women, on the other hand, are supposed to be nurturing. Myra Hindley transgressed in two ways. She both killed, and she killed children. Because of that she has become a kind of demon we can tell each other stories about. I think one of the things that played into the hands of the tabloids was that awful picture, taken shortly after her arrest, where she's shown as an incredibly brassy blonde with a very stern, very unpleasant expression. The effect of that photograph is probably incalculable in creating the myth of Myra Hindley, as a kind of demon figure of the late twentieth century.'

The impact of the photograph has not been on the lawyers, probation officers or Home Office officials, of course. Its power is in the media and its influence is on public opinion, that volatile but weighty force that is now the Home Secretary's touchstone.

I talk to Bridget Rowe, editor of *The People.* She is in no doubt that Myra Hindley should never get parole, and she is confident that she is speaking for her readers. She insists it is proper to refer to Myra Hindley as 'an evil monster' for that is what she is. She expects to return to the subject if the issue of the European Court of Human Rights comes up. And indeed the week before the transmission of our programme she launches a poll in the pages of *The People* – 'Should Myra Hindley ever go free?' Unsurprisingly the feature is accompanied by that terrible photograph. Inaccurately, a week later, the follow-up column claims: 'She appears tonight in a heartfelt television plea to the nation.' Over 40 000 readers responded to the newspaper's call line: 39 452 said Hindley should remain in prison; 624 said she should go free.

Louis Blom Cooper assesses the influence of such public opinion on the Home Secretary:

'He is probably thinking to himself, if I were to release Myra Hindley what would be the political implications of that? There is a very large constituency out there that will regard my decision as being wholly unacceptable. As a result there might be political implications. He might even think that it could bring a government down. I don't think it would, of course, but he might well feel that. He's a political animal and therefore affected by those kinds of considerations.'

I have spoken with lawyers and debated the role of public opinion in this matter. But *Heart of the Matter* asked 'Can we *forgive* Myra Hindley?', a question framed in moral terms around a major Christian duty. So I have also spoken with Christians.

Father Bert White has been at Cookham Prison some eight months. He is Roman Catholic Chaplain to prisons and hospitals in the Medway area. He is clearly a good man, steeped in faith, and although his manner is soft, his views are unwavering. Even under torture I can imagine he would quietly and consistently refuse to betray what he believes. He is gentle in voice, gentle in demeanour. As prison doors and keys clang around us, he is somehow cocooned from the noise and harshness. He explains to me how he regularly gives Myra Hindley communion, how familiar she is with the breviary, the church's calendar, the lives of the saints. She is prayerful and quiet. She has even, on one occasion, asked that they pray together for Ann West. He reiterates over and over the central theme of his case for Hindley's parole, and indeed the theme of his entire ministry: the need for forgiveness.

'We pray: "Forgive us our trespasses as we forgive..."' It is the very phrase Ann West has told me she omits when she speaks the Lord's Prayer. Forgiveness, he insists, is really the only way to go forward to heal the situation:

'I find it very hard to forgive people in my life. I'm not saying I'm good at it, just because I preach it. But I know it's true in my heart...

'We're talking about something that happened thirty years ago: we're talking about a woman who has repented, who has confessed. We're talking about whether people can change. There is always redemption. Now that might be unpopular. I'm not responsible for its unpopularity. I preach it and I'm being faithful to the Gospel.'

I put it to him that not to forgive the most terrible wickedness is to express a common hatred of sin. It's not only understandable, it's even commendable. He gets as excited as his meek temperament will allow:

'One of the things I find hard about this lack of forgiveness is that it doesn't go anywhere. It just perpetuates the hatred, the revenge-seeking, and the violence. On a practical level, it doesn't actually move to a new place. And what forgiveness does, if it's done properly, is say the spiral of violence stops here.'

It is possible that Myra Hindley has confessed and been forgiven by her God: it is possible for some in our society (I recall the 624 who voted for her release in *The People* poll) to forgive her. But should she not, in accordance with her repentance, accept the terms of her crime and punishment and be willing to expiate her guilt for the rest of her days?

'She will repent for the rest of her days. She obviously will never forget what she's done... in her own mind, in her own conscience, in the way she looks back. But she also looks forward. If we're becoming a society that just bays for blood, that seeks revenge, then we have to ask ourselves, where is the role of justice?'

It is as we are concluding our interview with David Mellor that murmur of an impending storm reaches us.

Supporters of Myra Hindley's bid for parole have learned that our programme will include a contribution from Ann West. Some of them feel this betrays our promise to be scrupulously balanced in our handling of the subject, and they say so in no uncertain terms. But they are not aware of how we will edit or write the programme. After all, we have taken great care to set powerful emotions in context in order to prevent them sweeping aside the calmer arguments of reason. So we feel such allegations are misinformed and misjudged.

We proceed with our plans to visit our final witness, who will tell her own remarkable story of Christian forgiveness. But, before that, the production team check out the allegations made against us. First, we had always spoken openly of our intention to interview Ann West. There had been no attempt at secrecy, and indeed, after I had interviewed Andrew McCooey, he had enquired how that earlier interview had gone. I said Ann West had been very distressed and I thought she was probably very ill.

Our programme deals in Christian forgiveness and the extent to which it underpins our system of justice and can be subverted by tabloid hysteria. Ann West, who is a Christian and a Methodist, had been pressed on this very issue. Far from influencing public opinion, we had set out to examine the extent of its influence on the judicial system, and the power the tabloids have to keep hatred alive. Satisfied in our minds that our project was on course, we set out to meet a remarkable woman.

Her story, though terrible, does not in any way parallel Ann West's. Lesley's murder was peculiarly sadistic, and subsequent events – the long wait, hoping for her return; the gruesome process of identification; the tape of her daughter calling out 'Mummy, Mummy' – piled suffering upon suffering for her distraught mother. However the programme aimed to examine what it is to forgive. In that sense only is it appropriate to tell this other story.

Beth Ellis is an actress in her early sixties; she lives in a small, sunny flat on the ground floor of a house in Kensington. French windows open onto a long narrow garden, the sort of garden that takes a good deal of planning to make it attractively disorganized. Roses climb on trellises; there are herbs; a small statue, interestingly arranged brick paths. Indoors, comfortably soft sofas, knick-knacks, pictures, and the photograph of a young man on the wall. It is Beth's son, Adam. But Adam is dead, murdered six years ago as he fished quietly in the local canal, hit by a brick in a sock, then a knife to the heart. There was no apparent motive. His murderer, a young man called Christopher, was caught, tried, and is now serving his sentence. He will be out after ten years. Beth hopes to meet him. For Beth is now a Christian and living out her sense of Christianity in the view she takes of Adam's murder: 'Adam was very loving and very caring. He also kept talking about God and church and the Bible. But I didn't want to know then.'

From the age of sixteen he'd been diagnosed schizophrenic but he was all right as long as he took his medication. Beth felt close to this vulnerable son, watched over him more than his years warranted. It was on *Newsroom South East* that she heard West London police were trying to identify the body of a young man found on a London tow-path. At that very moment, Adam's girlfriend Sheena was on the phone enquiring Adam's whereabouts. Beth knew, and the grief began. 'For weeks, months afterwards, I kept seeing him. It was extraordinary. A young man with narrow shoulders and glasses on the end of his nose. I'd think, that's Adi.' She hadn't wanted revenge. 'It never entered my head. I was just desolate, disbelieving, confused with this enormous sense of loss.' But then she began a journey that has taken her deep into the faith that sustained Adam and led her to forgiveness and a renewed life for herself:

'I became a Christian completely involuntarily. I said to Hugo [her other son], "Look, we've got to go to this church because Bruce [the curate] has been very good and looked after the funeral and just out of courtesy we must go for a couple of weeks." And I was just blown as if by a clap of thunder. And so was Hugo. Forgiveness came fairly naturally in a way. Not having been a Christian, and knowing Adam was, I knew Adam would want me to forgive. I knew he wouldn't think it a betrayal. Otherwise it makes Adam's death meaningless – if we went on grudging and being resentful. There would have been no redemption. I know that my anger is not going to bring Adam back, but I also know, because I'm a Christian, that Adam is OK.'

Nonetheless she had waited daily for the verdict in the trial of his killer:

'The police phoned and said, "You'll be pleased to know it was murder. He's got life." I just collapsed in tears. It was a relief it was murder. Adam's life would have been trivialized if it had been manslaughter, an accident. Inside me was that very deep primeval need for justice.'

Adam's killer, a 34-year-old Irishman called Christopher, will be due for parole one day. That does not preoccupy Beth at all: 'I don't think it matters what I want. If he comes out, he comes out. That's the law.' What does matter to her is that he might have changed: 'I would love to think he has somehow come to some sort of healing, some sort of repentance and reconciliation. And if that was the case I would love to meet Christopher.' But suppose he were still a mindless young thug, what then? 'That would be very, very difficult. Mind you, the Bible does say love your enemies. Anybody can love their friends. It takes an extra bit of grace, a bit of help' – her eyes turn upwards to where that help might come from – 'a bit of help to love enemies. So, I'd hand that over...' Again, the gesture towards her God.

I must emphasize that Beth Ellis is in no way dour or pious about expressing these feelings. I am moved by the contrast with Ann West, and only wish some of Beth's peace of mind could be given to Ann. I ask whether she takes such an attitude because she's been told it's her Christian duty?

'No. It comes lightly to me. I think I've just been blessed with a letting-go nature. I don't hang on to grudges. I think it's partly a matter of temperament. But then as a Christian I realize the greatest witness of all, Christ, hung on a cross – with people spitting and throwing things – and said, "Forgive them, Father."'

There is also the memory of what Adam would have wished: it is her way of keeping him with her: 'I know that somewhere there's an echo saying, "Good on you, Ma. Great. You know that's the way."'

Beth Ellis is walking proof that forgiveness is good for you. Her life is busy, full of Christian commitment. Her heart may always be heavy with loss but it's her belief that the killer should not claim two lives:

'I didn't want to be a victim as well as Adam. I didn't want my life to also be destroyed. He killed Adam's life here. But my life is still continuing. How could I possibly do anything worthwhile with my life while I was going around in this lather of unforgiveness? That's how I feel.'

This is the redemption we have sought. Now our programme can be seen in its rightful perspective, not about the politics of Myra Hindley but the forgiveness of Myra Hindley. But no one has seen the programme yet. And there are those who are actively trying to stop it.

Important decisions are made in every cutting room. On this occasion we were more aware than ever that the balance between raw emotion and reasoned argument must be meticulous. We set about it, using the professional judgements and skills in which we are trained. Programme-makers – especially those on *Heart of the Matter* – know that no single view of a case must be given unqualified free rein. Each argument, the passion of each case, must be openly scrutinized. Our objective is that after the programme's transmission those who have watched it will fall to discussing among themselves the rights and wrongs of the issue. We know this happens.

But others were fearful. The Hindley camp was now deeply concerned. While we were gathering daily in the cutting room, Andrew McCooey, Hindley's lawyer, had written to the BBC Religious Department to ask that his contribution and that of the Reverend Bert White be dropped. The request was referred to the Legal Department of the BBC which called for a full briefing. A significant factor here was that both had signed contributor release forms. These forms set out the terms of the contract entered into by each interviewee and the BBC. In signing, the interviewee agrees that the interview that has taken place can be used for transmission. Neither McCooey nor Bert White had raised any objections at the time they signed those forms. And, indeed, they were not now objecting to what they were asked or what they said, but rather to the fact that their contribution would be in a programme in which Ann West also appeared. Yet, at the time of signing, both knew Ann West was to be included.

David Astor, a supporter of Hindley's campaign, had also written to the Religious Department, setting out in strongly worded terms his fears that Ann West would inject tabloid hysteria into the programme. He was, of course, right to fear the tabloids. As our encounter with *The People* had shown, they are powerful campaigners for Hindley to remain inside. It was exactly the validity of such influence that the programme was seeking to examine.

Finally, as the programme reached completion, and the commentary – vetted and revised – was due to be recorded, McCooey appealed even higher, to the Director General of the BBC, John Birt.

Again he explained that he had 'obtained authority from his client' to appear in our programme, but feared that Mrs West's inclusion would not allow a 'proper reasoned debate' to occur. He expressed his wish to disassociate himself and Father White from the programme. I went ahead with the commentary recording.

The programme was transmitted two weeks later. The next day the phone at my home rang. It was Lord Longford calling to congratulate me and all the team on a remarkably fair piece of work. We had no response from the lawyer or the priest. Before we embarked on our filming, the production unit of five had taken, secret to ourselves, a vote on what we each thought should happen. Now, as the programme finished, we voted again: two of us had changed our minds.

I think there is not the remotest possibility of Myra Hindley being released in the near future. No Home Secretary could countenance the outcry such a move would provoke. Public opinion is against it. And if the tabloids do exploit the story, retelling over and over the appalling details, while at the same time professing to take a higher moral tone, that is not to say they create public opinion. Certainly they play on its basest instincts; certainly they would appear to use Hindley stories, plus that photograph, to boost circulation. But there is also, in the public at large, genuine abhorrence and horror at what Hindley did.

Hindley is not in pain. She is not deprived of the necessities of life, dispensed with some consideration for her comfort and wellbeing. Early in 1995 she was transferred at her own request to Durham Prison. An accident, in which she broke her leg, put her in the hospital wing there. If her renewed faith brings her daily comfort, that is not too bad a life. Perhaps when she is an old woman, and those she has injured are no longer vocal, society might be willing to let her end her days in freedom.

The Voice of the Victim

One of the continuing dilemmas of our time is what to do about the increasing crime rate. No developed or developing society I can think of has been able to check its growth or has any cogent idea of how to stop individuals wanting to break the law. Perhaps, among still unknown tribes lurking in the Amazonian forest or the remoter enclaves of New Guinea, rebellious young males are successfully persuaded to conform by means of initiation rituals or rites of passage. If so, the closeness of their communities, and their small numbers, will keep any latent disruptions modest in scale and easy to handle. Certainly, for the rest of the world, increasing crime – the breaking of rules set by any society to be obeyed by all its members – is an endemic problem to which no one has any plausible answers. And it is certainly the case that even those hypothetical Amazonians, once exposed to money, drink and modern communications, will follow the global trend of increased lawbreaking. It may be that the only cure for crime is the absence of opportunity – and there is now universal opportunity.

There is also a great deal more law to be broken. Victorian mothers who wrapped a lump of laudanum in a hankie for their crying baby to suck were not behaving illegally. Branwell Brontë bought his opium regularly from Haworth's respectable high street chemist. Today, as Teresa Gorman MP knows, anyone putting a mock Jacobean porch on a listed Tudor building can be found in breach of proliferating local planning laws and brought to book. Twenty years ago, at a local grocer's shop, I was served by an elderly man with dirty fingernails whose cat sat on the cheese. Asking for half a pound of Cheddar meant dislodging the moggy – nothing more than a mild inconvenience at the time: now such circumstances might well constitute a prosecutable offence. I make no judgement on the matter. I am happy that there are laws governing hygiene in shops: I naturally prefer my cheese without cat hairs. But within the last fifty years we have become hedged around with rules, laws, controls and prohibitions governing every aspect of life – property, health, education, transport, sexual behaviour, social attitudes. All of them are intended for our own good, collectively and individually.

So when, today, another local grocer tells me that boys are now buying boxes of eggs to throw at old ladies' windows, I'm not entirely surprised. Being spontaneous is almost impossible outside the civically authorized adventure playground.

There is a rite of passage familiar even in developed societies that deals with the aggressive impulses of young men, and that is war. It was always the young warriors of the tribe who were sent to burn off their high spirits in contests with other groups of young warriors, supposedly to redress wrongs concerning boundary, property or family. But war got bigger and deadlier. The First World War left a million British military dead – the flower of a generation. Such an enterprise hardly recommends itself as a way of taming the young. Yet, among those calling for firmer discipline, there is still a certain nostalgia for the military remedy: boot camps, short sharp shocks and the benefits of National Service. John Major's call to reinstate compulsory school games is but a dilution of this impulse. Where else, after all, was the Battle of Waterloo won?

Ostensibly the most crime-free countries are police states. I walked the streets of Moscow in 1970 alone at night with total confidence – apart from a realization that my street map was useless as I couldn't read Cyrillic script. Asking for help from a passing stranger held no terrors. In the Moscow Underground I saw someone drop a cigarette butt, only to have a passer-by stop them and insist they retrieve it. In Argentina, too, when I was there soon after the military dictatorship, a woman could confidently stroll the streets on warm summer nights without a shadow of fear. The trouble is that in such countries it is often the state itself that is committing the crimes: drug traffickers and thieves may be caught, but there is also a deadly tradition of kidnapping dissidents, rounding up the disaffected, torturing, imprisoning and even executing without trial. Islamic states which impose the theocratic law of the Sharia present a different problem. Brutal punishments such as stoning to death for adultery and amputation for theft may keep the crime rate down, but are regarded by enlightened values as barbaric. What's more, in Middle Eastern States other factors contribute significantly to the low crime rate: the relative prosperity of the people and the threat held over an immigrant labour force, that if they break the law they will be immediately sent home. It is also the case that certain Islamic states are notorious for tyrannical repression, widespread corruption and nepotism. With freedom comes the choice of whether to break laws or not, and the need to decide what punishments are stringent enough within humane constraints to keep society stable. From that equation springs a whole series of current dilemmas.

Crime is everywhere condemned as a social evil, yet neither the strategies of reform nor retribution are holding it in check. Over the years *Heart of the Matter* has examined the paradox.

It is January 1995 and we are heading for California, which has lots of crime and lots of punishment. Indeed it is the state, above all others, that is spearheading the move across America to get tough on criminals.

In 1994 there were already one and a half million Americans behind bars, just over half of them blacks though blacks make up only 12 per cent of the population. The prison population has tripled in fourteen years and continues to grow. California is proudly leading the way. Between 1952 and 1984 the Sunshine State built twelve prisons; between 1984 and 1994 it built sixteen. There are plans to build twelve more. California currently imprisons 126 000: its penal policies take up 7.5 per cent of public spending. In March 1994 the Californian Assembly passed a law, known colloquially as 'three strikes and you're out', from a phrase familiar in baseball but used in penal terms to mean that after three felonies a criminal will be inside for life. Critics claim this will add a further quarter of a million new prisoners to the state system at a cost of over 5.5 million dollars. California faces the dizzying prospect of an even greater number of its citizens – lawyers, police, prison guards – being employed to convict and control an ever increasing number of lawbreakers, at an ever increasing cost to its taxpayers.

As we take off from Heathrow, prisons and prisoners are making headlines all around us. 'Prison chief slams jailers' proclaims the *Daily Express*. Apparently the warders at Parkhurst don't want to be cross- examined about the escape of three IRA prisoners who made off three days earlier and haven't been seen since. Also that day's papers report that at a prison in Humberside IRA prisoners have put aerosol cans in an oven to cause mayhem. How much more mayhem can Britain's legal system take? The Home Secretary, Michael Howard, clearly favours the Californian solution: more prisons and a tougher time for regular offenders. Perhaps the unemployed can find career opportunities as prison guards, in what is clearly destined to be a growth industry.

The 'we' on this occasion are myself and the senior Scottish judge, Lord McCluskey, who only six weeks earlier had sent up a rocket or two from the discreet pages of Edinburgh University's magazine *Edit*, where he might have expected his views on the judicial system to prompt a civilized and scholarly exchange. But if that's what he was hoping for, he should have reined in his rhetoric, for within days national headlines were shouting 'Judge champions thirst for revenge' and 'Our right to exact revenge'. The *Guardian* republished Lord McCluskey's article in full, setting before a wider public his view that juries should have a say in the sentencing passed on those they've found guilty. Only then, he maintained, would the broader public feel they had a real voice in penal policy. 'People commonly think,' he wrote, 'the present system is failing to do a worthwhile job. It doesn't deter, it doesn't rehabilitate, it doesn't satisfy our primitive desire to see wrongdoers suffer.'

It was that phrase 'primitive desire' that earned the headlines. Whatever images of unthinking retribution this conjured up, Lord McCluskey went on to make matters worse:

'I would be opposed to introducing primitive or fancy penalties such as public flogging, the stocks, the branding or tattooing of persistent recidivists or the imposition of humiliating tasks upon those convicted of certain types of crime. But it would be arrogant of me to say that because certain punishments are not to my taste, or offend my bourgeois sensibilities, they should never be inflicted, if the judgement of the people is that they may be appropriate.'

Thus, while asserting that he himself was not a hanger-and-flogger, Lord McCluskey had managed to convey the opposite – that the possibility of such sentences was exactly what he was seeking. Clearly this is a judge of a disposition to find Californian penal ways congenial; which is why *Heart of the Matter* is taking him along.

Not surprisingly it is with a certain sense of apprehension that I arrive to meet him in the VIP lounge of Virgin Atlantic. What can I expect from the author of this bellicose prose, which smacks of golf-club colonels fulminating through ample moustaches into their ample brandies? In the event, I am relieved to find that John McCluskey fits none of these clichés, except perhaps for a Scotsman's discriminating taste in whisky. He is a dapper, neat man taking a sybaritic pleasure in the indulgences on offer from the airline for its waiting travellers. He has had not only a haircut at the hands of the red-nailed beautician but a foot massage as well. I find later he has already enjoyed a morning swim. Such delights of the flesh sit oddly with the buttoned-up repressive hinted at by the papers. And indeed Lord McCluskey proves to have far more confidence in the judgement and good sense of ordinary people than in the broadsheets which he feels have misrepresented him.

He reminds me, as I question him about the article, that he had also written:

'Jurors are very good at divesting themselves of their prejudices and making sound judgements on the basis of the material presented to them. So I would not expect such people to adopt the primitive attitudes that tend to be reflected in tabloid newspapers or in Yes/No opinion polls.'

My heart warms to him as he explains his belief that judges have too much power and not enough options. Back in 1989 he himself attempted to involve a sex attack victim in the sentencing of her assailant. A 25-year-old-married woman had suffered a horrific sex ordeal at the hands of a man who pleaded guilty. Lord McCluskey had postponed sentencing in order to ask for the woman's opinion as to what it should be. This highly original notion was roundly condemned by the Court of Appeal, who declared that consulting victims was getting into dangerous 'uncharted territory'. But Lord McCluskey is not afraid of uncharted territory. He persists in his view that victims should have greater rights, that they should be given the chance to make a statement to the court as to what the particular crime has meant in their lives. This specific idea, the victim's statement, is what has persuaded Lord McCluskey to accept our invitation to California. In Californian courts every victim has their day. Lord McCluskey plans to see and hear how the system works there, and then plans to return directly to set his findings before the British House of Lords.

We arrive in a San Francisco buffeted by wind and rain and no warmer than London. We walk, as planned, towards the lenses of the television cameras waiting to record our arrival. This is our loyal crew, flown in ahead of us. Deftly they catch in close-up the metal message tagged to our luggage trolley: 'Welcome to San Francisco'. One shot, in television, can be worth a paragraph of words and we are in America's most punishing state.

After the prolonged hanging about that characterizes the making of television and has driven many talents despairingly into careers in print journalism, we enter a stretch limo, within which are already nestled a tripod and camera, portable monitor, sound boom and the three persons operating them. Up and down the freeways we drive as I recite my opening statement to camera in gruesome close-up, my skin chalky and dehydrated from eleven hours in the skies, and my brain phrase-dead from in-flight movies.

Four times I deliver the same words, while producer and cameraman debate whether the vistas of San Francisco glimpsed through the car's window give the right impression. 'Does there need to be such attention to detail?' asks the bemused judge at my side. 'We work to the highest professional standards,' I respond pompously, but I too have my doubts. I am seriously flagging by now and take a bath before dinner still wearing my earrings. It's been a long day.

One of the reasons we have come to California is to tell the story of Maggie Elvey, an indomitable woman, typical of members of the victim support groups that are gaining power across America. In alliance with the prison guards' groups, they now constitute the most potent force driving the penal system to adopt increasingly punitive measures.

We fly into San Diego and drive in swirling rain to Maggie's house 15 miles outside Vista, itself one of those scattered settlements that seem to be all suburb and no centre. The house itself is a modest, sprawling bungalow, unfolding into one continuous living space, meandering through sitting area and dining area, extending to kitchen area, projecting through desk area into television area. Noise in any one area would disturb all the others. I decide the invention of rooms was a good idea.

Maggie is small and dumpy: she wears white sneakers, grey leggings and a large cotton top. She is in her mid-fifties and nervously excited by our visit, or so I deduce from her continuing light laughter, which she seems able to slot in before, during or after anything she says. Maggie has a tragic story to tell, and she has told it many times. She has become a star telling it. She will tell it to us, yet again. Telling it has made her famous, a heroine and icon of the emerging victims' pressure groups. Telling it has become her life, her mission, her crusade. The thought occurs that it has given her life purpose and significance. And that is a cruel thought because it is the story of her husband's murder.

In 1993 Maggie and Ross had been married twenty-nine years. Modest people, they'd first met when Ross delivered potato chips to the milk bar where Maggie worked. Over the years Ross had had a series of jobs. Throughout the 1950s he was with the US Naval Reserve; then he found work with a finance company, then in dry-wall construction. In the 1980s he took a partnership in a gun shop, 'but partnerships don't work'. In 1989 he purchased a gun shop of his own from a widowed friend on the main highway through Vista. He was an expert with guns, building custom guns for clients, a keen member of the National Rifle Association. But guns would be his undoing.

On the late afternoon of 28 April, Maggie is getting ready for an evening out – the sixty-second anniversary of her Beta Sigma Phi in Escandido. Ross is alone in the gun shop, preparing to lock up, when two young blacks – one just under sixteen, one just over – come in through the unlocked premises, attack him, smash his skull repeatedly with an iron bar and make off with seven guns. Careless, amateurish young thugs, they are seen leaving the premises with their haul. The police, alerted, pick them up within half an hour. Meanwhile Maggie returns from her celebration to find Ross missing. Her answerphone calls her to the hospital. Ross remains in a coma for forty-one days, with Maggie and his family in anxious, tearful attendance. On the forty-first day Maggie gives her consent to his life-support system being switched off. During that time she has taken snaps of Ross lying bruised and stricken, snaps that will feature later in her court appearance.

Victims in America are seeking to sway justice in their favour, and Maggie was to do so more dramatically than most.

There were to be two trials: one of the juvenile Damien Miller, fifteen years and eight months at the time of the crime; and one of Kris Kirchner, whose extra six months meant he would be tried as an adult and could be given a life sentence without parole. It is that sentence, particularly the 'without parole', that Maggie Elvey works towards. She puts all her grief and rage and dislocated energy into achieving it. Her means – as she sees it – are the two appearances she can make at the trials to give her victim impact statement. Court procedure allows her to speak after the verdict and immediately before sentencing. She devotes herself to making that impact as strong and vivid as possible. It consumes her waking thoughts, it activates her latent storytelling skills, it mobilizes all she knows or can observe of how to influence public opinion. She becomes the voice of her grief:

'It was a gruelling experience. I lost many hours of sleeping, thinking of what I wanted to do. I took little pieces of paper and wrote in different categories what Ross's death had done to my life, the children's lives, to our business, our livelihood. A sorority sister put it on computer for me. Then we redid it, probably about fifty times. Then I rehearsed and rehearsed it and when I got up in court it just flowed.'

Maggie Elvey's statement was indeed a powerful document. It ran to some twenty-eight pages and included thirteen photographs – among them five gruesome colour enlargements of Ross's appalling injuries which she held up for the court to see. It took Maggie over half an hour to read, and she warned early on she would not be cut short: 'If my statement is too long or I offend anyone, I'm not going to say I'm sorry, because no one here will be offended worse than I have been by this brutal murder of my husband.'

The statement is written as a letter to her dead husband, but with the narrative fluency of a novelist she shifts direction with fierce dramatic effect:

'Dear Ross,

'I don't know if you ever knew what was happening to you on April 28th, 1993. I'm sure you never had a chance to. I pray you didn't. I will try to tell you what I think happened to you that day and how it has destroyed our lives...

'First, Ross, excuse me while I tell Kris and this court about you, since you are no longer here to speak for yourself... What kind of person Kris and Damien have murdered. I will be one of your character witnesses...'

The story of Ross then unfolds – popular, handsome, active, a good friend, a good worker, loyal, resolute, life-loving, an all-American guy. 'He enjoyed camping, gunsmithing, music, dancing, gold prospecting, his family and friends. Ross was loving, caring, too trusting, easy-going, a dedicated family man and worker. He had respect, remorse and valued life. Ross cherished life and nature...' Clearly a paragon of a man.

Then we are back with the events of the murder and how Maggie returned from the sorority night to find the answering machine flashing. When she got to the hospital Ross was already in surgery. She didn't see him until the next day:

'Ross, your head was wrapped in bandages. Blood in your nose and ears. Blood on the pillow from the back of your head. Your eyes were so swollen, black and blue. I'd never seen eyes that swollen before. Your whole body was so swollen due to the trauma... Your room was filled with beeping, flashing machines.'

This is dramatic enough on the page, but imagine a widow reading it in a hushed courtroom before judge, jury and the media. Maggie went on:

'I watched you, my once strong husband, wasting away. Family and friends tried to exercise your muscles just in case you would come to. The first time you partially opened your left eye, your son came running out to the waiting room. "Mom, come quick, Dad opened his left eye. He will be okay." Your left eye was the only one that ever partially opened but you were not conscious. I never saw your blue eyes again.'

And on the forty-first day, after medical advice and counselling, Maggie had to make her momentous decision – 'No Life Saving Procedures. It's a decision, Kris, that I will live with for the rest of my life. Would you have come to, Ross, and been okay or would you have been a vegetable forever?'

Maggie then describes the grief of Ross's immediate family. His daughter Leslie: 'She was your auburn-haired, green-eyed little girl. You were real proud of her. She had you for less than twenty-eight years. . . She is having a very rough time with the loss of her very special Dad.' His son Kevin: 'You won't be around to share life's daily ups and downs or trips to the gun range to shoot together. You helped each other with car repairs. You won't be here for all the special events to come in Kevin's life – birthdays, holidays, weddings and children.' His seven-year-old grandson: 'He sits on the top of his slide in the back yard and tries to call to you, Grandpa.' His four-year-old granddaughter: 'When we tell her you are in heaven she wants to drive there to see you.'

Maggie then itemizes her own losses. After her battles for medical welfare and some sort of business security, she returns to the tear-jerking parade of intimacy, painful enough to hear but heartbreaking to deliver:

'I've lost you, my husband of almost twenty-nine years, my best friend, my lover, companion, dance partner (and, boy, could we dance!)... my gardener, electrician, plumber, mechanic, handyman, painter. My security and my income are gone. Our dreams of retirement and travel, of growing old together are gone too. I miss our nightly conversations while doing dishes together... I miss your snoring, our Sunday outings... I miss your hugs, love and affection. I was allowed to do my things as you were. We shared our two worlds as one.'

Maggie has mined the rich sources of emotional expression so much a part of America's popular culture – from greeting cards, to films, from ballads to advertisements – and tapped with native skill the rich, juicy, soft-hearted core of American sentiment. And so to the final page, one might almost say the final curtain:

'I know you are in a much better place, Ross. You and Bob, your dad and grandfather are hunting and fishing in green fields. Your mom is making you biscuits and gravy for when you get home. Give Mom and Dad a hug. I miss you all. I see a lonesome dove sitting on our back fence from our bedroom window when I arise. I wonder if you have sent us your angel. If I had only known it was our last walk in the rain, if I had only known I'd never hear your voice again, I would have memorized everything you said, so on lonely nights I could think of them once more. If I had only known it was my last night by your side I'd pray a miracle would stop the dawn. And when you'd smile at me I would look into your eyes and make sure you knew my love for you goes on and on.'

I imagine you could have heard a pin drop. American courts are, we know, places of high drama, and Maggie Elvey had one more sensational gesture to make. Her letter to Ross finished, she addressed the court directly. 'Kris Kirchner could one day go home to his family,' she declared, 'but that's how my husband came home to me,' and she slammed a small wooden box on the courtroom table. Ross's ashes.

'It was incredibly emotional.' This is the judge in the case telling me. 'I took the opportunity to look at the audience and there wasn't an unmoved party, and that includes the media.' Indeed it did. Television pictures of the dramatic moment were soon on Californian screens. The defendants' lawyers were stunned, too: 'When the box hit the table I was dumbfounded. My gut feeling was to say something comical, about the absurdity of what we were doing. But I held back.'

In the event, Judge Lisa Guy Schall went on to pass a sentence of life without parole on the guilty seventeen-year-old. It was what Maggie Elvey had wanted and had worked for. But had her statement swayed the judge's sentence? Judge Lisa Guy Schall is perfect Hollywood casting for a Californian woman judge – slender and leggy, silk shirt, good jewellery, choosing her words with immaculate attention:

'The victim impact statement was emotional, and it clearly made a difference in the minds of the people in the audience. Was it the pivotal reasoning for what I finally did? No. I knew Mrs Elvey. She had been involved in the case from day one. She had made her feelings very well known. But I also felt I did what was right, irrespective of her statement. The fact that I ended up imposing a sentence she agreed with doesn't necessarily mean I did it only because of what she said or did. The outcome is exactly the same, but we got there by different roads.'

Ross Elvey's killer, Kris Kirchner, sixteen at the time of the crime, faces life without parole. Moreover, it would require a prison governor or a change in the law even to make his sentence eligible for review. Lisa Guy Schall may disclaim the direct influence of Maggie Elvey's statement in her court, but as an elected judge she fully acknowledges that, since victims' statements were introduced in the late 1980s, victims rights' groups have gained enough political clout to swing the whole climate of opinion in California towards harsher sentencing: 'There's no doubt about it. Changes in the law have paralleled the rights of victims' movements and have made sentencing harsher. There's been a public outcry from victims' groups and they're supported by the electorate.'

Judge McCluskey is distressed by a good deal of this. It is not what he wants to see in Britain at all:

'What they allow in California is that the victim may come to court as an advocate, sometimes even a passionate advocate. I don't think myself that is the way we want to approach the matter. I think passion has a role in the conduct of legal proceedings, I think we have to concede that. We're not conducting an analytical experiment in a laboratory. But when it comes to determining what to do with a person in court, one has to approach that in a balanced and just way.

'In America you can have members of the public appearing in court to cheer on the victim, as it were. You can have television cameras focused on the judge and maybe the judge is up for re-election. Now this appears to me to be a dangerous combination of circumstances. That's not the way I'd like to see us in Britain approach the matter. I want the victim's statement to be a written document prepared by an independent official and presented to the judge. That's all.'

What worries Judge McCluskey is the politicization of penal policy in America. Victims' groups are proliferating: MADD, Mothers Against Dangerous Drivers, Survivors of Murdered Victims groups.

'This alarms me. We must try to keep penal policy rational. Otherwise we end up with a situation like California, one of the richest states in the world, which has proportionally the highest rate of imprisoned population in the entire world, more even than Russia, Turkey, countries we think of as having severe penal policies. What hope for us then?'

Things are not over for Maggie Elvey. There is no doubt that for a victim to make a statement in court acknowledges their suffering and their involvement with the crime in a way that is both just and therapeutic. This would no doubt be the case in Britain too. The very writing of her statement led Maggie to bring forward into her consciousness all the things she loved about Ross. This must surely be good for her. Yet there is a risk of such involvement going too far. Being a victim has given Maggie a status she never had. She appears on radio and television, she addresses groups. She has become a career campaigner, channelling her unleashed energies into lobbying in the state capital, Sacramento. Her car bumper has the sticker: 'Someone I love was murdered'. Ross's death may have taken over the rest of her life.

Over dinner, the production team speculate about her testimony. And her passionate single-mindedness. There have been clues scattered through the day that perhaps her married life wasn't quite the golden idyll she had painted so dramatically in court. One of her children had remarked idly to me, as we drank coffee while the camera was being set up, that they hadn't known how to break the news to their mother that fatal night because Maggie and Ross weren't on speaking terms. On a closer reading, Maggie's own account suggests as much:

'When I got home that evening, Ross, you were not home yet which was very strange... My first thought was that you had left home because we had an argument that Monday because of something you had said. On Tuesday 27th... I remember that Ross had said he was sorry for what he had said on Monday, but I wouldn't accept his apology... but we always worked out our differences.'

Heaven knows, plenty of couples have troubled, combative relationships and are happy to keep them going. But could Maggie, even unwittingly, have misrepresented to the court the nature of her marriage in order to influence the sentence? Which of us would not? Could the passion that drives her be partly fuelled by her guilt and grief at that quarrel she can now never make up?

Kangaroo courts and lynch mobs were condemned years ago because it was clear that those hurt by crimes often simply want revenge. Considering their grief and sense of loss, that is not surprising. But it is not the way in which to conduct a legal system. As Lord McCluskey insists, legal procedures must be logical. Behind the public frenzy about crime currently sweeping America there lurks the shadow of mob rule. What's more, when victims display their suffering as dramatically as Maggie Elvey, those who strive for a balanced assessment of the situation can easily be portrayed as insulting their grief.

Maggie's story and the complexity of her motives are of more than merely psychological interest because she has powerful allies. Maggie is working to have the death penalty extended to under sixteen-year-olds. She wants harsher prison conditions – fewer gyms, televisions and conjugal visits. I accuse her of wanting revenge – 'I don't want revenge. But why should they live better than we do on the outside? And have all the free benefits? Better law books than some of our attorneys – free medical that a lot of us don't have. And get all this for murdering somebody!'

Our next stop is Sacramento, where we visit one of Maggie's allies: Don Novey, President of the California Correctional Peace Officers Association (the CCPOA), known as the Godfather of the Crime Victims Movement. He has certainly hitched their wagon to his star, funding their leading lobby group and offering facilities and resources to others. 'I think they want justice. I think they want a voice in the courtroom. If that's revenge, then so call it – revenge.'

There is no mistaking the clout of the CCPOA. Since 1991 it has had its own purpose-built headquarters: three million dollars' worth of post-modern offices, grey walls, pale blue wall-to-wall carpeting. The interior has the discreet feel of a bank, or a very upmarket health club, with staff gliding unobtrusively along still and silent corridors.

Yet, even as we set up the cameras in this calmly neutral setting and await Novey's arrival, we spot startlingly overt evidence of their political allegiance: a shooting target in the cut-out shape of a life-size Bill Clinton stands beside a conference table; on its lapel an 'I love Newt' sticker. Along the corridors framed 1940s Norman Rockwell posters proclaim 'Freedom from Want','Freedom from Fear'. None of the folksy figures is black or Hispanic. Round another corner, framed cartoons: 'Clinton doesn't inhale, he sucks'; 'Charles Manson supports Dukakis'. Suddenly a small, hunched man shuffles past. Trousers slightly flared, short at the ankle, slip-on shoes, a trilby pulled low. We fail to recognize our interviewee. He, however, sensing the soft Left of the media, will be ready with combative answers to my questions:

'The victims of America have probably been the most deprived, neglected element in our society. They're shunted off when court proceedings are taking place. Now it seems to be the cause of the nineties, the victims' movement. It's near and dear to my heart and also our membership's heart. We understand the predatory criminal more than anybody else.'

The CCPOA campaigned vigorously for the 'three strikes and you're out' law: 'The street police, the citizens, the victims of California have had enough. People that were selling drugs to little kids, child molesters, armed robbers, rapists were back on the streets in less than two years on average. The public had had enough.' But to get life imprisonment, automatically, after a third felony? He tips back the trilby which he keeps on throughout the interview. 'Break my heart! These are career criminals. I guarantee you these individuals have been arrested nineteen, twenty, twenty-five times, and they've plea-bargained their arrest down to county gaol so it doesn't go on the record. They're career criminals and they're preying upon society.'

The CCPOA puts money behind political candidates. And, bearing in mind that Judge Lisa Guy Schall may some day face re-election, I hazard a rather obvious guess that it must be hard to get elected if you're soft on crime in California.

'Correct! Darn it, there was such advocacy in the seventies for inmates' rights! My God, we've got to reverse roles! What's this country coming to?' Don Novey's conversation proceeds by exclamations. His favourite, 'Break my heart!', greets every question of mine challenging such harshness. So the CCPOA had been behind the Republican successes last autumn? He's pleased to have wrong-footed me. 'We endorsed thirty-two Democrats in California the last election: twenty-seven won. We did strongly with Republicans as well.'

Perhaps, I suggest, in my tentative English way, you get a lot of murders in America because people have the right to carry guns? I had mentioned to Maggie that perhaps it was the fact that Ross ran a gun shop that put his life at risk. She had dismissed the notion as irrelevant. Likewise Don Novey:

'It's not a matter of just gun control. Thirty per cent of all murders in America are done with clubs or axes or knives. So if they can't get a gun they'll do it some other way. It's an attitudinal thing within society. It's a reflection of people not being held accountable and responsible for their actions, from youth on. It's not just here, it's world-wide. It's a sad scenario.'

Does he have any theories then about what makes people killers? 'I just think that when the good Lord puts us on this earth, there's one half of one per cent that just doesn't like their fellow human beings. And they're vicious: and they've got to be put away.'

This hardly amounts to a theory of criminal behaviour, and Don Novey admits as much: 'I'm just a layperson, I'm not a doctor, or scientist or anything like that.'

However the uneasy fact is that neither doctors nor scientists have come up with a plausible theory that has brought about any consistent, long-term reduction in crime. The unequivocal hard-line view is that crime is a fact and the thing for societies to do is address its punishment. The so-called softer line seeks the origins of crime in the character and background of individuals, and the way those individuals have interacted with the world around them. Such an approach in itself implies a withholding of judgement while complex and unfolding relationships are examined. It currently engages criminologists, social workers and theologians, who for their pains are labelled 'soft' on crime.

Taking a hard line with villains – lock 'em up, treat 'em rough – is an easy populist option. But it has not made California a particularly safe place to be. Even those who champion it will eventually be driven to realize that it is not enough. After all, we have been this way before. Hanging, transportation, the stocks, did not make Victorian England a conspicuously savoury place.

The really hard option is to take on board what's called the 'liberal' view – i.e. a commitment to long-term solutions rather than quick-fix remedies. This approach requires an open mind, a continuing and patient engagement with what is going on, an alertness to the complexities of how a human being is shaped by both nature and nurture.

My experience in America tells me that the hard line wins votes. Its theory has the intellectual weight of sentimental melodrama, its heroines and victims over-simplified, even by themselves – and an electorate eager to hiss and boo designated villains. But what happens when the play is ended?

Postscript: On the day of his return from California Lord McCluskey debated the matter of victim impact statements in the House of Lords. In expressing the view that such statements should be written rather than oral he sited his experience in America. After a strong debate the amendment to the Criminal Justice (Scotland) Bill proposing such statements, was withdrawn. Lord McCluskey expects it to be back.

Mad or Bad

In February 1992 I looked at crime from a different perspective: I went to talk to the mother of a murderer. Primrose Kirkman brought up seven children but only one of them – Kim, the second – turned out to be anything other than you would expect to find in a Staffordshire farming community. Kim, however, had turned out very bad indeed. He violently attacked a number of women and finally killed a young woman who had sought his help. But what makes Kim's story so worrying for us all is that he committed this murder on the very day he was released from seventeen years in psychiatric hospitals and clinics. *Heart of the Matter* asked was he simply 'bad' – aware that he was doing wrong and callously indifferent to the fact? Or was he 'mad' – mentally unwell to such an extent that he wasn't in control of his impulses and actions? Should he have been punished with a term in prison or given treatment as a patient in hospital?

It sounds an easy enough choice – bad or mad. But rhyming monosyllables can't convey the nuances of definition and the convolutions of theory I was to encounter as we put the programme together. What *was* clear was that from the age of seventeen Kim had been described as a psychopath. I was to discover that such a definition doesn't get you far. But sadly it was all the Kirkman family were left with when I visited them on that wet winter afternoon.

They made the production team welcome with tea and such, in their cosy home, with its horse brasses and open fire. But there was a tension in the air, for I was here to ask about a tragedy that had followed a course neither police, psychiatrists nor any of this apparently normal family could have predicted.

Prim – the name seemed curiously apposite – was wearing a trim silk dress speckled with daisies. She had a locket round her throat. It held my attention. A locket holds the picture, sometimes the hair, of those we love. Perhaps Prim had a picture of Kim there? Kim/Prim: the similarity of their names struck me. Were they as close as rhyming words? Asking a mother about how her son came to kill is not easy. The room fell quiet; there was none of the usual jostling and joking from the crew. I held Prim's attention and she gave it to me, facing bravely my insistent rooting after details, her piercing pale blue eyes never flinching as she sought yet again for explanations. With Prim's help I pieced together the stages of Kim's life. Her flat Staffordshire vowels trawled his name painfully through her account, her expression bemused, sudden frowns – half-questioning as though together we might yet alight on an answer as to why things had happened this way.

Psychiatrists were to be plentiful in this programme so, taking my cue from where they begin their enquiries, I asked Prim about Kim's early years.

'As a baby he was too good to be true. He didn't cry. He didn't cry at all. He was a very quiet little boy – he liked his own company a lot. When he was three or four he used to play on his own. If he was naughty, I smacked him and he had to go to bed. And he just used to go.'

When Kim was thirteen he went to school at Uttoxeter. He'd suddenly grown very tall for his age, and was teased for it. He wasn't a very bright scholar, it later transpired, and was bullied a good deal: 'He did grow up a little bit too quickly. His body grew quickly, not his mind. He was still a little boy, really.'

Then when he was fourteen there was an odd incident. Local children were playing up the lane and they found a pile of shoes – all of them women's shoes. There were also some clothes belonging to a neighbour's daughter. It came out – and Kim admitted – he'd collected them all together. The shoes belonged to different members of his family.

'I said, "why have you got the shoes like, Kim? Why the dresses and things?" And he said, "My head makes me do it." He always said that when he was young: "It's just my head; it make me do it." He was always sorry for what he'd done. Always.'

The police came: the phrase 'shoe fetish' was used. Neither helped much. And then things got worse. Again down the lane near his old home, Kim attacked a girl who lived nearby with an umbrella. She wasn't seriously hurt and ran home crying to tell her parents. Kim's brother Greg arrived just afterwards and went home to tell his mother. Prim again tried to wheedle an explanation: 'I said, "Why did you hit her with an umbrella, Kim?" I said, "Don't you like her?" And he says, "Yeah, of course I like her. It's just something as makes me do it."'

But there were more incidents. 'I used to think he seemed quite strange. I'd say "Have you been doing anything, Kim?" He did sometimes seem very strange.' Mrs Kirkman got to know the signs. 'It made him moody. The time he hit the girl down the road, he just went to bed, he just stayed in bed.' But no one in the family, then or later, had ever seen Kim lose his temper.

It was after a series of attacks on women that a care order was issued and Kim was admitted to his local psychiatric hospital. At the age of seventeen he was admitted to Broadmoor with the deadly label 'psychopath'. He was to remain in special hospitals until he was thirty-five years old.

So what is a psychopath, and are they born or made? The legal definition set out in the Mental Health Act 1983 reads: 'a psychopathic disorder is a disability of mind which results in abnormally aggressive or seriously irresponsible conduct. This does not mean mental illness.' Not, then, in the programme's terminology, 'mad'. The *Shorter Oxford Dictionary* is even more ambivalent: 'mental disorder considered apart from cerebral disease.'

I begin asking around among forensic psychiatrists for clearer guidance on how we know and identify psychopaths in the community. According to Dr Derek Chiswick at the Royal Edinburgh Hospital:

'Some 80 000 people are sentenced every year by the courts for criminal violence. Because only a tiny number are examined by psychiatrists, it's impossible to know how many of that 80 000 may have a psychopathic disorder. Everyone charged with murder is examined, but for all other crimes it is entirely discretionary. So we don't have a complete sample.'

This is already worrying, but it gets worse. It is up to the psychiatrist to decide whether someone is a psychopath or not. So I asked Dr Chiswick for the checklist of characteristics:

'The checklist isn't very helpful because it depends heavily on persistent violent behaviour. There are other features which are much softer, and much less reliable – such things as showing callous disregard for the feelings of others, an inability to learn from previous behaviour, a shallowness in relationships, an inability to make sustained relationships. A lot of those are very difficult to define in any clear way and are often the subject of disagreement between psychiatrists.'

Already the word 'psychopath' is looking a bit vague. Martin Scorsese's film *Cape Fear* is opening as we begin our interviews. From its publicity and that of other terror movies, it seems that popular culture has a clearer concept of 'psychopath' than the medical world. No one is concerned, as Robert de Niro or Anthony Perkins stalk their victims, with what the medical explanation might be. Though it's interesting that in Hitchcock's *Psycho*, an early landmark of the genre, Anthony Perkins is not killed – as befits any aggressive killer in movie ethics – but led away, clearly raving mad.

So can the term have any specific meaning, if it simply gets used to describe anyone regularly committing violent crime? For, although the definition is inexact, the consequences are very exact indeed. If the psychiatrist decides you're a psychopath, you go to hospital for treatment. If the decision is that you're not, you go to prison. With remission of prison sentence for good behaviour, the chances are that you'll be out on the streets sooner than if you'd been classified as psychopathic. It makes me shift uneasily at the thought of all those 80 000 violent crimes whose perpetrators don't even get examined, let alone recommended for treatment. No wonder the Chairman of the Home Office enquiry into what went wrong over Kim Kirkman declared, 'The classifying of those with personality disorders ... is useless.'

Let me bring you up to date with what happened to Kim. We left him in hospital, which implied that he would be treated and possibly cured, and if cured he would be different, and then eligible for release. Dr Chiswick explains that this would be the case for anyone with schizophrenia, for example, because it's possible to monitor actual improvements in the condition.

'But with psychopathic disorder we don't have the technology to understand when someone is cured. We take decisions about patients living in an institution, as to whether they are safe. But life in an institution is very different from life in the community. So it's harder to determine whether a patient is cured.'

And so it proved.

Kim Kirkman was first in Broadmoor, then Ashworth Hospital – and then, in 1989, as a prelude to release, spent twelve months at Reaside Rehabilitation Clinic. Throughout his seventeen years inside his mother and family had kept up their visits. In the later years Kim had begun to speak to them of coming out, of wanting to be out. At Reaside things improved dramatically. Mrs Kirkman saw great developments in his character – 'He was joking, he could stick up for himself, he did a lot of swimming, very good at carpentry. He wanted most in his life to get home, get married and have a family and of course it was coming true.' For in Reaside Kim had met another patient, Mandy, and become engaged. The Christmas of 1989 Kim spent four days at home with family, friends and Mandy. In April 1990 Mandy was released into a mother and baby home where she gave birth to their daughter Natasha. Kim was allowed to visit her occasionally. Together they were decorating the flat they'd be moving into after Kim's release. Then the day came. Kim – proud father of a two-month-old baby, devoted to Mandy, with a spanking newly decorated flat to live in – was finally released on 1 June 1990.

But his mother, always sensitive to whatever meagre clues Kim gave to his well-being, was worried:

'I could tell by his face that there was something wrong. He aged ten years in so many months. It was all happening a bit too quick for him really. When he was going to be released the social worker came to see me and I asked her why they'd kept him in a secure hospital all those seventeen years. "Well," she said, "a psychopath could turn into either a murderer or a rapist." "In that case," I said, "I want Kim to stay where he is until I know for sure he's going to be all right." But there is no knowing for sure.'

On the day Kim was released, a young woman, Elizabeth Ward, who had the flat directly above Kim and Mandy's, came to ask for help with a plumbing leak in her lavatory. Kim went willingly to see what he could do. What happened next has been reconstructed from Kim's subsequent confession. The lavatory was an old-fashioned type with the cistern high above. Elizabeth climbed up to show Kim where the problem was. It's thought her shoes fixed his attention. He reached out, she pushed him off, and then he beat her to death with the hammer he was holding. That night the murder was reported on the local television news. Kim's brother Greg noticed it was at the same address Kim had. 'I never thought for a moment it was him: it never entered my head.'

Kim was taken to Winson Green Prison. At the moment of greatest significance in his life, the day of his liberty, he had destroyed it all and taken an innocent life too. It can hardly have been something he wanted or planned. It lost him Mandy, his daughter Natasha, and in the end his own life. In September 1990 Kim Kirkman hanged himself.

His mother tells me the family weren't surprised:

'We knew he was very depressed. Greg had been to see him on the Saturday and he said Kim was extremely depressed and he wasn't talking. We tried to get in touch with his solicitor, but we couldn't. I suppose they're busy, aren't they... On the Wednesday he committed suicide, before any of us got a chance to see him again.

Two deaths and several families distraught. Yet for seventeen years Kim's infirmity had been contained. Mad or bad? How about sad? 'I don't think they should have let him out personally. I know that sounds cruel towards him but at least he would have been safe, secure.' This is his own mother, opting for her son's permanent incarceration. What others involved with Kim's case thought was not easy to discover.

There was a major enquiry following Liz Ward's murder. It found that 100 people, including the Home Office, had been involved in the decision to release Kim Kirkman. The report exonerated them all but drew attention to the problem of diagnosing a psychopath.

Because psychopathy is not a medical illness with verifiable physical symptoms, it can never be monitored for recovery in any absolute sense. Dr Chiswick, psychiatrist, again:

'We're not sure if we can cure them or not. We're not sure about identifying the signs of improvement and we're not sure what improvement within hospital means in terms of safety out in the community. The problem with such people is that unless they choose to disclose to you aspects of their feelings, aspects of their thinking and functioning, their ideas about their behaviour, you have no way of knowing these things because outwardly they appear perfectly normal people.'

This is a perfect Catch 22. To cure psychopaths you talk to them and gauge from what they say whether they are cured or not. But psychopaths are known liars. Any statement from them – 'I am well', 'I am feeling better' – is *ipso facto* suspect.

And so it proves. Many psychopaths have a great capacity for convincing and persuading their carers that their preoccupations with violence have vanished. In Kim Kirkman's case, he managed to persuade 100 people this was so. Possibly even himself.

As treatment isn't reliable, it becomes all the more urgent to find out what causes psychopathy. Again, information is not exact: 'Sometimes there may be genetic influences, sometimes environmental factors play a part, sometimes physical factors, perhaps a brain injury, something like that.'

I asked Brian Thomas-Peter, a forensic clinical psychologist of Reaside Clinic, where Kim had been for a year before his release, about the background of such people:

'It's extremely common among personality-disordered people to find disruption in their background, people who have broken families, who've been the subject of sexual abuse, have learned to distrust relationships, too poorly prepared for multiple parenting. A common feature of such people who've been in care is that they've moved on from one place to another without any real security. A lot of relationships come and go and they fail to establish empathy with individuals; they fail to see things from another person's perspective, fail to consider the implications of their behaviour on others.'

With the growth of psychiatry, it has become something of a cliché that explanations for the sort of people we are can be found in our early nurturing or lack of it. But in political or social terms it's a mistrusted cliché. Plenty of people, the argument goes, have a disadvantaged background and still manage to grow up into wholesome, law-abiding citizens. And within whatever limitations, individuals still retain freedom to make moral choices and must be held responsible for their actions. Brian Thomas-Peter has a 'yes' answer and a 'but' answer:

'Yes – when you're working clinically with people they must know they are responsible for their behaviour. But that doesn't mean that the rest of us aren't also responsible to a degree. A child who has been abused from the age of three, has fifteen care placements before their fifteenth birthday, who's failed to establish caring relationships, then indecently assaults a child – someone who's a victim, in that moment becomes a perpetrator. And it's at that point we come in. At Reaside Clinic we pick up the damage that accumulates in people who have very disturbed personalities.'

Increasingly, however, some psychiatrists are declaring that psychopaths cannot be cured – at least not cured enough to let them go free. And they object to hospitals being used as prisons simply to lock people up, rather than give them treatment with the possibility of a cure. There is thus a damaging tension between hospitals and prisons. Brian Thomas-Peter:

'I think perhaps a hybrid between the prison service and the health service is needed. We have to integrate the treatment programmes that happen in hospitals and in prisons into the community. We must hold on to these people for years. Short-term interventions are completely wrong.'

This plausible objective, however, could in effect infringe people's civil rights. If a psychopath goes to prison, with good behaviour he will be out within a specific number of years; if he goes to a hospital, his stay could go on and on. Thus the apparent punishment is harder, in the sense of being longer, in the hospital than in the prison. Here differing values have to be assessed and choices made. If the choice is made to favour the safety of society, then it has to be acknowledged that certain individuals could be held longer than might be necessary – simply because we do not currently have the means to assess exactly how long *is* necessary.

All this is a long way from Kim Kirkman, and further still from California's strategies of revenge and retribution. But they all beg the question of what has gone wrong in the lives of people who become killers. How does a child acquire a conscience? There is universal agreement among psychiatrists and theologians to whom I put the issue. Doctor Brian Thomas-Peter of Reaside Clinic:

'It's about discipline, early discipline. It's also about consistency and taking the perspective of a third party, understanding the implications of what you're doing to someone else. These are values that are learned very early in life. If you fail to learn them somewhere between the ages of seven or ten, it becomes increasingly difficult. Once you've failed to acquire that conscience, you can deal with things by understanding that acting outside the rules is not in your best interest, but that's not the same as feeling that something is wrong.'

Perhaps more children are reaching the age of seven without that consistent and close relationship that is at the heart of discipline and parenting. It appears to have been true of the two boys found guilty of the murder of James Bulger. But was it true of Kim Kirkman? From meeting and talking with his grieving mother I find it hard to believe it was so. He had, after all, taken his own life. Had those last terrible weeks – plunged in depression and loss – also been a time when Kim felt genuine remorse, and knew what it was to have a moral conscience?

Since Kim's death there has been greater interest in the genetic factors affecting human behaviour. There is much wild talk of there being a gene for criminal behaviour. While this notion remains no more than a fantasy at present, any perceptive parent will know that some children are born with a greater tendency to aggression than others. And it is a wise family that disciplines their more spirited children in a different and appropriate way.

The mapping of the human genome, now going forward in laboratories around the world, will identify and describe the entire genetic code that makes up the human race. It is a momentous undertaking, as important for science as the discoveries of Galileo and Darwin. It may well reveal how the genetic make-up of each individual predisposes us to certain ailments, to certain character traits, and thus to certain moral propensities. We may well find the nature of our humanity more mechanistic than we like to think. It is a prospect that travels much further down the path that the behaviourists and relativists have already signposted. It might ultimately raise the question of whether anyone can be judged wrong or wicked any more in the sense in which we currently make such judgements. And to what extent does 'good' have intrinsic and independent moral worth? Might any value system – that of Jesus or of Hitler – be equally valid and explicable in the determinism of the double helix? This is a nightmare vision for the twenty-first century to grapple with.

But somewhere in the future there may emerge an explanation for Kim Kirkman. Mad? Not in any observable sense. Bad? Not willingly so. In the end the person who found what he did most terrible and baffling was clearly himself. We can only be sorry.

'He couldn't live with the fact that he'd murdered Liz Ward. And he couldn't live without Mandy and his baby – there's no way he could live without them.'

'Do you think about him a lot?' I asked Prim.

'All the time. He's never away from me. Never.' She gulped and for the first time blinked her pale blue eyes and looked away.

Clash of Ideals

It would be hard to imagine more different ethical world views than those held by Quakers and Muslims. They are at opposite poles, both in their concepts of God and in how they believe religious principles should be applied in society. The Quakers – pacifists and against capital punishment – reject all violence and ideas of retribution; whereas the Muslims live under Islam, a system of rules for both moral behaviour and the government of society. The Sharia – the cardinal law of Islam – advocates an-eye-for-an-eye punishment, and sees retribution as God's justice in a fair society.

But there is one thing they have in common: a conviction that their religious view of the world should be carried into every part of their lives. Many of those from both polarities demonstrate considerable courage in doing just that. Nothing could therefore demonstrate more clearly the practical and ideological problems that arise in today's pluralist culture than an encounter between two such diverse belief systems.

That encounter began on a hot summer evening in May 1988. In the Acropole Hotel, Khartoum, in northern Sudan, three British aid workers were having dinner together. Clare and Chris Rolfe, both Quakers in their early thirties, on their way to work in a Sudanese refugee camp with their two children, were dining with Sally Rockett, who also had strong Quaker sympathies. Indeed it was their commitment to helping others that had brought all of them to this part of the world. In 1982 Chris and Clare had been to Somalia to work with Quaker Peace and Service in a refugee camp. They stayed four years, pioneering the idea that what refugees really need is not handouts and food parcels from the West, but opportunities and means to help themselves. Chris and Clare lived in the camp alongside the refugees, planting vegetables and such round their own little house. They wanted to see just how rough and difficult life was for the 60 000 people camped in meagre huts over the sandy hillsides. According to friends, they were immensely happy and fulfilled in their work.

Sally Rockett, too, was drawn to work in the developing world. She'd already done a tour of duty in Nepal and since January 1988 had been working for the World University Service in an East Sudanese camp. So round the table were gathered a group of idealists, willing even to bring up their small children in difficult circumstances in order to live out their belief in Christian charity and commitment to other human beings.

At that time another young idealist – 22-year-old Imad Ahmed – from another culture entirely, was committed to a secret Palestinian terrorist group. He sought to further his cause by violent means, to strike at Western interests in the Sudan. That evening he put on a Sudanese djellaba and entered the Acropole Hotel carrying a bag. It contained a tennis racquet and 5 kilos of explosives. He went up the stairs of the hotel and, from an overlooking balcony, hurled the bag into the dining room below.

The reverberations of his action were felt in, of all places, Budleigh Salterton, a sleepy little Devon resort, the epitome of peaceful England, blessed by the calm uneventfulness of rural life. It was there that Ken and Ruth Rockett, Sally's parents, had a small bungalow where they took pride in their rose garden and the worthwhile work being done by their only daughter. The equilibrium of their lives was such that they didn't at first appreciate the significance of what they heard on the news:

'We had seen the news and the report of the deaths of the family of four, the Rolfes. But there was news also of the death of two Sudanese and some other British people. I don't think any worry crossed our minds. Then, about a quarter to eleven at night, there was a knock on the door and a young policewoman there.'

The pain of coming to terms with Sally's death was hard enough. But suddenly an unimagined complication was thrust upon them, turning their private grieving into a matter of public responsibility.

Under Islamic law the families of those who are murdered are allowed a say in the punishment of their killers. This is exactly what America's victim support groups are campaigning for, but for the Rocketts, used to remote, impersonal, consistent British justice, it was extremely disturbing.

Once the terrorists were caught, tried and found guilty, their fate lay in the hands of, among others, this modest and thoroughly English couple. The Sudanese Embassy in London explained to them the three options dictated under Islamic law: they could choose pardon, blood money or death. Suddenly the parents of a young woman committed to Quaker values were given the power of life or death over her killers, and embroiled in Islamic principles of morals and law.

Sudan's political life had become increasingly dominated by Islamic fundamentalism. Since Britain and Egypt pulled out in 1955, the Republic had been riven by conflict. Seventeen years of civil war between the Muslim Arab north and the Christian African south had impoverished its people. Brief episodes of democracy had given way to ruthless dictatorships, and through it all the grasp of Islam had tightened. In 1983 the Sharia, Islam's body of law, became that of the Sudanese state.

In 1989 yet another military coup deposed the democratically elected Sadiq El-Mahdi, the moral climate hardened and the harshest controls were put in place. Independent newspapers and political parties were banned. Alcohol was forbidden. Harsh punishments, such as amputations and flogging, were reintroduced. Women had to cover their bodies, sometimes even their faces. The civil wars, combined with famine, killed over two million people. Hence the refugee camps where the Rolfes and Sally Rockett were hoping to do good. They had certainly chosen a hard path, knowing the risks and the dangers. Sally's mother and father tried to imagine which choice she would have wanted them to make:

'We were given about forty-eight hours to make the decision, have it ratified, have it signed by a local solicitor and posted express to reach the Sudanese Embassy in time.' Clearly some quick reasoning had to be gone through. The whole process was a shock for the

Rocketts. 'We don't normally think in this way. It's become a dreadful problem. We've thought over it, round it and through it; we've talked to people, and we can't resolve it satisfactorily for our own peace of mind.'

To discover just how different the Islamic tradition is from our own, I talked to Dr Hesham El Essawy of the Islamic Society for the Promotion of Religious Tolerance. First he put me right about the phrase 'an eye for an eye'. Often seen in the West as brutally retributive, he explained it was originally conceived as a way of limiting retribution:

'The Koran was revealed to pagan Arabs at a time when they were living in tribes in desert lands. There was so much pride among these tribes that if, say, a slave from tribe A was killed by a person from tribe B, then retribution from the proud tribe A meant they would kill, say, ten of tribe B. When the Koran came, it said, "No, we won't do that. Take vengeance only on the killer." In this, Islam echoes the Judaic law of the Old Testament in its concept of qisas, the punishment fitting the crime, an eye for an eye.' So, far from being barbaric, Dr El Essawy sees such a law as civilizing society's impulse to seek excessive revenge.

Not so for the Quakers. Punishment for punishment's sake is not their vision. The Quakers, more properly called the Society of Friends, came into being as a Christian group in the religious turmoil of the seventeenth century. They have no creed, no liturgy, no clergy, not even an officiating minister. They come together in meeting houses for silent prayer, in total equality, in the most humble setting. Their pacifism stems from their belief that God is in all of us – therefore you must not destroy the divine in others.

David Gray, of the Society of Friends, explains the Quaker view:

'When we have offended, we need in some way to be able to make restitution to those we've offended against. Formal punishment can be one of those ways but only if it leaves room for communication. The death penalty certainly doesn't – it's a dead end – and frankly Quakers aren't interested in dead ends. I happen to think total pardon is also a sort of dead end. It says "go away, forget about it". And it seems to me that the Christian faith, let alone Quaker faith, is about forgiveness and restoration.'

It is this degree of compassion that impresses Keith Ward, now Regius Professor of Divinity at Oxford University, and one of the Church of England's foremost theologians:

'Basically what Quakers do is take Jesus's teaching in the Sermon on the Mount pretty straightforwardly. So when Jesus says, "If anyone hits you on the cheek, turn the other cheek, do not resist", they take that very literally. My own belief is that the Quakers have the best religion in the world but it seems to me that it will always be a minority faith. It requires so much of people, to be utterly non-vengeful, utterly compassionate at all times and never – although the law gives the right to vengeance – to insist on having it. No society could live by such principles. Once you're dealing with criminals and terrorists you're into a more classical Christian tradition, which, as with Islam, builds social principles on the basis of what will allow people to live together in a harmonious society.

'The fact is that retribution has its place in the Christian tradition and of course there are many Christians in Britain today who would say that we aren't retributive enough. Indeed, let me put a stronger argument: that if you don't believe in retribution, you are not actually honouring the responsibility and the freedom of the individual. If you say "someone has done this because they're sick" you take away responsibility from them. If you say this is the price you will pay if you do something evil, you give them responsibility. In a sense you can see that as honouring human freedom. So there is a serious argument for retribution. And in both the Old Testament and most of the Christian tradition, capital punishment is not wrong.'

So where did that leave Ruth and Ken Rockett, agonizing over the decision they had to make about Sally's killers? Back in Budleigh Salterton it soon became clear that each of the three options involved many qualifying considerations:

'Our immediate reaction was that we just wanted them to be pardoned, but not to go free. A total pardon would be complete nonsense. From what we knew, the terrorists are completely unrepentant, they say they have no regrets. These people are geared to go out and kill again. So we are responsible for other people who might be killed if they bombed again. They would be doing it on your permission, and you would therefore be a murderer yourself, would you not?'

So, no pardon.

The second option, blood money, sounds ancient and tribal. In the West it's known as compensation. After tragedies such as those at Lockerbie, Zeebrugge, King's Cross, bereaved families make claims against those who are legally responsible. How much they get is often determined by international agreement. Within Islamic tradition, compensation for a Muslim's murder was once fixed by law at 100 camels. Today there is instead a statutary sum, although there can be much bargaining over the final price. The families of the two Sudanese killed by the Khartoum bomb wanted to settle for blood money. The Rocketts rejected it:

'We think that Sally's life is not worth any finite sum of money, so we couldn't agree to it. We did have the thought that money might be taken from the organizers of the crime and put to good use. But for ourselves we couldn't accept money where Sally's death was concerned.'

And yet they hesitated.

'We understand one of the Sudanese killed was a waiter who was breadwinner for his family, and we heard the family were completely destitute. Obviously, if we say "no blood money" we don't want to commit his family to poverty.'

That left the third option – execution. Ruth and Ken's thinking about this was perhaps not as absolute as their Quaker daughter's might have been. Ruth tried to draw up her own equation:

'We realized that Sally was going to do certain things in the world, and that's been cut short. It's a great pity the world has lost that. There are people today who say we should have capital punishment back for certain crimes and I have given some thought to whether terrorism is one of those crimes. But I find it almost impossible to think how I would feel about myself if I said "go ahead and kill them". I think in the end one can't terminate a life.'

The Rocketts decided to reject all three options.

'We stated we were satisfied with none of the three and that we'd prefer to have these people prevented by a term of imprisonment long enough to ensure that they never did any such thing again. But the choice of imprisonment was the one option the court could not offer. In the event, the situation was left open, with the Sudanese judge having the right, in the interests of safety, to finally rule for imprisonment.'

Since sending their reply to the Sudanese Embassy, the Rocketts have heard nothing. What happened to their daughter's killer remains unknown to them. Whether the family of the Sudanese waiter received blood money is also a mystery.

This remarkable story highlights a philosophical quandary of our times – relative values, relative as between different cultures and relative in terms of our own internal moral landscape. The prevailing liberal view is born of eighteenth-century enlightenment which brought rationalism into matters of ethics and morality and unseated the absolutism of church teaching, divine revelation, church tradition and the divine right of kings.

The separation of religion from politics had begun. Drawing its strength from both the enlightenment and the Judaeo-Christian tradition of individual conscience – whose ideals Muslims share – liberal humanism became the basis of the prevailing secular world view. In political terms, liberal democracy was seen as the enlightened way forward, superior to other political systems – dictatorships, for example, or self-perpetuating oligarchies.

Today, in a time of multiculturalism and plurality, such a view is viewed by many as imperialistic and out of date. We live, it is argued, in a world of diverse cultures and who are we, of the white man's Europe, whose exploits caused so much devastation and anguish to the cultures we colonized, to claim the superiority of our own value system above others? This view is held with particular vigour by religious fundamentalists, who see in the abandoning of God's law the start of the collapse of values in the West.

By the 1960s, many people assumed that religion had lost its force. The Church of England – in espousing biblical scholarship that challenged or dismantled a number of traditional Christian beliefs – was seen to have secularized itself, some would say sold out. By the 1980s, however, religion was back on the world stage in a new and powerful form: fundamentalism. In his book *The Revenge of God: The Resurgence of Islam, Christianity and Judaism in the Modern World*, Gilles Kepel charts how fundamentalists of all faiths are seeking to abandon the secular world and draw their communities back into theocratic states. This is as true of ultra-Orthodox Jews in Israel (insisting their airline El-Al does not fly on the Sabbath) as it is of the Christian Right in America (seeking to sway the choice of presidential candidates), and Islamic countries (who are increasingly giving their religious Sharia the force of law).

All these movements reject the secular state and its values as a failure. Dr El Essawy again, speaking of cultural values prevailing in Britain:

'You make the laws you think are merciful, but have we got mercy, have we got justice? The answer is no. You can't walk the streets at night and feel safe. Is that stability or security? Is this a great civilization that we're building with our secular law? I think we should re-examine the divine law.'

The divine law is absolute and admits of no human amelioration. It also has a chilling clarity. Dr El Essawy defends to me the penalty in some Islamic countries of amputating a thief's hand:

'If a surgeon removes an organ because that part is diseased and it's going to harm the rest of the body, then that action is not barbaric at all, it's a very merciful action. That is how we should look at punishment. They are protecting the entire body from a diseased part, lest it be overwhelmed by it.'

In countries where fundamentalism holds power, the values of secular humanism and its liberal political outlook are rejected. Sudan is such a country. There is no liberal tolerance, no pluralism, no multiculturalism. Apostasy is punished by death. Those with other cultural backgrounds – businessmen, embassies – are constrained to live as far as possible by Muslim values. In 1993 the Right Reverend Peter el-Birish, suffragan to the Anglican Bishop of Khartoum, was sentenced to a public flogging for committing adultery. He received eighty lashes to the back of the legs and upper torso.

This clash of value systems poses a major dilemma for liberal societies, of which the options presented by Sudan to Ruth and Ken Rockett were a small example. How can we continue to uphold our non-judgemental belief in the plurality of value systems, when such a philosophy calls on us to recognize, in parallel with our own, political and ethical systems which consistently challenge and seek to subvert that very liberal tolerance we proclaim?

In odd, oblique ways these conflicts have emerged as we have made other *Heart of the Matter* programmes.

On one occasion one of our researchers, herself a Muslim, was sent to Birmingham to investigate on our behalf the existence and extent of arranged marriages by Asian families. She came back with plentiful information but refused to put it at the service of the programme: 'I share many of their values,' she declared. 'Why should I turn them over to be criticized by white liberals who don't even have a commitment to their own religion?'

Again, when we were making a programme about genital mutilation – widely and inaccurately called 'female circumcision' – I went to interview the Nigerian novelist Buchi Emecheta, putting to her the barbarity and brutality of the ancient custom still extensive across the broad central belt of Africa. She rounded on me with fury for denying her culture the right to its own practices, and mocked, with her broad laughter, what she called my deplorable imperial superiority. Then, in the spirit of mutual tolerance, she feasted us on wine and mince pies. It was Christmas after all!

Our answer to such challenges is always the same. Let us set before our viewers the full facts and the divergent views of different cultures, as far as we can ascertain them, and give the audience the freedom to make their own individual judgement, that individual judgement being the essence of the liberal values we seek to uphold.

Climate of Hate

These are the stories of two men: one who was hated and one who incited hatred. They appeared in different programmes but were each the focus around which we set out the reality and the arguments that surround racial hatred. Since I began reporting moral dilemmas in 1988, one of the most significant developments in global culture has been the intensification of hatred between different groups of people. Sometimes that hatred is of whites for blacks, as exemplified in Britain by the rise of the British National Party, with their election slogan 'Rights for Whites'. Sometimes it is between ethnic groups, as in the former Yugoslavia, where petty demagogues have stirrred up hatred between different races who were previously living harmoniously together.

The point about Bosnia Hercegovina is not that it has always been a hotbed of racial hatred but that, while holding the memory of their different histories in mind, Muslims, Christian (Orthodox and Catholic) Serbians, Croats and Bosnians had been able to live in peace with each other. Such old hatreds as there were, were triggered into action by deliberate political manipulation.

Sometimes the hatred has been of the host nation for its immigrants. In Germany, Turkish workers established there for decades have been finding their homes attacked and burned and their lives threatened. Again, self-seeking neo-Nazi groups have managed to establish an effective network among the young and disaffected, despite German laws that ban the swastika and make it an offence to deny the Holocaust.

There is a tide of hatred running in the world. It always begins locally: the claiming or reclaiming of a boundary here or a frontier there; the desire of one tribe to gain power over another. And, while it takes leaders to identify grievances and formulate policies and slogans, it is a troubling fact that people seem willing to respond eagerly to simplistic political ideologies and the emotional appeal of banners and rhetoric.

Heart of the Matter has on several occasions examined what it is that brings hatred so easily into being. Is there some vast well of untapped evil within us all that, in response to the right call, will deliver even the most apparently sane individual up to a life of barbarity and cruelty? I hope not. But I fear the power of demagogues and their ideologies to unleash powerful feelings and then distort them: the terrorism of Islamic fundamentalists; the fanaticism of American anti-abortionists who kill doctors; the mutual loathing of Hutu and Tutsi – all attest to the power of rhetoric and rumour to stir hatred into bloodshed. Searching out the roots of why this happens is one of the most important tasks the civilized world can undertake. Meanwhile *Heart of the Matter* tries to bear witness to what is going on.

Kenneth Ighavbota is a Government statistic, a victim of racial hatred. Between 1988 and 1992 there was in Britain a 77 per cent increase in racial incidents. These are not the heated claims of political pressure groups or lobbies. They are ice-cold official police and Home Office figures. Things are getting worse, not only for black and Asian communities but for Britain's Jews, who find their cemeteries daubed with swastikas and their students threatened. So great is the problem, the idea is now being widely canvassed that crimes of violence motivated by racial hatred should carry a heavier penalty than others. In June 1994 the House of Lords debated an amendment to the Criminal Justice Bill to that effect. Its intention was to send out a clear message that our society will not tolerate racial bigotry. But might such legislation actually inflame conflict? Would it be practical? And what about violent crimes against the old, against women, against gays? Where would it stop? *Heart of the Matter* set out to weigh up the arguments.

Which is how I came to be visiting a tower block in Deptford on a wet afternoon in May 1994. The River Thames curves wide and slow below Ken and Patricia Ighavbota's sixth-floor flat. The day is grey and drab and the wind cuts round the side of the building, biting into exposed flesh. Even so, as I huddle indoors, I have just time to see how, given sunshine and trees in leaf, this would clearly be a very attractive corner of South-East London. The flats, though tiny, aren't run down, and Pat and Ken's windows look out at the curving silver loop of water below.

We have come to hear Ken's story. But that won't be easy. Ken, who has been badly beaten up twice by white youths shouting racial insults, now suffers chronic anxiety. He's fearful even to go out and has withdrawn into himself, scarcely sleeping, eating or taking interest in anything. His distracted wife, Pat, takes him regularly to see a psychiatrist at a mental health clinic. Nonetheless, Ken has agreed to talk to us, braving the formidable array of television equipment and, worse, a number of white men of whom he now lives in fear. It will clearly be an ordeal for him.

Ken comes into the room gently, moving slowly, not smiling. He is very tall and, were his face mobile and animated, good-looking. But his expression is dead, his eyes lifeless, the muscles of his face still. They have been still for a long time. Even as he tells his story, his quiet voice has no modulation, no passion. Somehow that makes it even more poignant.

Ken joined London Transport in the 1980s:

'My ambition was to be a train driver. It was my life, you know. I had to work my way up from the start by becoming a leading railman, then a guard, and then a driver. I thought it was a challenge. And I was almost there – I was just going on a course to become a full-time train driver.'

The second racial attack ended those ambitions. But already, four years earlier, Ken had been the victim of a major assault:

'I was on Tower Hill Underground Station, doing my job. I was a leading railman working on the barriers, collecting tickets, when, at about seven o'clock in the evening, a train pulled into the platform downstairs. I heard it. Many passengers came up, going through the ticket barriers. Everyone left the ticket barrier except one man. I went to assist him. He said his ticket was jammed in the machine. I opened the machine up, got his ticket out and found it was the wrong ticket. I told him so and he got really mad, wanted me to let him out. I said to him, you have to go and pay your excess fare. And he got really vulgar, you know. He spat at me. He was calling me names. But I got on my radio to try to call my station supervisor. And when he saw that, he jumped on me, punched me. Then it wasn't long till some of his friends outside the barrier jumped over. And they all beat me up. Five of them... White? Yeah. I didn't insult them, I didn't do nothing. I was just doing my job.'

For Ken his job was everything. It's hard to imagine anyone being so happy to work for London Underground. But he was. And that's why he went on:

'You see, I loved my job so much, I tried not to let things like that get to me. I thought the best thing was to go back to work the following day. But it was very bad and I collapsed at work. My manager arranged for someone to bring me back home and my wife took me to hospital.'

Ken was off work some three months but always eager to get back:

'I thought the best way to get over this was to go back to the same environment and then maybe that would help my wounds heal quicker. But I still found it difficult. So after a couple of months I applied to go on the trains, to become a guard – I passed the exam and was posted to Morden on the Northern Line. Then I promised myself I was going to be prepared. After the first assault I was going to be prepared for the next time it would happen. I would be very prepared next time.'

In the event it made little difference:

'On 6th December last year, I was doing my job as a guard. My train pulled into the southbound platform. I opened the passenger doors, the passengers got on and off, and I closed the doors. I was just about to give my driver the starting signal when I saw this white man running beside the train towards me. I stopped. I didn't give my driver the starting signal because I felt here was another passenger needing my assistance. Maybe he needed my help or wanted to report to me an incident. He ran straight towards me. I was standing by my guard stool. And he just pushed me. Really hard. I slipped and fell back into the train and hit my head. Then this guy jumped on me. At this point some of the passengers had got up and were screaming at him. He jumped on me, he stepped on my testicles and it was really painful. One of the passengers came to help me to my feet. The man couldn't take the screaming from the other passengers. He ran back out, through my guard's door, and this time he knocked me down for a second time. And this time the pain was really unbearable. I stayed down.'

Finally Ken was on his feet again and still struggling – even then – to do his job correctly.

'I thought to myself, I must try the best I can to take this train a couple of stops, to Camden Town where I can get relief. Because if I stepped off the train at that point there would have been serious delays. I felt, even if I have to crawl, I will get this train to Camden Town, which I did.'

Ken has delivered this fluent account completely deadpan, emotionless. On the sofa beside him sits his wife Pat, holding his hand and clearly moved. The attacks on him have ruined both their lives.

'I keep thinking it will happen again. I used to trust everyone but now I find it very difficult. At first I found it difficult even to trust my doctor... I don't go out any more. I get very frightened. I think someone's going to jump on me. I feel very, very insecure. I could have been killed that day, you know.'

The assaults have ruined his beloved career. 'I could have been training now as a driver... my initial ambition. That hope of mine has been dashed to pieces now.' His marriage, too, is at risk: 'The relationship between myself and my wife has gone. A complete standstill. She has threatened to leave me several times. Only my doctor has kept my wife beside me.' He says it without feeling. But it is clear that somewhere he feels it very much.

Pat's feelings are brimming from her eyes. 'I just want my husband back, I just want him to be the same person. That's why I keep on trying.' Her account of how they used to be, reveals to us an unimagined Ken:

'He was an outgoing type. He liked swimming a lot, went to the gym three times a week, played snooker. He loved music before. Now it doesn't interest him. I don't sleep with him any more, because I don't want to upset him. He wants to be left alone.

'After the second assault he couldn't sleep at night. He was waking up, having nightmares. He was carrying a knife everywhere. He wanted to be prepared, to protect himself. He won't eat. He won't let me open the door for anybody. He just wants to be in the bedroom all day. No television, no music, no nothing. He turned to me and said, "I'm scared. I don't know what to do, I'm scared."'

Now, lurking unspoken between them, is the risk of suicide.

'I've had to give up my job to take care of my husband. I couldn't leave him alone indoors. When I wake at night, he's downstairs, standing by the window. Now when I go to bed I lock the entrance door because I don't know what he's going to do.'

This total and private tragedy should not have happened. But does it warrant making crimes involving racial hatred subject to extra punishment? The first problem would be establishing racial motive. Ken's psychiatrist, Dr Lipsedge, who has made a special study of the psychological effects of racial crime, has no doubts:

'If you're living in a climate where you may be singled out, not because of any personal or moral quality within yourself, but because of the colour of your skin which is unchangeable, it increases your sense of vulnerability. It would be unrealistic to prosecute everybody who says unpleasant things. But it's when there's a clear link between verbal abuse and physical violence that the person will be psychologically damaged in the way that Ken is.'

But surely white people on the Underground get attacked too?

'Yes, but as you're being hit and kicked and spat on, being also called a nigger and told to go home is a psychological assault which has profoundly damaging effects, which white people being attacked by white people simply do not experience.'

There is a huge risk attendant on the idea of imposing heavier punishments for racially motivated crimes: the risk of exacerbating racial hatred still further by such discriminatory sentencing. Brenda Almond, of the Department of Moral and Social Philosophy at Hull University, feels it would do more harm than good:

'Our legal traditions in this country have not concerned themselves with people's thoughts, but with people's actions. I think we should be very careful about policing thoughts. It would certainly increase racial feeling because in every violent crime the first thing people would have to look at would be: "were different races involved?" Then the prosecution would have to try and unearth evidence for a racial motive. That would seem to me to produce quite the reverse effect from that intended by the good motives that no doubt lie behind such a proposal.'

Unmesh Desai, a lawyer who has spent fourteen years in London's East End and sixteen years involved with the anti-racist movement, agrees with Brenda Almond. 'It's working-class communities who suffer the brunt of racist attacks. They have to live side by side with white people in inner-city ghettos. Unfortunately a section of the white working-class sees black people as a scapegoat.' He believes hate crime laws would only fuel their resentment. 'What victims of racist attacks want is the existing laws prosecuted effectively: they want firmer sentences. They are not out there clamouring for special extra penalties.'

The question of equality before the law is a difficult one. Is it properly served if some citizens live in fear simply because they're black or gay or Jewish? Surely not. And yet would added penalties for hatred end up creating a hierarchy of punishments, meted out according to the colour or race of the victim? And where would this leave the little old lady, who happens to be white, hit over the head for a few pence? Would it be fair to say a crime against her merits a lighter sentence than the same crime committed against others? What matters is to understand, identify and defuse the motives behind all aggressive crime and those whose statements incite it. That's how I came to be talking to David Bruce.

Dave Bruce is a force to be reckoned with, a force on the edge of

British politics that we would be ill-advised to ignore. Dave is a racist, a long-standing member and official of the British National Party (BNP). He's been involved in right-wing politics since the 1960s.

'We are racist because we believe in standing up for our own people. We're not going to shy away from that. It just shows the potential popularity of our views, that governments have had to pass three or four Race Relations Acts to suppress our point of view'.

In June 1993, 2000 people marched in Croydon against racism and racist crimes. The focus of their concern was the BNP: they were calling for it to be banned, along with the militant group Combat 18 (so named because the first and eighth letters of the alphabet, A and H, are the initials of Adolf Hitler). Ken Livingstone explained why:

'Even if they don't actually urge people to go out and kill specific individuals, they create the climate in which people are triggered to go and do that. So there's got to be a much firmer response from Government.'

If society feels it needs Race Relations Acts and might even need to ban a political party to suppress certain ideas, then *Heart of the Matter* felt it was worth examining those ideas and the policies they give rise to, in detail. Our programme was called 'Freedom to Hate'. So I spent a day with David Bruce, listening to his story and how the BNP wants to change the country. In the event, it wasn't detail I got so much as repetition. But repetition is a powerful campaigning technique, especially on a one-issue platform. What became clear was that David Bruce's political point of view had been shaped almost entirely by the bitterness of personal experience.

'I was first attracted to the BNP because of their policy on immigration. I saw the change that took place in Willesden as a result of mass immigration.' It's clear from the start that, in referring to immigrants, Dave means non-whites, blacks and Asians mainly, though he would probably oppose Turks, too, and even have doubts about swarthier Latins. But he has no problem with descendants of white settlers in India, Rhodesia (his word) or Hong Kong 'returning' here, seeing them as 'our own people'.

'Willesden was a rough, tough, white working-class area, then we had this influx of immigrants. There was no hostility at first. Curiosity. Then more and more arrived and attitudes changed.' Dave is in his fifties now and he is speaking of the post-war years. The political climate was different then. The British had just won the war. At that time it was acknowledged, even celebrated, that the term 'British' (defined by the Empire) encompassed West Indians, all the peoples of the Indian sub-continent, as well as those of Britain's African colonies and large chunks of the Far East. They were proud of their part in Britain's victory, and many were eager to come and work here. With post-war reconstruction underway, uncontrolled immigration provided a source of much-needed labour. It was also a time of social transformation, with the Labour Government funding huge public housing developments, and council tenants moving out into improved housing and new towns. Dave's family missed out on these opportunities.

'Where I used to live, 206 Chapter Road, upstairs was a family with about five kids. We were on the ground floor with three.' Clearly they were eligible for rehousing. It didn't happen:

'When my father was alive we went on the council list for housing, to be moved out to one of the new towns. We got to about fourth or fifth place. So we were all due to get a council house somewhere like Hemel Hempstead or Stevenage. Then my father died: we went straight down to the bottom of the list. If my old man had stayed alive another two years...'

Suddenly the speculation turns to pain. 'My old man had a bloody awful life!'

Dave was refused even the modest improvements enjoyed by others in Chapter Road. It rankled:

'When you see over a period of years your friends, your neighbours and people you know going, it does affect you. Most of my friends and neighbours went: they moved to Harrow, to Wembley, places like that. In a street where once upon a time I knew everybody – suddenly I was surrounded by strangers.'

We take Dave Bruce back to Chapter Road to see it as it is now. Red brick, bow-fronted houses, solid nineteenth-century villas, face on to a tree-lined street. The corner shop is colourful and bustling, run by Asians. I'm eager to hear why this street, where he lived some twenty-five years before, embodies memories of such happiness for him, memories so intense that he feels paradise was lost when it changed. Are his politics rooted in something as powerful as a sense of a childhood betrayed? As we stroll up and down the summer pavement in the early evening heat, heads are thrust from windows, groups of boys, idling, take an interest in the filming. A young woman with a child tends a windowbox brimming with geraniums. They are all black.

'At this time of night when I was a kid, there'd be people going up and down, going into shops, talking, doing things. Now it's nothing. It's nothing.' What had once been a little row of shops was indeed boarded up. Dave sighed with the nostalgia of it all – the names came back to him with the clarity of childhood:

'That was a bootmender's... There was an upholsterer's there... Arthur Osman's shop sold ice lollies... The Williams' had a very thriving fish and chip shop... That was a wet fish shop over there. We had a bakery too. Old Tom, the greengrocer's. I always remember those days, I remember the pomegranates. We'd sit around spitting the pips out for hours.'

Which of us, I wonder, who've been sent out shopping by busy mothers, do not think nostalgically of chest-high counters, the buying of sugar in blue bags, and lumps of cheese cut with a wire. I can offer up a litany of such shop names myself: Claytons, the grocer's; Leathers, the corner shop; and the Co-op store where on pain of punishment I must not forget our dividend number. I remember it still. The fact that they have all gone – swept aside by supermarkets, changed lifestyles, new eating habits – still gives me a pang of regret for passed times. But it has not fuelled a political hatred for such changes. Nor do I attribute such transformation to a single cause. Of course, it's true life opened up its opportunities to me; to move away, to travel, to 'better myself'. But if it is also true that the BNP attracts no-hopers, then it's time someone addressed those disappointed hopes. For the disappointments continued. Dave attributes his failure to get a job on London Transport to the immigrants:

'I went for a job on London Transport three times and three times I got rejected... They don't give you a reason. I can only guess that when I went for a job – I'd had about five or six jobs by that time – they might have thought, "Well, you're not going to stick to this job either." But how do they know? It might be just the job I was looking for.

'What is actually galling is that I put my full record down and somebody comes across from the West Indies, or Asia, who has basically no track record at all, no job record, and he gets the job and I don't.'

By the 1960s Dave Bruce was involved with right-wing politics, and today supports the BNP policy 'Stop Immigration, Start Repatriation'.

'I remember my town, my area, my country as very much a white nation. As far as I'm concerned, that country, that area, that street, I don't relate to any more. All right. Put it down to nostalgia: but is it wrong to wish that things were as they were as a kid?'

'You can't turn the clock back, can you?'

'We intend to try. It's not going to happen overnight. Nobody's suggesting that the BNP will come to power on Monday and by the end of the week every immigrant in this country will be gone. It's got to be a gradual process. What's going to happen is you get two or three MPs selected, then a few more. Now I think the Asian community, which is very astute when it comes to business matters, will say to themselves, "If this escalates, we don't have a future here," and they'll make plans to go back home before the British National Party actually take power.'

And if they don't?

'Their rights will be progressively withdrawn, and eventually British people [meaning whites] will progressively replace them in their jobs. We have three and a half million unemployed. It cannot be beyond the wit of this country to train people to take their jobs. And those people who have worked in hospitals, schools, transport over here – obviously they'll benefit the countries they're returning to.'

The Asian corner shops and newsagents will have to go, although 'adequate compensation will have to be paid. But it's a price we're prepared to pay. Also we're quite prepared to continue aid to India and even increase that aid to help them accommodate immigrants returning from Great Britain.'

'But supposing...?' I persist, hoping the absurdity of his proposals will become apparent, '... supposing compulsory repatriation triggered a parallel repatriation of white settlers to Britain?'

'I think that would be a good price to pay. But in practical terms it won't happen. Those particular people are needed in other countries, for the benefit of the countries themselves. Let's suppose every white man left South Africa. What would happen to South Africa?'

I try another approach. 'Many blacks and Asians were born here, educated in schools here: aren't they part of our society?'

'You argue that because they're born here they're British. I would argue against. Suppose your parents happened to work in India and you were born in India, would you regard yourself as Indian? If you were out in a bazaar somewhere in India – Calcutta, Delhi – and you had a row with a shopkeeper and he told you to go home, go back to England where you belonged and you said, "I was born here, I'm as Indian as you are," he'd either fall about laughing or probably belt you on the head.'

'Have you been to India?'

'No.'

It would be easy to dismiss Dave's simplistic political outlook. He confuses race with nationality or citizenship. He even gets that wrong: are we an Anglo-Saxon or Celtic people? Well, which? He disregards Britain's history as an imperial power whose objective was to make peoples of many countries subjects of the Crown and in so doing grant them citizenship. Over-simplified, one-issue conflicts have an increasing appeal in a country where major parties overlap in their efforts to woo the middle ground. The BNP fielded thirteen candidates at the last election. At a council election on the Isle of Dogs in 1993, the BNP polled nearly 20 per cent of the vote. They may not be destined for power but they keep the Tories up to the mark on immigration control, hearing their own voice in Winston Churchill's remarks on immigration, Lord Tebbit's comments about who you cheer on in Test Matches, even John Major talking about 'England's country lanes'. According to Dave, 'Margaret Thatcher virtually included National Front policies on immigration to get herself into power.'

He gets distinctly more belligerent when I ask about BNP activities in the East End. Surely marching, proclaiming as they do 'Rights for Whites', has escalated the violence? He denies it entirely – and then concedes almost immediately:

'What happens at our rallies, where there's opposition from the Left, the violence, the aggravation and the threats always come from them. If you say we're aggressive, I'll point out that our young men are not the sort of people to stand by and let themselves be walked over. If they get involved with reds and the reds come off worse that's their hard luck. But when the reverse happens and our people are attacked we don't go whinging about it. We accept it's part and parcel of what we're involved in. When reds attack us, our boys will defend themselves as best they can.'

When I suggest that his party could be banned, Dave – who quite happily contemplates the idea of using physical force to drive blacks and Asians from these shores – is outraged. But he also takes comfort: 'You don't ban a political party if you're not worried about it. It would mean this government is weak and frightened of our potential.'

The whole question of banning a political party is a very difficult one for a liberal society. Clearly freedom of speech doesn't mean freedom to say anything at all. The law constrains our right to speak libel, blasphemy, obscenity, official secrets, to incite to racial hatred or to cause a breach of the peace. The Public Order Acts declared: 'A person who publishes or distributes written material which is threatening, abusive or insulting is guilty of an offence if he intends thereby to stir up racial hatred or racial hatred is likely to be stirred up thereby.' In 1986 John Tyndall, leader of the BNP, served six months for just such an offence. The prosecution of laws already on the statute book should indicate conclusively that hatred and incitement to racial crimes will not be tolerated. But this message is not going out, perhaps because not enough prosecutions are brought.

Banning a political party damages democracy itself. Indeed, democracy is based on balancing extremely distasteful views with the regular and effective expression of moderate counter-views. But when I seek to debate with Dave Bruce the point at which he would feel banning a party was justified, the whole hinterland of his political opinions is revealed:

'If a Nazi party said it was against Jews and approved of Hitler, should it be banned?'

'I don't think any party should be banned, whatever its views.'

'Not the Nazi Party?'

'Not any party. I wouldn't ban the Communist Party.'

'Even a party that *championed* genocide?'

'Genocide is obviously a terrible thing. But a political party that stood up on a platform and said, "We want to wipe out half the world", how far would they get?'

'How far they would get' is exactly what concerns us. Certainly too far for the Bosnians, Croats and Serbs, and the Tutsis of Rwanda. The way David Bruce shrugs off the notion of genocide suggests either wilful ignorance or a callous disregard for the dangers that lurk beyond his yearning for a white Britain. 'Ethnic cleansing' might easily become a BNP slogan. Nonetheless I persist.

'But this country fought the Nazis because of their policies. How do you feel about that?'

'I regret the last war. It's a war we should not have got involved in. I think with hindsight we could have avoided that war. All the last two wars have done is leave millions of Europeans dead on the battlefields of Europe. But once the war was engaged, my attitude is "my country right or wrong".'

It is frequently proclaimed in BNP literature that the Holocaust was a myth. Such literature is rarely prosecuted. Bhiku Parekh, Professor of Politics at Hull University and formerly Deputy Director of the Commission for Racial Equality, thinks the liberal conscience is too squeamish about not wanting to ban the BNP:

'There is a mythology among liberals that takes two forms. First, that if you ban an opinion, you'll drive it underground. And second, you'll then turn such people into martyrs. Neither form applies. After all, we are all constantly driving ugly impulses underground in our own heads, and an individual can never become a martyr unless the thought for which he stands has moral dignity.'

When our programme was transmitted, a number of people, even some of our own unit, were critical of our giving the BNP so much coverage, indeed any coverage at all. I don't regret it for a moment. If we are to defuse in time these forces moving in our community to destabilize it and cause injury and grief, we must understand the motives and resentments that fuel them. Talking to Dave Bruce taught me a good deal about the trigger points of discontent.

A society going through change cannot afford to neglect those who stand to lose by that change – in housing, in jobs – without expecting them to be bitter and angry. That bitterness is a fertile recruiting ground for no-hopers, who seethe with resentment at any apparent 'favours' instituted to safeguard the rights of minorities. That bitterness also marks out exactly where trouble will arise in the future. Immigrants to this country are here by right of British passports, their children by right of birth. Not surprisingly, such immigrants build up communities together, sharing an initial strangeness to British ways, and later a common background in race, religion and culture. These communities seek to live by British ways, but they are also seeking more and more to cherish their own ethnic identities. The days of integrating into some amorphous melting pot are over. The vigorous identities of minority groups can cause social discord. What happens when Asian girls, expected to observe the tradition of arranged marriages, fall in love outside their own circle? How are children, brought up in Muslim schools to believe in the strict tenets of the Koran, to relate those values to the secular world around them? France's attempts to ban Islamic students from wearing the scarf have prompted riots. The careful balancing of special interests within the greater good is an ever-shifting complex of tensions. Those tensions are with us for the future. Dave Bruce has put me on notice that there are people actively seeking to exacerbate them.

After the programme was transmitted, I received a letter headed in gold – 'Der Recht Weg, ist Der Richtige Weg' (The Right Wing way is the right way) – and carrying an exhortation 'Love the White Race'. 'We are a Nordic tribe and Nordic people are white.' The letter came from Greenford; the head office address was Munich.

But there is hope at the end of this unhappy chapter. It comes in the form of a Boston police officer. Deputy Superintendent William Johnston looks as you'd expect a Boston cop to look – big and brawny, with a goodly girth and the broad jovial face of a Boston Irishman. He has been in the Boston force for many years but more recently has headed up the Boston Community Disorders Unit, a department set up in 1978 to deal specifically with hate crimes. The CDU now has twelve full-time investigators, its own suite of offices in the police building, and the backing and resources of a city shattered by race riots in the 1970s when Boston schools were forcibly integrated and trouble spilled out across the city. Shocked by what could happen in one of the East Coast's most decorous cities (Harvard University is just up river, downtown exudes a leafy affluence) the city authorities resolved to take strong action. They went in to fight for the victims of violence, and Bill Johnston's department has been doing so ever since. There are lessons here for many of Britain's city police. I flew into Boston to see how the CDU operates.

Americans are articulate people, and Bill Johnston is a more fluent talker than any police spokesman has a right to be. He lectures on this subject right across the States and his office walls are patchworked with civic awards and gratitude – so the sound bites come easily and, because he cares, they carry conviction rather than glibness. But *Heart of the Matter* digs deeper than first exchanges. Gradually Bill relaxes and begins to speak less as he might to a city dinner and more as a man among colleagues.

'You know when I just arrived at this unit, and people came in saying "that man called me a nigger", or "this man called me a gook", I said to myself, "Jesus, compared to what's happening in the rest of the city – with the homicides and the rapes – they want Billy Johnston to investigate name-calling?" I didn't understand all the whining and crying over these mickey mouse crimes. But dealing with these crimes – not just as a police officer but as a man – I've found them absolutely devastating. And the response of the police at the start was wrong. They questioned the victim: "Well, what did you think when you moved there? What were you doing in that community anyways? What were you doing in that neighbourhood?" They were making it the victim's fault! Now those questions are no longer asked. And one of the biggest changes in the last ten years, police officers on the street are now identifying hate incidents themselves. That is really major!'

Given the behaviour of some members of the Los Angeles Police Force, it certainly is. But Boston boasts that its deliberate policy of targeting hate crime has helped avoid the sort of catastrophe that blew up in Los Angeles.

So how does it work? A number of American states have had hate crime legislation for some ten years now. All such legislation focuses on the constitutional rights Americans enjoy under the law. In that sense it is a law that protects all those who might be attacked because of their difference from others.

'A lot of people still think these are special laws for special people. But the civil rights law belongs to all of us. "Please allow me to live in my home without someone breaking my windows." Is that a special law for special people? I don't believe so. "Please allow me access to church, to work, my child access to the playground without being assaulted or called names." Special laws for special people? No.'

But attacking buildings and people is against the law anyway?

'The unique thing about hate crime is you're targeted because of your difference. If I'm on the street and I get robbed, there's a whole lot of things I can do. I can say, "I won't go to that area, I'll make sure I have protection, I won't carry money" But if you're assaulted because of your difference, then you're carrying it around with you. Within our Massachusetts law, there's no one group singled out – by race, religion, sexual orientation. Its message is simply that you cannot violate the constitutional rights of another person. And every time we protect somebody else's rights we protect our own.'

Britain does not have such constitutional rights, so the merit of this universality doesn't apply here. Hate crime as proposed in Britain would be linked to racial attacks. In that sense it could be criticized as one law for one group, not for any other; whereas the American hate crime legislation protects not just racial groups, but gays and women.

Bill Johnston has his own memories of what being a group with a difference really means.

'I remember when I was working as a decoy, being robbed, the difference when I was robbed coming out of a straight bar and when I came out of a gay bar. From the gay bar there was always a beating as well. And when they were arrested – the question: "He's only a fag, what are you arresting me for?" As though fags are less than human. Now when I'm looking at these crimes, I ask "could this have happened if everyone was the same?" If the answer's "no", then there's a good chance it was a hate crime.'

That this law is greatly feared was demonstrated to us by a case then going forward. It concerned an incident in the Old Colony Housing Project in a run-down area of South Boston. Eighty-five per cent of public housing in Boston is for minorities. The scope for conflict is great and Irish Catholic traditions here are proud and fierce. A white girl, Patrice Russo, of just such an Irish Catholic background, had been going out with a Hispanic boy, Manuel Rodriguez. Her white friends didn't like it. By a blinding coincidence, when I went to visit them, *West Side Story* was being shown on television. They didn't see the parallels: perhaps only outsiders can.

On a February night a group of white youths who'd been drinking had gathered outside Patrice's flat and made trouble for the couple. When Manuel came out to protest he was hit by a bottle and sustained two minor cuts on his head. Patrice's mother called the police. When they arrived, so did the CDU. No waiting to follow up hate allegations until later. Immediate action is essential. It reinforces the confidence of the victims, and terrifies the attackers.

Michael O'Connell was one of sixteen boys arrested. He feels, with the CDU called in, he won't stand a chance:

'They're one-sided. They do what's politically correct. They're not interested in white rights being violated. Perhaps the city of Boston believes it will ease everybody's feelings, but we couldn't possibly get a fair trial in front of a judge now because he's out to do what the CDU think is right – just convict the white people to appease the minorities.'

Bill Johnston again:

'We can make the price of hate extremely high. When you're dealing with haters, you're dealing with cowards: they don't want to pay the price of hate. So we can make that price extremely high. Assault and battery with a dangerous weapon is a ten-year felony. Civil rights violation assault – that's also a ten-year felony.'

If he'd been found guilty, Michael might have ended up paying that high price.

'If I'm convicted, not only can I do time in jail, but if you have civil rights on your records, it's like being a leper, a social leper. You won't get jobs. I won't have the same opportunities as everyone else. I'll be blacklisted.'

That crowd of some twenty white boys may have a long time to regret piling on a single Hispanic. Billy Johnston speaks confidently of getting convictions. So, what sort of evidence turns an ordinary assault into a hate crime?

'Ninety per cent of our cases are brought through confessions. The decent people within those communities are going to come forward because they know the impact these crimes have. It isn't the use of words we're after: under the first Amendment you can say what you want. But nigger, wog, spick, tyke – those words help us to judge what follows. Such words show there might be more going on than straightforward assault and battery. Research has shown that with normal assault 7 per cent of victims need hospitalization. Where there's assault because of difference, 30 per cent of victims need hospitalization. There's that extra kick, extra punch, because of the difference. So they are different crimes. The real problem is racism, and if we keep on classifying these crimes as assault and battery, we're not addressing the root problem. In the event, fifteen boys admitted the harassment and accepted injunctions that put them on parole for up to three years. So the matter did not go to trial. Michael O'Connell is the exception. He persistently refused to admit to the crime and has now gone missing to avoid accepting the injunction. The police have, so far, not been able to trace him. And there the matter rests.'

I think back to Ken Ighavbota and the assaults he suffered, both fuelled by foul racial abuse. None of his attackers has ever been caught. Had they been, and had we had similar laws to Boston, they might be languishing a long time in jail.

In more reflective mood, Bill Johnston explains why he believes it is of the utmost importance to nip signs of racism in the bud:

'Let me tell you about haters. They start with words. They know that words can hurt, but words can't kill, but as cowards they step back and they wait. They wait to see what the reaction from the community is going to be. Is anybody doing anything, anybody saying anything? No. It escalates. Now it's assault and battery. Again, are the police investigating? Are they concerned, are they treating us as a threat? No. Is the media there? No. Now it's assault and battery with a dangerous weapon. At each point they wait to see what the response from the community is. Finally it escalates up to a point where someone dies. Now what do we as a society do? We point the finger and blame the hater. Yet at any point we could have said, "This will not be tolerated." In fact, it was us to blame.'

This analysis seems thoroughly plausible to me, the more so as it is delivered by a front-line Boston cop, not the usual image of radical political correctness in action. Bill Johnston drives me round the streets he knows, points out where families were harassed and then protected. He is immensely proud of the CDU and does it justice in terms of public relations. Even knowing that, I warm to his outlook and his commitment. He is genuinely optimistic in an area of human behaviour that gives little scope for hope. But he is a hands-on tough guy. His ideas are grounded in experience and fundamental good sense. He has Michael O'Connell and his cronies wondering what happened to their position as cocks of the walk. And while this no doubt makes them likely recruits to America's extremist Nationalist Movement, Boston's CDU is monitoring their activities as well.

In 1993 there were 276 hate crime incidents investigated in Boston. How many might there have been in London that same year? Between 1992 and 1994 Britain saw fourteen people murdered by killers who hated them for being black. Britain has not yet had an eruption like the one in Los Angeles. But we are incubating the causes. Perhaps it would be wise before it is too late to take at least some advice from that no-nonsense unit on the streets of Boston.

The Case for the Cree

There was no road to this place.The aircraft flew low over an endless wilderness of dark green trees laced through with the sparkle of water, great tracts of water, sweeping rivers linking mighty lakes. This is a terrain where water is as much part of the earth's surface as land. Indeed that is why I have come. This is North-West Quebec on Hudson Bay, to my eyes a remote and inhospitable land virtually empty of life.

It may have no road but it has two names. The sprawling village that meanders inland from the sweep of curving sand is known to its Inuit villagers as Kuujjuarapik and to the Cree Indians who live here as Whapmagoostui. This is a place where two native cultures co-exist. Each has its own language, its own school, its own style of housing. I am to see them at a moment in history set between their more independent, nomadic past and whatever the future holds that will make them more like people everywhere else, with, who knows, McDonalds and Marks and Spencer warming the inner and outer man.

As if Kuujjuarapik and Whapmagoostui were not enough, this modest settlement has two further names. It's Poste-de-la-Baleine to the French; and to the English, Great Whale. The first white people here were seventeenth-century traders coming to buy furs and skins from both the Inuit and the Cree. (Inuit is the proper name for Eskimos and means 'man' in their language. Eskimo is said to be a term of reproach, meaning 'eater of raw meat', applied to them by Algonquin Indians. It is falling out of use.) The early trading posts along Hudson Bay were only open in summer months and interfered little with the aboriginal hunter-gatherer way of life. Small native groups might congregate for a while round the homes of their summer visitors, but their traplines, their myths, their closeness to nature and the immense spaces they enjoyed, remained untouched. Today they are fighting for their heritage. It is why I have come.

As the plane descends from lowering skies towards the airport it is clear that the place already has the universal characteristics of a settlement on the brink of development: raw, uncoordinated and shambolic. There are power cables looped between buildings, haphazard clusters of houses, a few white specks along the shoreline that will make sense later, a corrugated iron roof or two. And beyond, and into infinite distance, the wilderness of northern Canada; inhospitable and monotonous.

As the plane reaches the runway I spot two tiny figures on the ground – indeed the only two people in sight – and they are jumping up and down, waving frantically. I recognize, beneath their woolly hats, our researcher and production assistant who went ahead by a week to search out people and facilities for our programme.

We spill into the arrival shed, our camera gear in shiny silver boxes. There are hugs and cries all round: that mix of relief and solidarity shared by all small groups who suddenly come together far from base. Only recently we were taking for granted the cushioned calm of centrally heated offices. Here we are cold and raw. We look like gaudily plumed birds in our new anoraks, gloves, hoods and boots.

I survey the crowded arrival area – corrugated walls, cement floor. There are other anoraks arriving but they are big burly men with beards, noisy large people come to work on the project that is transforming the area. And there are Indian faces, some with large noses, some with narrow Asiatic eyes. One old woman, very small, is sitting on a bench holding a child. On her tiny feet she is wearing delicate moccasins of stitched sealskin. They look neat and appropriate compared to the clumsy intrusion of so many boots. A Cree woman with long dark hair has a baby slung on her back in a threadbare tartan blanket. She and her friend are smoking.

This makeshift airport – one large shed, one runway along the edge of the sea – was built by the Canadian government at the height of the Cold War. It was one of the front-line air defences, ready to alert the world if the Russians ever headed over the Pole towards

America. Once a toehold had been established on Hudson Bay, the settlement grew. Through the metal door of the hangar lies the world of the Cree, the Inuit and Hydro Quebec.

But, as I landed in the Canadian wastes that morning, I had other things on my mind.

Back home, in a hospital bed in Stockport, my father was dying of cancer.

He was eighty-seven and had been living alone for all his twenty-eight years as a widower. He had collapsed at his home some six weeks earlier and been taken to hospital with pneumonia. I was summoned, not unduly alarmed at this point, for he had always enjoyed robust health. At the age of eighty-five he had bought himself a new car. He regularly played golf, nine rather than eighteen holes being his only concession to age. His was a spry even wilful character, not someone a child thinks of as frail and dependent. But suddenly now he was.

Prompt medical care, his own resilience and my own bedside prayers willing him to live had brought him through a hazardous twenty-four hours. After that a colourful tide of friends and family lapped around his bed, cheering on a recovery we thought was a matter of days away. I took books and tapes, regaled him with the plot against Gorbachev from his precious *Daily Telegraph*. But the recovery faltered, then stalled. He couldn't take his food. And his jaunty eye, sparkling with the old charm when golf club cronies and their pretty wives jollied and petted him, glazed tiredly when the tray came round. Did he know?

We never spoke directly of his dying. But we talked of what was happening in oblique language, hinting at shared knowledge. In the past, at other deaths, we had talked together of how it might be: the half-jovial 'It'll be my turn one of these days' and the more thoughtful 'Don't let them mess me around, will you, Joan?'

I had said then: 'Don't worry. I'll be there going through it with you.' And that moment had come.

He spoke of my work of which he was intensely proud. But his interest was vague, rambling. I was losing him. And for me there were practical matters to be decided. Because each series of six *Heart of the Matter* programmes is made within a period of twelve weeks, schedules are tight and hours are long. Filming is arranged that way so that topical issues of the day can easily be included. In September 1991 I had already embarked on the autumn series and the visit to Canada was pressing.

This remote area of North-East Canada was then at the centre of one of the biggest ever battles between on the one hand the forces of development and energy generation, and on the other the combined forces of conservation and aboriginal rights.

Quebec's boundaries were extended by law in 1912 when the Quebec government acknowledged its obligations to the native inhabitants of the James Bay Territory, an area of some 135 000 square miles, as much as 20 per cent of Quebec. James Bay itself is a huge curving inlet, on the south-eastern side of the greater Hudson Bay, and the Territory extends inland from along its eastern shore between the 49 and the 55 latitudes. The native peoples, Inuit and Cree, lived by a regular cycle of hunting, fishing and trapping, an ancient way of life which they had inherited and learnt from their forebears, an existence infinitely subtle in its understanding of the natural life around them.

In 1971 the Quebec government approved the development of the James Bay Territory's hydro-electrical potential. The biggest of the planned schemes, the La Grande Complex, would extend over a drainage basin covering some 68 000 square miles. The Great Whale project further north – the one we are concerned with – is smaller but still involved some 21 700 square miles.

Having mapped this great wilderness of lakes and rivers, they realized just how much electrical power it could generate. It has long been, and remains, a dream of the human race to find a source of energy that will not pollute, will not run out, will not involve the devious diplomacy of international politics, will not destroy existing cultures or peoples. Here, in the virtually empty wilderness of northern Canada, enough clean energy could be generated not just to meet the needs of Quebec but also to provide for its neighbour, the ever energy-greedy United States. It must have seemed a heady, exhilarating idea from the start.

But even in the early 1970s there were those who could foresee problems. The company – Hydro Quebec – confronted them head on, setting up agencies and funding projects. They talked of interdisciplinary research and ecological monitoring. They encouraged studies, shared costs, wrote papers, observed, measured and reported. They were strenuous in their efforts. They visited, explored, talked of environmental impact, and reminded themselves of those fifty-year-old obligations to 'native inhabitants'. Some of my fellow anoraks arriving that day in Great Whale may well have been such seekers after a solution. For a solution would be had.

In 1975 the go-ahead was given. The signing of the James Bay and Northern Quebec Agreement allowed the construction of the La Grande Complex to begin. This was to be the biggest hydro-electrical project the world had ever seen.

Very soon mankind would be dynamiting and re-routing, blasting and shaping some of the oldest rock on earth, dating back some 2.5 million years. The Canadian Shield is what remains of an ancient mountain complex worn down since the dawn of time by wind, water and ice. The going would be tough, the impact brutal.

By 1991, when I arrived with the *Heart of the Matter* team, the project had run into trouble at Great Whale where a groundswell of protest from Cree Indians was threatening to stop the building of a road. That 1975 Agreement had been significant for the Cree. They had profited directly: some 225 million dollars given to Cree and Inuit organizations as well as local bodies set up to provide them with education, healthcare and social services. Shrewdly, the Cree and Inuit turned these compensations to their own advantage, getting educated, sending their young people to Canadian and American colleges where they soon acquired the latest thinking in native politics.

They returned to make things sticky for Hydro Quebec.

So the white man's world and values had already infiltrated the area at every level. Their strategy for energy was in place, their agreements with natives had done much to buy off their objections, and the aboriginal peoples themselves, in accepting the money and compensating services, had accepted the standards of those making them. Where then was the surviving spirit of the Cree? They might be consulted but they also had to be persuaded. They might be compensated but they could also be bribed. This was a moral thicket for everyone. My own eagerness to tell this story was at its height when the phone call came, telling of my father's collapse.

I have my own dilemma.

I sit by his bed, holding the leathery hands in mine. I have loved this man for over fifty years and we are at the edge of parting. The burden is like lead on my heart.

I talk quietly with the doctor in the adjacent visitors' room. The provision of coffee and the reluctant start to the conversation signal alarm. But what is 'alarm' in a situation with death already in sight? I ask how long. The words stick in my throat, literally, so they come out huskily. 'No, not immediately. He'll probably live until Christmas.' It is now September. I decide to go to Canada.

I have made a bread and butter pudding, a particularly good one, rich in eggs and double cream. The offering is of far more significance than a supplement to hospital food. My father is forced to refuse it. Such are his impeccable manners, sustained even in the face of hospital indignities, that it pains him to turn aside my gift. 'I just can't, but thank you, thank you.' It is the last thing I give him. I leave the hospital desolate and pack for Hudson Bay.

It is only when I am on the plane that I realize I am taking him with me. A rich, somehow joyous melancholy has settled on me in which I feel in deep, almost continuous communion with him. I know the withering hulk of his many years is tossing among the sheets to find some comfort; but here on the plane his alert and enquiring spirit, deeply rooted in my own identity, is pulsing in my mind. I land, hugging my sadness to me.

As we set out for our first day's filming in Great Whale it instantly becomes clear who lives where. The Inuit houses are two storeys high, entered via an outside staircase to a door some 1.2 metres off the ground. The Cree houses are bungalows, spread in suburban rows across the bare sand. Cree houses, sand-coloured like the earth on which they nestle, are a neat, flat intrusion on the landscape. The Inuit houses, in contrast, have their top floors painted shrill red, bright cobalt blue. They stand resolute and tall in the thin clear air. Such racially distinctive housing shocks me at first. Haven't liberal values taught that there shall be no discrimination? Aren't we looking at housing apartheid here?

The explanation goes back into the very nature of each culture. The Inuit people come from the land to the north: barren rock, where only the most tenacious mosses lurk in the hollows. Theirs is a snow culture and when they took to settlements they lifted their houses above the snow. The Cree come from the land to the south, where the rock has enough soil to support spruce trees, abundant mosses and ferns, lichens and scrub. Their impulse is to live below the trees, within their environment rather than atop it.

But wait a minute! Didn't Indians traditionally live in wigwams and Eskimos in igloos? Whatever happened to them? The answer is simple. The Inuit I meet explain the igloos: they still build them occasionally, when they are out on trapping expeditions. But an ice house gives poor return for effort. It is hard labour cutting solid blocks of ice, and the houses don't last much more than twenty-four hours. Then you move on and build another, while your last residence simply melts back into the ground. What a perfect ecologically sound dwelling. What a nightmare for Inuit archaeology.

The Cree still build their wigwams; they're known as *mitshuaps*. They rise some 4.5 to 6 metres, a conical arrangement of up to thirty timber poles sheathed in skin or canvas. But now they stand in the spaces behind the bungalows, for all the world like ethnic garden furniture, an accessory without a role, the last remnants of Cree culture, reminding them of what was once raw, and rough and theirs.

I feel regret at the sight of them. Somehow I had hoped to find the Cree standing resolutely by their ancient way of life, making no compromises, conceding nothing. Admittedly they would have had to live in the raw wind, eat the meagre rations their skills gave them, enjoy no comforts, or medicines, the caresses of modern living. For us their stand would be romantic, emblematic of ancient values. But what would it be for them?

Robbie Masty heads a Cree family and strives to keep alive what he has learnt from his forebears. He is broadset, with hefty shoulders. He is at home in the wilderness. I interview him beside his *mitshuap*:

'Our Creator gave us this land to live on. Nothing more. He provided everything: the animals, the plants for our medicine. It's just like a garden. When we need something we just go out there. It doesn't cost us anything. And if our garden is lost, our culture will be lost too. This is important for us and for people to understand what we are. Every chance we have we spend time at our camps. That's the time when I start to teach my kids what it is to be an Indian: how to survive, how to use our own language and traditional ways of doing things.'

'I don't believe anybody owns the land here but the Creator. He gives it to us to live on and protect. White people do hunting for sport. But not us. We hunt to survive; to eat what we kill. We don't waste anything. White people, if they kill a caribou or a moose, they take the head off as a trophy. We don't do that.'

Just a few hundred yards from Robbie's bungalow and his *mitshuap*, his 'garden' is seriously threatened. The hydro-electric project involves diverting so much water that the average annual flow of the La Grande river has doubled since it began. In winter the flow is eight times as great.

Areas where Robbie once tracked and trapped, fished and fed, have flooded. And there is worse to come. For all their scientific research, Hydro Quebec misjudged the effect of one sudden and deadly consequence: mercury. When forest and vegetation is submerged it gives off methylmercury which enters the food chain. Mercury levels in fish in the area are already naturally high because of the nature of the rock. Even in lakes not affected by the hydro-electric scheme, mercury levels exceed those laid down by Canadian marketing standards. Along comes the scheme and makes things dramatically worse for those who depend on fish for their diet. The Cree are particularly badly affected because they fish inland, away from the vaster space of Hudson Bay. Some of them now go 50 or 60 miles further than their traditional routes to find fish, beyond the reach of all the threatened changes.

None of this was predicted when the construction got underway in the early 1970s. With all the technical know-how that went into the scheme, this major side effect was under-estimated. And there's nothing the aboriginal peoples can do about it. Except feel sore. Except feel that no one asked or cared, or took enough trouble, or worried. No wonder they are protesting.

Robbie still hankers after the traditional ways. And we are prepared to take the camera along with him. Around eleven o'clock at night, just as we are all settling into our timber beds in the rough-built single-storey timber hotel, a cry goes out along the corridor... 'The geese are flying, the geese are flying'. Stirring in my bed I sleepily imagine that I have wandered into a Chekhov play, and wake to the unhappy discovery that Robbie is rousing us all to go with him to hunt geese. This is the season of migration and goose is now on the Cree menu. I peep through my window into the total blackness. It is freezing cold, pouring with rain and gusting an icy wind. The party intend to travel on small all-terrain vehicles of amazing toughness, heading directly over the bumpy rocky surfaces towards their camps.

I call into play the excuse of every on-screen presenter faced with prolonged hours of discomfort: 'You won't be needing me in the shots, will you?' The director concedes that I may stay behind. I conceal my relief by cheering them vigorously on their way, running around in my flannel nightie taking snaps of everyone in the most preposterous assortment of weather-defying clothes. Then I sneak back guiltily to my warm bed and a Jilly Cooper novel about the antics of people in television. I feel I could add a chapter or two.

For almost twenty-four hours I have no work to do. Emma, the PA who's stayed behind too, comes with me on a long walk around the entire settlement. The wind chill factor is high, but the morning is bright. The red and blue Inuit houses line up along the shore. Were these sunny latitudes, these homes would be prized indeed for they command the broad sweep of Hudson Bay, white sand fringed by tough green grass.

Standing out from the green we see again the white specks I had spotted from the plane. As we approach the beach we identify some dozen scattered rectangles of white fencing, each about 2 metres square. I feel an uneasy stillness settle on me. I know what they will prove to be. Of course, I recognize them: they are graves. Inside each little picket fence there are garlands and wreaths of plastic flowers, gaudy and cheerful in this barren waste. These are not flowers and ferns from Robbie Masty's garden, or even the traditional way of making a grave. These flimsy flowers are cheap supermarket trash flown in by traders to meet a new need, a need they are creating to match their own values.

I read the dates on the small white crosses. Many are people in the prime of their years. I reflect on their end in this place that was their home, and the end that is nearing for my father back in England. Soon another grave will be at my feet.

Not far away we find a church. And here we discover that Christian missionaries first came to the area over a hundred years ago. Most of the Cree are Anglicans. But, having struggled to bring Christianity to the Cree in colonial times, many Canadian churchmen are now listening to the faiths and beliefs of aboriginal peoples. The Reverend Peter Hamel, who I meet later in Montreal, explains the support he now gives to the Cree cause:

'In Canada we're beginning to realize that the spirituality of aboriginal people has much to teach us about the Judaeo-Christian tradition. For example the aboriginal view of the land allows the land to rest. Now we have that idea in Leviticus; that people rest on the seventh day to allow the land to rejuvenate. But we've turned that round to signify only in human terms. Aboriginals think of the land and people as one. The aboriginals have lived in harmony with the natural world for thousands of years, and their whole life is integrated with the ecosystem, the habitats, the cycles of the year, of fish, of birds and it's out of their relationship to the natural world that their society has evolved. It's an understanding of life we long ago rejected in the interest of getting more material possessions.'

I think of those wreaths again and the ethnic garden furniture and decide that the Cree and the Inuit have lost much for some pretty tawdry gains.

Later that day a bedraggled band of hunters and programme-makers staggers back to base. Their city spirits are chastened after only twenty-four hours away. They tell of sleeping on hard rock in icy temperatures, of walking to hunt goose, then seeing their booty cooked slowly over a wood fire that filled the *mitshuap* with smoke. They speak of hunger barely satisfied and the ordeal of driving full tilt across the rocky landscape. This is the only glimpse we get of the harshness of Indian life as it once was everywhere, and as it survives in the occasional excursions made by Indians now gathered in settlements and living lives more Canadian than Cree. Conditions in these latitudes can be very hard indeed, well beyond the capacity of civilization-softened folk to tolerate.

But there is surprising comfort at hand. The only other hotel around, the Auberge Sinittavik, has a chef to grace the most starred of restaurants. Indeed, that's exactly what he used to do. Martin Cameron was a chef at Quebec's prestigious Château Frontenac and now cooks for the anoraks and sweaters who race for places round his four or five formica-topped tables. Restaurant and kitchen are one, and seeing Martin prepare lemon meringue is like watching a cross between Michel Roux and Anton Mosimann at work. But what brought him to La Grande, to cook in cramped quarters for a heavy-booted clientèle here to talk hydro-electric?

He explains in a gentle, modest voice that he could not stand the pressure of high level, noisy, competitive restaurant behaviour. I think of Marco Pierre White and understand instantly. Here, Martin is free to be the dedicated but reticent chef he clearly is. In sight of his hungry guests, his fingers fly, the pastries and pies take shape, the soups and sauces bubble, the oven opens upon dish after dish of fantastic food. I have often imagined that when quizzed for my favourite restaurant by some trendy food column, I would cite the Auberge Sinittavik, Great Whale, as my first choice.

What Robbie Masty and the Crees all fear is the coming of the road and the dangerous temptations it will bring in its wake. More cars, goods, development and tourists will destroy the few remaining shreds of their declining culture. That is why in the spring of 1991 they actively began their opposition to its construction. So it is time to fly some 120 miles south to a Cree village on James Bay in a part of the Territory already brought within the network of roads the scheme has mapped out.

Chisasibi is home to a Cree community that formerly lived on Fort George Island, a few miles offshore. The Cree themselves decided to move and chose the new site. Hydro Quebec and others funded the change and the setting up of houses and the community centre-cum-shopping mall that is the social focus of the settlement. It takes only one look to realize that Indians who are seriously trying to limit the infiltration of other values must indeed stop the road being built. Chisasibi is awful.

Chisasibi cost Hydro Quebec forty million Canadian dollars and the Federal Government ten million. For what? An alien way of life centred on a Western-style shopping mall that has quickly grown shabby and strewn with litter, so different from the fastidious care with which the Cree have always treated the wilderness. Clearly it has thrown their culture into crisis.

The environment is immediately recognizable to us and our New York camera crew. It is a prototype in miniature for inner-city neglect. The community centre comprises a single covered walk-through space with shops, a post office and civic offices set above it. The walls are rough grey cement, the steps the same. Drink cans lie discarded on the ground; old paper wrappers and bits of debris blow in the wind. Young people are drifting around, casual, indifferent, bored. Many people here have no jobs. Many are on welfare. It is an appalling indictment of civilized values that they have brought the Cree to this.

Most insulting of all, and indicative of official insensitivity, someone has erected a monumental metal sculpture in a wasteland of open space. It is nothing less than a grotesque parody of a *mitshuap*: 6 metres of sheet metal twisted to mock the elegant simplicity of their primitive homes.

This is a cash economy and the Cree have joined it. They are shopping, pushing supermarket trolleys, pausing to talk, holding plastic cups of machine coffee. I had flown out of Great Whale sensing the passing of Cree culture: those tawdry wreaths on the shoreline graves, the *mitshuaps* in the bungalow backyards. Now, at Chisasibi, I feel the game is up. The Crees are integrated Canadians with no more than fond memories of their past, a past receding so fast they can only snatch at its essence on special hunting weekends. Nothing more than that. And then I meet Helen Atkinson.

Helen is Cree and serious about it. She is petite and neat. Her long black hair frames golden skin, black eyes, a narrow mouth and deeply dimpled chin. She wears spectacles, sits at a desk and has a college education. She is one of those fighting for the survival of Cree values:

'I see modern Western technological society as being totally separate from nature; they see nature as something to be exploited. All their housing, their buildings, their cars, everything is to protect them from nature. I see people who are scared to deal with nature.

'Now, when you're living with nature, it's so powerful and so subtle you cannot help but be spiritual. You're not above it. You're part of it. What I learned from my elders is that each thing has a spirit, each thing has a life; even rocks have a life; water has a life; trees, plants, animals, everything has a spirit inside it. And why we never rose above nature is because we say we come from the same spirit.'

I ask her how much damage the hydro-electric scheme has done to this spirit.

'Oh we were a very sick community. There was lots of vandalism, a lot of violence, drinking, drugs, family break-ups... disintegration.'

The most poignant indicator of this disintegration is that the Cree literally lost their bearings within their landscape.

'Things were very predictable in nature; things had cycles. And the Cree would predict, by changes in nature, every little thing that would happen.'

Again I think back to that summons in the night, 'The geese are flying, the geese are flying.'

With the scheme their power to predict died. The development totally changed the nature of the land. The water levels changed. The weather changed. And the psychological effect of losing this power of prediction has been immeasurable.

At Chisasibi the Cree made a simple deduction. It was the road that had brought these troubles. They would stop the traffic. And so they did. Operating at night only, they set up a blockade and searched incoming cars for alcohol, which they then confiscated. This is strictly illegal, but the Cree are dedicated to their cause. We have our car searched. I meet Natasha, a young girl in her late teens. She and her friends used to drink too much:

'It seemed there was nothing to look forward to. There was all this destruction about, and it was so depressing. When we were drinking we seemed merrier, but it just caused more problems. That's why I don't drink any more.'

Helen Atkinson is a leading figure amongst the Cree. She is seriously organized. We sit in her office discussing plans for lobbying the purchasers of Hydro Quebec power. Can New York City, desperate for electricity, afford to buy it from a source that a major ethnic group is claiming has destroyed their way of life? Helen explains her hopes that the prospect of a buyers' boycott will strengthen the Cree case. She shows me anthologies of Cree poems, published accounts of their way of life. She talks of lobbying the United Nations, of embarrassing America if it goes ahead and buys electricity at the cost of ethnic peoples. She is quietly resolute, almost stern in her beliefs. I begin to think the Cree lobby has a chance.

But then within hours I stand at the site of a major excavation. Huge cliffs of white rock loom over the shattered landscape, a tumble of angular stones newly exposed to the air reminds me of some daunting avant garde sculpture. It lacks the natural fall and grace of nature. This change is actual. How can the forces of Cree conviction defy all this? The pylons, the already created new reservoirs, the investment, the implacable forces of development. The Cree and Inuit are few against such strength. The answer is they can do so only by becoming part of the change themselves.

That evening, as I contemplate the destiny of the dying Cree culture, there is a call from England. My father's condition has suddenly deteriorated. They fear he may not last more than a few days. My sister's voice is flat, devoid of hope, resigned. My scalp goes cold. This will be it: the great parting. I stand in the overheated corridor of the little hotel, a million miles from all that matters, and let the phone line hang limp.

There is still one interview left to do. Hydro Quebec have a spokesman ready, briefed, informed, prepared, media-trained perhaps. I am febrile with conflicting tensions: half eager to be gone; half eager to pin him down, test him, dissect his answers, make him answerable to the Cree. My mind is hectic with grief and the knowledge of grief to come. But I am here. I can scarcely contain the chaotic energy within me.

I pace his crisp white office in a Montreal skyscraper. There is wan autumn sunlight and golden leaves. Outwardly I strive to be gracious, professional, trim. Inside I boil with rage at my impending loss. Between the two, he looms, this man of Hydro Quebec, my adversary; the destroyer of forests and waterways; of traplines, and lives; of Cree poetry and Helen Atkinson's heritage. I attack and harass. We skirmish and hedge. I cite with passion the evidence of five days in Hudson Bay. He parries with statistics, with reasoned argument and long familiarity with fact and detail, with conviction courteously expressed. And then I flee to the airport. Sighing into my seat, I smile wryly at the impartiality that's expected of me.

Well, that's how it felt at the time. In the event the man from Hydro Quebec gave a clear and confident account, even mixed with pride of what Hydro Quebec were doing – for Canada, for its aboriginal peoples and for the global environment:

'Do you want global warming? No. Then hydro-electricity is the answer. Do you want acid rain? No. Then hydro-electricity is the world's best option. Do you want to melt the ice caps and displace hundreds of thousands of people? No. Then hydro-electricity is essential. Chernobyl? You're better off having roads to Great Whale.'

He presses the point that change is inevitable and that Hydro Quebec have not been the initiators of contact with the Inuit and the Cree. Given that there were fur traders in the seventeenth century, missionaries in the nineteenth, airforce defence systems in the twentieth, it's inevitable that aboriginal peoples will increasingly come under the influence of the more dominant cultures to the south. 'It's not a hydro-electric development problem: it's a clash-of-civilizations problem. OK?' insists their spokesman. 'It's not the complex as such. It's the arrival of airports and various means of communication.'

He's both right and wrong. For the problem at that moment is the road. It is being built specifically to further Hydro Quebec's scheme. The land is inhospitable, the rock itself not only some of the most ancient, but some of the hardest on earth. To force a network of roads through such resistant terrain would be uneconomic if it were merely to bring consumer goods to a scattered population numbering not more than 16 000.

One day tourism may come this way – but shooting, trekking, challenging the great outdoors will not bring people in large enough numbers to justify such extensive road building. It is the project itself that has created the need for the road and made it economically viable.

Yet Cree and Inuit contact with civilization did indeed begin long ago. Even where there is no road I have seen how much these people relish the products flown in to Great Whale. In an Inuit home, centrally heated to the pitch of a hothouse at Kew, I saw freezers, televisions, a CD player, microwave, cooker, washing machine, tumble-dryer. They jostled for space in the living area, spilling into the hall. The child's bed was heaped with small mountains of fluffy toys and cushions. Outside, the wind might lash and temperatures plummet, but inside was as bright and cosy as an American sitcom. It was slightly false in the same way, too.

Yes, Hydro Quebec is both creating jobs and paying compensation. Many Inuit and Cree are happy about that. And the company has brought more than goods: it has brought education and health.

The James Bay Agreement of 1975 set up the Cree School Board which is run entirely by elected representatives of the Cree Community. It has broader powers than any other School Board in Canada: it can determine the curriculum and school calendars, choose textbooks to preserve and transmit the Cree language and Cree culture, decide the numbers of Native and non-Native teachers. Strangely, French is the second language taught in such schools. English remains the second language only of Crees over the age of forty.

The final irony is that the Cree people themselves are on the increase. Better healthcare has greatly reduced Cree infant mortality. It fell 50 per cent between the mid-1970s and the mid-1980s. The Cree people have grown by almost 50 per cent in only thirteen years.

With health, social security, protection against the perils of the climate and the terrain, these people are on the march as never before. More and more Cree are now part of a Canadian population whose need for energy has set the forces of destruction against their hunting grounds and traplines. The price has been high. They have been forced to accept the money economy and political discourse of Quebec.

Hydro Quebec simply reckoned without the fact that some Inuit and Cree would continue to think in traditional rather than capitalist ways: respecting nature above money, seeking equilibrium rather than job opportunities. And it is their passion that is sustaining the opposition.

Knowing that the ancient Cree way of life is doomed, but that the Cree themselves live on, transformed, I fly home. I fly to my father's death. And I witness another sort of transformation.

By the time I arrive he has lost the power of speech. Whatever his final words might be, he has already said them. There will be no more. He is propped on pillows, his hands inert, listless, in his lap.

His eyes move slowly, without effort but without purpose. When I come into their range he responds with everything left to him. The eyes refocus, his shoulders hunch, he makes a sound. I am there. He knows I am there. Our pact, never formally agreed, always understood, is fulfilled. I am going through it with him.

And then the last dramatic moment of his life. Four weeks earlier my son's wife had borne their first child, a boy, my father's first great-grandchild: perhaps he had been hanging on for this moment. They arrive at his bedside. Very gently my son places into the arms of my father, my first grandson: four generations, two of them at the extremity of their years. My son smiles: I smile. My father is beyond smiling, but not beyond knowing. The dribble of saliva on the baby's lip is as glistening and fresh as life itself. There is no sadness at all; no tears. My father, I sense, is liberated into his death.

The next day, the light in his eyes died.

Postscript: It is three years later that I see *mitshuaps* again. They stand in a wide circle surrounding a green field on top of a hill just outside Monmouth. They are the homes of New Age travellers who have come together for a weekend-long country fair. I am reporting the dilemma of travelling people – New Agers, gypsies and the like – who want to espouse values at odds with those of the settled community.

As the camera crew and I move across the field, we become aware that we are alone. Elsewhere the crowds jostle and talk, smoke and gossip. But here there is an attempt to treat the green space as in some way sacred; to let nature be itself. How odd it is that as ancient values are overrun in one area of the globe, they seem to re-emerge spontaneously somewhere else. Do the Cree have much in common with New Agers? Not much. But enough to signify that power and development are not all that people want. There are other values.

Whose Church?

In the beginning it was easy:

> Gentle Jesus, meek and mild,
> Look upon a little child.
> Pity my simplicity,
> Suffer me to come to thee.

I sang the little hymn solo in the school nativity play, and when my voice wobbled on the last line it was not in anticipation of any doubts about my faith. I had more immediate preoccupations. I was tinglingly aware that parents, teachers, distinguished guests in their hatted ranks, were watching, judging, offering their approval and then, at that instant, threatening to take it away. I was eager to please, and knew – as the alarmed hush that greeted my wavering voice showed – that any deviation from the familiar line was error, and in need of correction. I was seven years old at the time and taking my conditioning well, like the cod liver oil and malt swallowed daily to keep me healthy. Even today I still keep a jar of that dark viscous brew at the back of the kitchen shelf, ready, at a moment's whim, to conjure up what childhood felt like. Perhaps I still have that child's simple faith, too, stowed at the back of my memory to remind me of how my world was then.

I grew up in the 1940s. It was a time when hierarchies were clear and unchallenged. Children were subject to their parents, their teachers, to grown-ups in general and in particular to those in authority – doctors, policemen, judges and clergymen. At the very top, further up even than MPs, lords, ladies, and the Royal Family, was God. God had his own immediate circle – glorious beyond all imagining – the angels and saints, all the good people who had died and gone to Heaven, the Holy Family and His son, Jesus, whose birth had in its way brought to light my musical ineptitude. God also lived in a different, much nicer, place.

People in the earthly hierarchies had power, but God had very great power indeed, by virtue of his supernatural identity as creator and judge of all things. Order was all-important, and God had emerged from chaos to create order. Order was accepted as the prime need. I knew and had my place in it. It was quite comfortable in fact.

But there was one particular aspect of God which made him complex – I would have said 'contradictory', but it didn't do to be critical of so much power. For some reason God had suffered a very great deal. Of his own choice he had come to earth as his son, Jesus, preached that we should all love one another, and then been treated in the most appalling way: arrested, tortured, rejected, reviled and, by the vote of the mob, sentenced to a prolonged, agonizing and public death. This was all done to save us – that is, me – because we were so wicked. I knew about being naughty of course (stealing some sugar – wartime rationing still prevailed long into peacetime – and then being thoroughly smacked for it). But that was clearly defined by time and place and could be said at the end of the day to be over. God's blame was, to a child, non-specific, everlasting and a very great burden. I learnt then to feel guilty, without quite understanding why.

Jesus, of course, had not stayed dead. Because of his power he had leapt from the tomb, told all his friends he was now alive for ever, instructed them about how to found Christianity, and then flown up into Heaven in radiant light. There was something else that emerged from this thrilling story. Both God and Jesus knew everything about me, watched all I did, and, despite that, still loved me very, very much, with a love far beyond even that of my parents. This was love indeed. Those then were the elements: power, suffering, guilt and love; a matrix of high-octane emotions that would fuel my life and my choices ever after. They are no doubt still at work today.

Jesus, now safely restored to Heaven and the company of all those who deserve to be at the same celestial party, was also still with us on earth. His particular places were the parish churches and cathedrals of the Church of England where I learnt to feel awe and mystery, to appreciate beauty, and where I felt able to talk to my secret all-powerful friend who both loved and forgave.

This talking was called 'prayer' and was intended to be part of daily life. I took my lead from soupy Victorian paintings that showed a golden-haired child of indeterminate sex kneeling, head bowed, beside a bed heaving with the lush comforts of feather mattress, frilled pillows and flower-sprigged eiderdowns. I yearned to dramatize my own spiritual encounters in this romantic way. But my bed was narrow and trim; the bedroom icy cold. I proposed to my mother that I should say my evening prayers at her knee, and to do so without disturbing her I would bow both knee and head on the hearth rug before the open fire, in the only room in the house that was heated.

I knew I had my mother cornered. She could scarcely refuse her daughter's offered pieties, but the evening's entertainment – listening to the Home Service on the wireless – would be severely disrupted by a six-year-old calling down blessings on legions of aunts and uncles, the remotest cousins and acquaintances. We compromised: I was to pray in silence; she would turn the radio volume down. So it is that early memories of my prayer life are interlarded with extracts from *Monday Night at 8 o'clock* and *The Adventures of Paul Temple*. Perhaps my eventually joining the BBC was in part due to the effect of that memory. Perhaps for a moment Lord Reith actually was God.

I made other mistakes, too. In 1940 I consistently and with some grief to myself prayed that Hitler might win the war. I had misunderstood the text 'love thine enemies, bless them that persecute you', and childishly believed that if you loved someone, you wanted to give them what they most wanted in the world. Yet I knew there was some paradox here that was beyond me. After all, was I not daily required to carry my gas mask whenever I left the house, against quite real fears that the Germans would attack with chemical weapons? I spent many nights in air-raid shelters, with the boom of guns defending Manchester loud in my ears. Yet the man who was masterminding all this damage was the nightly beneficiary of my prayers. I told no one.

Indeed, I told no one for thirty years, by which time God and history had sorted things out.

I tell of these naivetés to show how constantly the concept of God and my access to his power and love were in my mind. This was all very reassuring and I grew up with a coherent faith that made a continuum of what I believed to be true and how I behaved. The Christian story endorsed a moral code that prevailed in the world around me and made it work. I came to identify Christianity with morality. What's more, the constant repetition of prayers each Sunday, the swelling tones of the organ, the major chords of familiar hymns, the young voices, even the regularly boring sermons, when I scribbled in the back of *Ancient and Modern* or read lists in the *Prayer Book* of all the relations I couldn't marry – all this confirmed in my child's eyes that in such places dwelt the truth and the truth would remain unchanged for ever.

It was not to be. Both I and the church I knew, the Church of England, have changed. My teenage years brought doubt and D. H. Lawrence. I began to notice that God's imagined disappointment with me when I sinned had much in common with the roller-coaster of approval/disapproval by which my parents sought to control my behaviour. Most immediately this applied to sex. In those days the only acceptable route to sex was marriage. Everything else had to be concealed from the adults at all costs. Marriage I knew to be one of the greatest of church sacraments. Yet I could not fathom how the ecstatic fumblings that might precede it were smutty and sinful, whereas the very same impulses indulged on the other side of a marriage service were a glorious and liberated union of flesh and flesh.

If God, who was watching what went on down the lane with disapproval, was reserving his blessing for the bridal night, what kind of distinction was he drawing and why? And why had he endowed me with such powerful urges if only to insist that I frustrate them in order to please him. It all sounded very parental, and I was now beginning to be at odds with my parents. What's more, I was being taught to think for myself. And to teach thinking is to teach scepticism.

I left the Christian faith of my childhood where it was, and walked away. But I know it still has a presence where I left it, on the shelf if you like, with memory's cod liver oil. I can reach back into it and feel comfortable there. I joyfully bring it into my present life at moments of high intensity, at Christmas, at Easter, and at major rites of passage for those I love. On such occasions I find that, while my faith is much as I left it, with all the warmth and comfort of the intimately familiar, the Church itself has changed radically.

Today things are not as simple as they once were for the Church of England. It finds itself, like other human institutions, tossed this way and that by the prevailing values of society at a given time. These evolving values are familiar enough, but it is their confluence and the speed and range of their impact that creates such turmoil The increasing importance placed on individual judgement and personal autonomy weakens any claims to Christian obedience. The emphasis on democratic participation and accountability prompts the questioning of authority of all kinds. In the Church of England, religious practice can be shifted by decisions made by the General Synod, of which almost half, the laity, are elected members. Nothing divine or eternal there, beyond their own piety and prayers.

Then, in the world at large, rational discourse has, since the eighteenth century, come to be accepted as the basis for making sound judgements in matters social, political and economic. Religious explanation for the way the world is, based on supernatural revelation, has given way to scientific logic and evidence. En route this has undermined one of Christianity's oldest ways of maintaining discipline – the threat of judgement beyond the grave. People now find it hard to imagine how exactly such a transaction might take place. And finding it hard to believe, they stop believing.

What's more, within the Church's own ranks, the discoveries of biblical scholarship continually undermine the idea that the Bible is the revealed word of God. It is clearly a historical document, albeit one that has changed the world more than any other. Likewise, the creeds are not so much the definitive expression of what one is called upon to believe, but the recognized texts issuing over the centuries from assemblies of churchmen who at different times decided what was heresy and what was not.

Education has taught people to question. People have learnt that hierarchies are about power not virtue, and those in authority now have to earn respect. Other cultures have introduced other faiths, and once alien gods have become acceptable. It's clear that morality can exist separately from religion, that it is possible to live a good life without God. The voracious appetite of newspapers for news – everything from theological disagreements to scandalous vicars – lays bare the frailty of human endeavour. We live in cynical times and much of that cynicism is appropriate.

Among the turmoil of issues that confront it, the Church of England must now decide who it is for and whom it is to serve.

Once, things were the other way round. The historical origins of the Church of England lie in Henry VIII's quarrel with the Pope about his divorce. When the Church of England finally broke away from Rome, the act of defiance split the country's Christians, who were either Catholic or Protestant. And they were certainly one or the other – atheism was punishable by death. Catholic monarchs persecuted Protestant citizens; Protestant monarchs persecuted Catholics. Attendance at church was required by law and those who did not attend the Church of England could be fined or imprisoned. Only from the 1750s did parliamentary legislation begin to allow space for the individual conscience.

Nowadays, individual consciences have taken over. The Christian churches struggle to keep their members in line. The Pope regularly reminds the Catholic Church that it is, among other things, against contraception, abortion, euthanasia. Yet many Catholics deal privately and defiantly with these matters in their own lives. Rome's insistence on the celibacy of its priesthood and its ruling that women can never be ordained are now regularly challenged from within its own ranks. The Church of England has similar problems: what should those who claim to be members be required to believe and how should they be expected to behave? *Heart of the Matter* has regularly explored such questions. At such moments I have taken my simple faith off its shelf. And, hugging it close for comfort, I have sallied forth to tangle with the fine, sometimes convoluted, threads of church theology.

The Church of England has a unique place in the constitution of the country. It crowns the monarch; twenty-five of its bishops sit in the House of Lords. Its prayers are said daily before each sitting of the Houses of Parliament. At the same time, Church affairs are governed by Acts of Parliament. The ordination of women was voted through by 215 MPs, many of whom are non-believers. (Twenty-one voted against.) While only 1.2 million out of forty-eight million English citizens are regular church-goers, there is still a sense in which every church stands at the heart of its parish to serve the entire community. So who belongs to the Church of England? Who are its members? The defining moment is baptism. And there was, until recently, an assumption – common practice through the centuries – that all citizens, other than those of specific other creeds, were eligible for baptism in the Church of England.

This is no longer the case in many parishes. Parish priests have considerable autonomy on their own patch. They can, for example, decide to remarry divorcees. They can also decide whom to baptize. And different parishes are making different decisions about who to admit to baptism. In 1991 I visited the West Country to report on these discrepancies. There I met three parish priests living within 30 miles of each other who were practising totally divergent interpretations of baptism theology. But first I met a baby in need of baptism.

In 1991 Jack Dorrian was eight months old. When he was three months, his mother Debbie began asking round at various churches to see if he could be christened. Baptism would have made him a member of the Church of England, endowing him with the grace of God and welcoming him among those of the faith. Up to ten churches refused. It doesn't take a scholar steeped in arcane texts to come up with the admonition of Jesus: 'Suffer the little children to come unto me, and forbid them not. For of such is the Kingdom of Heaven.' So what exactly is going on?

The Reverend John Summers served for years in the Navy, as a navy chaplain. He is a brisk no-nonsense priest who clearly likes things ship-shape and well ordered. No doubt something of a naval rise-and-shine efficiency has carried over into his ministry at St Barnabas Church, Plymouth. He is typical of those priests pressing for more restrictive baptism:

'I felt, during my time as a naval chaplain and before, that baptism should not be devalued in the way it has been. A lot of weakness and flabbiness of the Church of England has been because anything goes. Believe what you like, nothing, or as much as you like. People come asking for baptism without really knowing what they're asking for.

'I think indiscriminate baptism, baptism on demand, is wrong. Somebody comes along with no contact, no link with the Church at all, with the idea, "Well we're born in England, so we are nominally C of E." It doesn't seem to stand for very much.'

To avoid such flabbiness among his congregation, parents or guardians must attend three or four meetings where they learn what the baptism promises mean: 'The service itself is very theologically expressed. It needs unpackaging, it's wrapped up in theological language that does need to be opened up.'

Jack Dorrian's mother wasn't prepared to go along. With a brisk dismissal of the priest's authority, and strong in the rightness of her views, Debbie is typical of a new assertiveness that refuses the insights offered by others and is swiftly sure of what she wants: 'It's no good giving me baptism classes now; my faith is established. I've got my own faith, and my own thoughts. I mean, I'm not a heathen, but I'm not running to church every week.'

What Debbie hasn't got is the theology. For John Summers that matters, and he gets stroppy when challenged: 'Are you saying I should encourage someone who hasn't the faintest idea what it means, or doesn't believe it, to stand up and say these statements which aren't true for them? I should encourage them in this hypocrisy?'

No baby can understand such matters, of course, and the fact that parents ask for baptism suggests they at least have an aspiration towards the Church for their child, and perhaps God, with his insight into the human heart, may be the best judge of that. John Summers doesn't leave it there:

'My experience, when people come asking, is that their motivation is mixed. Perhaps the mother-in-law is on to them, saying it's about time it is done. Others have funny ideas: You can't be married unless you're baptized. Some even say you can't be buried in consecrated ground.'

John Summers runs baptismal classes to sort out these misconceptions. It provides him with a rich recruiting ground for his congregations which have blossomed since he arrived at St Barnabas in 1981. He has introduced modernized, family services and conducts baptism not in some private family ceremony but within the morning service itself, taking the child round the baptized church, introducing him to his new, wider, family. He is insistent that the parents should profess the Christian faith before he will baptize their child.

The irony is that John Summers is promoting restricted baptism and thus membership, at a time when church attendance across the country is already falling. By requiring a qualification – the faith of the parents – John Summers is following the old advertising adage that to make something exclusive is to give it value. And in his church it's paying off.

His congregation has a preponderance of young people with young families who are responding to his call for regular commitment to church-going and church affairs. 'Our experience here is that this policy has been the key to the growth of the church. Because they've had an opportunity, through the baptism preparation, to discover something of the living God for themselves.'

His strategy of demanding more, cuts out those who don't want to enrol for the full tour of duty, but gets more out of those who do come aboard. It is a plan which could reduce the total numbers baptized but increase the commitment to a specific, narrower, set of ideas. It is the area of evangelical growth and fervour.

The Reverend Michael Malsom will have none of such constrictions: all are welcome to his church, Ascension Church, Plymouth. No questions asked. He baptizes many, catching the overspill of those refused elsewhere. And he glows with pleasure at the thought. He is a rubicund, Dickensian figure of a man, chubby-cheeked with a twinkling eye, an innkeeper, compared to the Reverend Summers' boatswain, welcoming all to the warm comforts of Christianity:

'I simply take the line that if they turn to me and say "please would you baptize my child" there is evidence of the work of God in that. Restrictive baptism says to others you do not belong. But God never said to anyone, you're not part of my creation, you're not in my love. If there are lost sheep we go and find them. We don't drive them out of the fold. We seek to bring them back in. The policy of the Church of England is to baptize children. And whilst the canon says that you may defer it for a period of instruction, you certainly must not put people off. In a way I'm not concerned with the parents. If baptism confers the grace of God then it is between the child and God, with me as the in-between minister. I cannot visit the sins of the parents upon the children.'

The Reverend Malsom's church is wide and sunny, rather like himself. He's been there twelve years and baptized over a thousand children. They don't often turn up in his congregations. But, as governor of three schools, he comes across them, he meets them in the wider community. His broad, welcoming, non-interrogational view of the ministry is strongly at odds with that of the next church I visit.

At All Saints Church, Taunton, the font is simply never used. The Reverend Alan Wright has an altogether more austere and exacting view of baptism. He's one of a number of clergy who depart quite deliberately from the rules of the Church of England, by refusing to baptize anyone until they're old enough to understand for themselves what the Christian faith is all about. Then he baptizes adults, by total immersion. Alan Wright is like his faith: austere of face and feature. A large man in a zipped-up cardigan, the reddish beard and steady eyes suggest resoluteness of character. The lowering brow is more indicative of troubled thought than celestial joy. He has listened to the still small voice within and it has told him to defy the ways of his Church. My question, as to whether he thinks the Church is in error, brings a forthright reply:

'Yes. Babies have been baptized commonly since about the third century. And the Church teaches that what happens at a baby's christening is the same as what happens to adults. Patently this is ludicrous, and we need to do something about it.'

What Alan Wright has done, since his ordination, is to have himself re-baptized by total immersion. This brought him into conflict with his Bishop, Bath and Wells. But Alan Wright claims he is responding to a higher authority. 'God is speaking to people and saying "You've got your practice of baptism wrong". Some people are hearing this.' He believes he is one of them. Unhappily for him, his former Bishop is not. That former Bishop was George Carey, now Archbishop of Canterbury.

The idea of certain clergy re-baptizing at ordination threatens the status of 'the one baptism' for which the Church stands. If you need to re-baptize, then what was the earlier ceremony actually about? Nonetheless the Reverend Wright now has a blue tiled immersion tank in a corner of his church. He clearly wants to recruit only the totally committed; and he judges people, not by the good life they might lead, the spirituality of their soul, but by regular attendance at services and being a regular part of his church community which is, not surprisingly, rather small.

The Reverend Malsom is appalled by such exclusivity: 'That way we'll finish up a sect like any other sect. A Lake Wobegon sect.'

The Reverend Wright deplores the policy of openness:

'Why join a club and never attend any of the meetings? ... I'm not happy functioning as a twentieth-century witchdoctor doing the religious things for people who happen to live in this area, for the people of the tribe. The Christian church is different from that.'

Debbie Dorrian might qualify as one of the tribe. She had felt that baptism was in some way meaningful for her son. The Church examined that meaningfulness in terms of theology and church attendance and found it wanting. Jack remained unbaptized.

So to whom does the Church of England belong? In the decade of evangelism there are moves to make it more exclusively for those who are fully committed believers. At the Synod of July 1991 an amendment to canon law was proposed in line with the policy of restricted baptism. It required that parents or guardians of infants should be 'willing and able' to make such promises as the baptism requires. That phrase 'willing and able' implies faith and observances on the part of the adults. The amendment was rejected.

Clearly if the Church moves towards restricted baptism, and thus specific membership, its status as the established church of the nation is called into question. The disestablishment of the Church is now countenanced by people with outlooks as different as Tony Benn and Lord Tebbit. It would, of course, require a Parliamentary procedure. No one is more keenly aware of this possibility than the Right Reverend John Hapgood, the recently retired Archbishop of York.

In January 1993, only a matter of weeks after the formal separation of the Prince and Princess of Wales, I went to talk to him about the significance for the Church if the future sovereign were to divorce and even remarry. The question of disestablishment was unavoidable. If Prince Charles were to remarry before his coronation, it is conceivable that the then Archbishop of Canterbury might refuse to administer the coronation oath, and instruct the Bishop to do likewise. Some other way of crowning the King would have to be found and the Church would be seen to have automatically disestablished itself.

Since the time of our conversation two things have happened. Firstly, the idea has been canvassed that Prince Charles might want to marry a Catholic (Camilla Parker-Bowles is thought to remain a Catholic, despite being divorced by her husband). Such a move would be an even more flagrant breach of the constitution and in the ensuing crisis the role of the Church as well as its Supreme Governor would be subject to convulsive change. Secondly, Prince Charles, in his televised interview with Jonathan Dimbleby, spoke of being proclaimed 'Defender of All Faiths' rather than 'Defender of the Faith'. Clearly, clouds once on the far horizon are coming closer.

As Bishop Hapgood sees it:

'We're in a particularly bleak time for religion at the moment. We live in a pretty individualistic, cynical and critical age. One can map the decline of churches and the growth of individualism. It doesn't mean people are less religious. What they tend to have is their own self-made and somewhat strange religion, concocted of various elements – some bits of Christian faith, some fantasy, some proverbial wisdom and so on. That's the sort of faith by which many people live, until it becomes inadequate. They then look around for something which they can identify as home. And many then look to the Church of England.'

Is it then as a catch-all for religious drifters that the Church fulfils its national role?

'Each citizen has rights in the Church. It goes back to the roots of the nation ... this sense of the Church belonging to the people and the people belonging to the Church. It gives many people a sense of religious identity, religious roots. We're talking about probably more than half the population. And this can co-exist with a pluralist society. You have a dominant culture within which different groups are accepted.'

On at least one specific issue the Bishop sees concessions having to be made: the coronation oath, the statement that binds the sovereign to uphold the Protestant faith above all others:

'I think it would have to be revised next time around. The religious make-up of the country has changed so much. If the coronation service is going to unify the nation, as it must do, then it must recognize that we now live in an ecumenical and multi-faith society.'

As accountability and transparency become the criteria of our institutions, the constitutional cat's cradle that has produced the tangled complexity of the Churches of Scotland and Wales and England is likely to be unwound. Bishop Hapgood fears that a disestablished Church of England would withdraw into itself:

'It would cut our links with these vast numbers of people in the nation who feel they have a relationship with the Church of England, although they're not paid-up members. I don't think there's any evidence from history that cutting links induces new vigour. I think one would see a withdrawal by the Church of England, and those who tend to look on the Church of England as just one denomination among others would withdraw into little assemblies of the keen and committed.'

And it is indeed the keen and the committed who have already denied Debbie Dorrian the right to baptize her son. In the end the reasons for an established church – its historic role, its constitutional function, its unifying value – may not be enough to sustain it. There are indications that forces of change are operating as powerfully within it as without. But change comes slowly to British institutions and we should not be surprised by the Church's capacity to ride out whatever storms come its way.

Personally I find the idea of disestablishment a melancholy prospect. The Church of England, a great national institution, brought low by non-believers, cynics, and the indifference of most of us to the great spiritual inspiration that once sent men to the stake for their God. The day thou gavest, Lord, would indeed be ending.

I Believe...

In April 1992 *Heart of the Matter* began to examine the faith of the Church of England. Easter was on its way. Indeed Easter Sunday was the date for one of our programmes. What more topical issue to examine than that of the crucifixion, the burial and resurrection of Jesus, celebration of the high point of the Church's year and faith? Samuel Beckett always insisted he was born on Good Friday, 13 April, a claim subsequently checked by his biographer and found to be less than the truth. Not the truth on his birth certificate at any rate. But Beckett withheld any denials, clearly taking some wry satisfaction in the notion that such a date of birth – commemorating as it does the death of the world's hope – in some way chimed with the tenor of gloomy resignation displayed by the characters of his mordant imagination.

I was born on Easter Sunday, a date in the Church's year of a diametrically different character – the day of Christ's resurrection, the revelation of hope, the dawn of salvation. This is only one of many differences between myself and Samuel Beckett, but I can imagine he might smile indulgently at my buoyant optimism and, considering my date of birth, opine that one can expect no less.

Easter is resonant throughout our culture, far beyond the observances of Christian worship. The first Easter coincided, and not by accident, with the Jewish Passover, being the occasion of Jesus' arrival in Jerusalem. Easter and Passover are both determined by cycles of the moon. Easter is celebrated as springtime breaks on the northern hemisphere; fluffy chickens and Easter eggs are pagan contributions to a Christian way of celebrating the new life of the year. The Paschal Lamb transcends both, symbol of Christ's sacrifice and God's chosen. Clearly the resurrection, and what is preached about it today in parishes throughout the country, is significant. As I began to ask questions, I found myself tumbling into Alice in Wonderland world. But then, what could be more appropriate at Easter than chasing after a white rabbit?

Our Easter programme posed the question: 'Are some Church of England clergy preaching the bodily resurrection of Christ to their congregations even though they don't believe it themselves?' Belief is what creates a church in the first place, and what holds it together through subsequent centuries. It is the first thing we ask of unfamiliar faiths – the Seventh Day Adventists, for example, who believe Christ's second coming is imminent, will be 'literal, personal, visible and worldwide' and only the righteous will be saved, or the Jains of India who believe in reincarnation, reverence for all life, and the avoidance of injury to any living thing. But beliefs are never static. They are usually set down at the outset by the religion's founder and his followers; the holy books written by them or about them by virtual contemporaries are then interpreted and augmented through the centuries by the traditional teaching of the Church.

Churches, being human institutions, often give rise to differing hierarchies each attempting to impose their own dogma. Those who lose out are branded as heretics and sometimes pay a heavy price. Today we live in tolerant times. Were it not so, many a fire might have been lit for the present incumbents of a number of quiet, English parishes. For the answer to our question – 'Are Church of England clergy preaching what they don't believe?' – is most certainly, 'Yes.' I went to meet some of them.

Our programme opens with the Reverend David Paterson greeting the dawn on Easter Sunday, with candle in hand and the prayer, 'May the Light of Christ, rising in glory, banish all darkness from our hearts and minds.' Moments later we see the Reverend Stephen Mitchell reciting the Creed at his Easter morning service: 'And on the third day he rose again in accordance with the scriptures...' Christ's rising from the dead is the central tenet of the Christian faith. The event is related in each of the gospels as the climactic moment in the Christian story: the proof that Christ died for us, but defeated death itself that we might live eternally. Neither David Paterson nor Stephen Mitchell believe in the bodily resurrection. Or rather, as they would put it, they believe it is a powerful myth. This has come as a surprise to many of their parishioners and is to come as a surprise to their Bishop.

But first I try to get to grips with what they do believe and why they feel entitled to be Anglican clergymen, drawing a stipend from a church whose followers assume their priests to believe as they do. Armed with my Sunday School religion, the Thirty-Nine Articles of the Church of England and the Creed, I set out to grapple with this new thinking that has so far survived within the Church I thought I knew.

David Paterson welcomes us warmly to the rambling, untidy vicarage of St Peter's in Loughborough. He is a large, amiable, shaggy man, marooned in a tide of books that have swept into his home and lodged on every shelf, cupboard, desk and chair. His life is about ideas, not decor. Dust and manuscripts lie in heaps, cushions bulge, chairs wobble; nothing has been renewed for a long time, except his active, questing mind, which leads us along some strange paths.

As the interview begins it's not long before I'm falling fast and, like Alice, glimpse books on shelves as I pass – Spinoza, Tagore, Pascal. To steady myself I decide to go for some straight questions and answers on a checklist of beliefs.

Q: 'Do you believe in the bodily resurrection?'

A: 'I don't think so. On scientific grounds it seems difficult to believe. If God means the sum total of everything that is, and if science is able to describe it, what place is there for this extraordinary idea that a dead body comes to life? On religious grounds it seems to be totally irrelevant, if not positively harmful.'

Q: 'Do you believe in the empty tomb?'

A: 'Oh no. I think it's a very powerful symbol.'

Q: 'How much of the resurrection do you believe happened as a real event?'

A: 'I think it's all interpretation. It's difficult ever to be sure, isn't it, that on the world stage the crucifixion was ever a real event. I think it was. But there is virtually no evidence outside the Christian text, which is strange. As far as the resurrection is concerned, that seems to me to be a spiritual event, not one you can write history about. It's much more profound than that.'

Q: 'When you use the phrase "risen Christ", what do you believe the word "risen" to mean?'

A: 'I think that's a very good question, and one I haven't really thought about. It is about our own rising from the dead, getting back to a more positive attitude towards life when we've been down in grief. It's about the sun rising every morning. It's about spring after winter. There's a very powerful metaphor in "rising".'

I feel as estranged from David Paterson's views on Christianity as Alice in Wonderland trying to get the Mad Hatter to talk of the world in terms she can understand. Like Alice, I cling persistently to what I know. I press on with my questions.

Q: 'Don't communicants of the Church of England believe in the virgin birth, Christ's mission, his teaching, capture, his trial, death on the cross and resurrection? It is, is it not, a set of beliefs?'

A: 'Some certainly do. I suspect the people who want an intellectual background for their faith and think they've got one, unfortunately have settled for the intellectual background they were taught in Sunday School and have never had enough faith to change it. [The shaft strikes home.] Such people think that faith is about having set, fixed, unthought-out propositions which they simply believe because they've been told it's true. I would want to unsettle that all the time.'

And that is certainly what he does. Many have left his congregation since he arrived at St Peter's twenty-eight years ago. He now ministers to around fifty; that's ten or twelve at any one service. But David is a good man – taking in, even housing, local tramps, embracing local people of other religions, members of immigrant communities. Perhaps he's simply in the wrong job. Others who think as he does become social workers, teachers, doctors. It doesn't occur to them to become parish priests because they recognize that they don't have what the world thinks of as the qualifications for the job.

But David Paterson is not alone. Some 30 miles away, at Barrow-upon-Soar, the Reverend Stephen Mitchell also disbelieves the Church's teaching that Christ rose on the third day. By now, strangely, my interviewing technique is becoming quite dogmatic, even truculent. While my own religious outlook is distinctly sceptical, I find myself speaking up for all those congregations I know to be seeking certainties and comfort in religion, and who expect to find leadership in their priests rather than a lot of convoluted theology that means they believe no more than I do.

I put my checklist to the Reverend Stephen Mitchell:

Q: 'Do you believe in the bodily resurrection of Christ?'

A: 'No.'

Q: 'Do you believe there was an empty tomb?'

A: 'There is in the story. But I still ask you what has speculation about what happened to Jesus's body in an empty tomb got to do with the way I live my life now?'

Q: 'Do you believe in life after death?'

A: 'I believe in life before death.'

Q: 'In this world?'

A: 'Yes, and having the blessing of, if you like, eternal life now.'

Curiouser and curiouser. What's more, Stephen Mitchell doesn't even accept my catechism checklist approach:

'I think there are two almost radically opposed views as to what faith is all about. On the one hand there's the idea that faith, saying "yes" to certain eternal truths, is like doing a questionnaire in a magazine. You go through statements: "Yes, that's true; yes, that's true." And when you turn to the back page, if you got eight out of ten right, you can say you're a Christian, and if you got two out of ten right, it's time to get out. That's nothing to do with faith for me. The question for faith is not, "Is it true?" but, "Does it bear fruit?" So I look back over faith as I look back over the history of art, and see a series of creative expressions. And we, if you like, have joined the painting class; we have to create our own authentic styles of faith today, which help us live valued and valuing lives.'

I am infinitely sympathetic to the idea of seeking in the ideas and creative expression of previous centuries, inspiration to guide us in our lives here and now. I am also aware that liberal theologians struggle to define what they mean by the truths of the faith in a world that thinks of truth as something that is scientifically verifiable or has historical evidence to support it. What puzzles me is why people who do not have exact beliefs remain parish priests, serving congregations who do. And what troubles me is the extent to which they may be deceiving Christian people of simple, uncomplicated faith. Clearly this worried Stephen Mitchell, too, and he made an attempt to put the record straight. The occasion he chose was a meeting of the Mothers' Union, early in 1989. The subject he chose to discuss: the divinity of Christ. It's not difficult to imagine what Alan Ayckbourn would make of such a combination. But the reality must have been painful indeed. Apparently when Stephen had explained to the meeting of women that he did not believe Jesus was divine, 'There was just a stunned silence. Then a few of us challenged him. But his defence was that Jesus never said he was God.'

Debate about the divinity of Christ raged early in the fourth century. The Athenasian Creed won out, and since then the divinity of Christ has been Christian dogma, though what that actually means is still debated. Stephen Mitchell takes these differences with his parishioners lightly: 'I'm happy for them to hold their view – but it's not mine. The Church doesn't stand still on eternal truths: it is constantly creating and recreating itself.'

David Paterson and Stephen Mitchell are not simple, maverick priests, each following a lone intellectual path. They are part of a network known as the Sea of Faith. Both were founder members of the movement formally created in 1989. One of its early moving spirits was the Reverend Don Cupitt, of Emmanuel College, Cambridge, and his ideas are still, for many, an inspiration and guiding force.

Sea of Faith takes its name from Cupitt's television series, itself named from Matthew Arnold's famous poem, 'Dover Beach', published in 1867 at a time when Darwin and biblical scholarship were felt to be undermining the religious certainties of Victorian life. According to the critic Lionel Trilling, Arnold, the great Christian humanist, strove 'to show the meaninglessness of all theological distinctions and by the establishment of a kind of natural theology, based on morality, to put an end to the dissidence and divergence of contemporary religious opinion.' Yet the mood of his poem is one of pained dismay:

> The sea is calm tonight.
> The tide is full, the moon lies fair
> Upon the straits...
>
> The sea of faith
> Was once, too, at the full, and round earth's shore
> Lay like the folds of a bright girdle furl'd.
> But now I only hear
> Its melancholy, long, withdrawing roar,
> Retreating, to the breath
> Of the night-wind, down the vast edges drear
> And naked shingles of the world.

In response to Matthew Arnold's despair, the Sea of Faith network seeks to renew faith for the twentieth century, meeting to explore and promote religion as a human creation: man as creator of God rather than the other way round. There are some 700 members in Britain, of many denominations and none, both clerics and laity. Some thirty, including David and Stephen, belong to the East Midlands branch, and thus come within the Bishopric of Leicestershire.

The time had come to visit the Bishop. I felt something of a heel going along to interview him immediately after being so courteously received at David's home. I felt as though, without naming him, I was shopping him to his boss. That wasn't how it was meant to be; but it felt that way. And I didn't know whether it was a sacking offence for a priest not to believe in the Creed.

It had certainly caused a fuss in April 1984 when the Right Reverend David Jenkins, then newly appointed Bishop of Durham, called into question the virgin birth, and drew an analogy between the resurrection and tricks with bones. A total of 12 000 people signed a petition to the Archbishop of York, protesting at his enthronement. And when the ceremony went ahead, and three days later York Minster was struck by a thunderbolt, there was much shaking of heads at such a sign of divine disapproval. But, as David Jenkins remarked lightly, it's unlikely the Deity would mistake both the date and the place. Bishop Jenkins survived in the hierarchy of the Church and did much to enliven subsequent debate and theology and remind the secular public that the ancient institution had plenty of life in it.

The Bishop of Leicester – the Right Reverend Thomas Butler – is most welcoming and then surprised. I sink into the yellow damask of a diocesan armchair and break the news that some of his priests don't believe Christ rose on the third day. Quite rightly, he first suspects the bearer of such news:

'I guess they may believe that the resurrection was more than a bodily resurrection. And if that is so, I agree with them. The resurrection certainly had continuity with what had gone before: they recognized Jesus' voice, the gleam in his eye. The person before them bore the wounds of torture. So it was the same old Jesus, but it was a glorified Jesus, an awesome Jesus.'

However – and this seems the crux of where David and Stephen differ from the mainstream – was this a vision of Jesus, seen in the mind's eye of the disciples, and not actually a dead body come back to life? The Bishop is clear and exact: 'It was a dead body come back to life, but transformed. More than a vision, or a ghost: a glorified body.'

To the suggestion that this is at odds with what I've been hearing, he is discreetly politic:

'If I began to receive letters from a particular parish saying we are quite disturbed about the preaching of our vicar, I would ask him to come and see me. I'm bound to say I haven't received such letters whilst I've been Bishop of Leicester.'

Nonetheless, he affirms for me that, while the Church of England is a very broad church – 'thoughtful holiness is our mark' – there remains 'a core of belief that it's our duty to preserve and pass on'.

The Church faces a dilemma. For some eighty years now, biblical scholars have been dating and analyzing New Testament texts.

They have uncovered much, the Dead Sea Scrolls being but a single high-profile example of the archaeological treasures that have come to light. They have questioned the disparity between different versions of reported stories, the political influences behind the formulation of dogma, the complex negotiations attendant on the writing of the creeds.

For some forty years, such scholarship has been taught in Church of England colleges, whose students emerge, buzzing with the latest in textual criticism and the history of the Church, to take up work in local parishes. But parishioners remain largely ignorant of these developments, perhaps even fearful they might shake their faith. Thus, two entirely different strands of thinking converge in the Easter celebration. And one strand, while ministering to the needs of the other, talks an entirely different language.

I recall that Lewis Carroll, Alice's creator and himself a devoutly Christian man, conjured up in Wonderland a world without order or coherence where Alice seeks constantly for answers no one is interested in giving. Perhaps, after all, seeking exactness and certainty in faith is as wrong-headed as playing croquet with flamingoes.

Postscript: There is a significant postscript to this story. Our programme was transmitted on 19 April. Ten days later, the Reverend Stephen Mitchell was called to talks with the Bishop of Leicester. Ten days after that meeting, he wrote the Bishop a letter of apology, regretting the pain and distress he had caused many Christians by what he had said and claiming it was 'unwise to think that a programme of this kind could do justice to the issues involved in proclaiming and interpreting the Christian faith today'. He went on: 'I do believe in the doctrines of the divinity of Jesus Christ, life after death and the resurrection of Christ.'

I had interviewed Stephen Mitchell for almost an hour. Whenever I had given him the chance to say as much, he had clouded the issue. These questions can, after all, be answered initially, quite briefly – yes or no. Any exposition can then follow. But Stephen Mitchell had hedged. This letter brought him back within the fold. Today he remains the priest at All Saints Church, Barrow-upon-Soar.

The Reverend David Paterson, too, issued a statement. His was altogether more judicious; not declaring outright what he actually believes. Instead this:

'I believe that I could, with integrity, affirm my vows as a priest of the Church of England .... since my understanding of them falls within the breadth of interpretation already established within the Church of England... Nothing that I have said on television, radio, the press ... has been intended to advocate any doctrine which in my view is contrary to those already held by other members of the Church of England.'

He expressed regret for pain caused, and his concern to promote 'a new and deeper understanding of the Christian message: resurrection, new life and hope'. None of this in any way contradicted what he had said in conversation with me.

Making both statements public, Bishop Butler declared he was satisfied and would not be taking any further action. The parish church councils had assured him that the ministries of both priests were valued by them.

For the Love of Man

Sex is a problem for Christian churches because sex is a problem for people. Sexual behaviour refuses to conform to the moral imperatives laid down by numerous cultures. And when any set of such rules is consistently broken by large numbers of people, the culture is thrown into crisis and a shift in the moral framework becomes inevitable. At the end of the twentieth century many cultures and religions are under such pressure.

The world's religions have always attempted to come to terms with sexuality by limiting the circumstances in which it is acceptable, such limits agreed by a particular society at a given time. The gods were often invoked to endorse such rules. And though in many cultures – Egyptian, Roman, Greek – the gods themselves behaved with reckless promiscuity, nonetheless the virtues of restraint, fidelity and devotion between men and women were almost universally praised.

The mainstream Christian theology of sex still confines it to within monogamous marriage, sanctified by God, for the lifetime of both spouses. In the Catholic Church, sex is always meant to allow the possibility of conception; the priesthood must remain celibate. In most religious traditions, homosexuality is regarded as unnatural.

However it is increasingly clear that this formula simply does not answer the needs of people today, the way they live, the freedoms they enjoy and the independence of choice and opinion they exercise. The secular and religious worlds are completely at odds over sexual mores, and many in the religious world are rebelling. Anglican Christians are seeking to remarry in church after divorce; Catholics are using birth control in defiance of the Pope. The exclusive male priesthood has fallen in the Anglican communion and will soon come under attack in the Roman Catholic Church, as will the rule of celibacy. Secular tolerance of homosexuality is now so widespread in the West that the Church appears one of the last bastions of prejudice. But that, too, is changing.

In February 1988 I began to receive letters from all over the country: from Anglicans, Methodists and Baptists. I had put myself on their grapevine, so I was not surprised by their arrival. But I was surprised at how many wrote and how much real suffering they revealed. The letter-writers all had three things in common: they were all ministers of Christian churches and they all asked me to keep their secret. The idea of men of the church being driven in such numbers to conceal an important fact about themselves from their church, their bishop, their congregation, is proof enough that something is wrong. It will not surprise you to learn that all these people were homosexual, and they lived in fear of discovery, for it would put an end to their life's work. The practice that disqualified them from the priesthood – active homosexuality – has been legal in this country since 1967.

Here are some extracts from what they had to say:

'Truthfully, it's not fear for myself but for the people that I serve, care for, and love so much. They would be very hurt. I have been a priest for many years, dealing with good people, caring for them, listening to them, being close to them in good and bad times, but I have never been able to tell them who or what I am. Being a priest and homosexual is like being a constant exile.'

'Secrecy carries burdens of guilt, frustration and fear...I feel great sorrow and anger at the tragic consequences of the Church's confusion on this matter, which is also reflected in society. I feel even greater sorrow because I feel too vulnerable to speak out about it.'

'The policy of my Bishop is very much to leave people alone, though I believe he has said that in the event of "scandalized parishioners" he would feel obliged to support them.'

'"Media attention" will unleash a torrent of hatred and personal abuse that few of us are strong enough to handle... Many live in tied houses, so the loss of job and pensions also means the loss of accommodation which is particularly threatening for those who are older or married.'

We embarked on a programme that asked whether homosexuality was a sin which the Church of England could no longer tolerate within its clergy, or whether it was a human condition created by God in the same way as heterosexuality. Would the Church make an absolute decision on the issue? And what would be the consequences of that decision?

The gay clergy who, speculation says, could constitute up to a quarter of the Church of England priesthood, believe homosexuality is an orientation, and part of God's created world. Traditionalists believe it is a sin and a perversion, citing Leviticus and several letters of St Paul, but not mentioning the gospels, or Jesus himself, who said nothing on the matter. The Church hierarchy, in trying to hold together such diametrically opposing views, finds itself jostled around somewhere between the two, struggling to find a form of words that will keep everyone happy.

In November 1987, the General Synod had debated a private member's motion that declared 'fornication, adultery and homosexual acts to be sinful in all circumstances'. It was brought by the Reverend Tony Higton, a vigorous evangelical of intransigently traditional views, who regularly volunteers to be the thorn in the flesh of the bishops. Higton, an ample cuddly figure with a halo of golden curls, is founder of ABWON (Action for Biblical Witness to Our Nation) which campaigns against such lapses from Christian exclusivity as services of multi-faith inter-communion. He deplores the fact that Anglican bishops attend. His forthright views brought him, in Mrs Thatcher's day, invitations to 10 Downing Street. Higton is not at one with the bishops.

The bishops responded to his motion by proposing an amendment. They were keen to tone down the absolutism of his language. But in doing so they gave birth to a phrase of distasteful ambiguity that in the event pleased no one: 'homosexual genital acts', they ruled, 'fall short of the ideal'. The amendment won a massive majority. A further amendment, seeking to make it effective, asked that 'appropriate discipline among the clergy should be exercised'. This was defeated. The *Sun*'s headline read, 'Pulpit Poofs Can Stay'.

Three months later, in February 1988, the Reverend Jeremy Younger went into the pulpit of St Mary's at Bow and explained to his congregation why he was leaving the ministry after eighteen years. His parishioners had not been in on the secret of his personal life as an active homosexual, although his partner had shared the vicarage for six years. The bishops, however, had known: 'I've worked with three bishops, and I've been open with them. I hadn't believed in being secretive. If I actually believe in the Christian Gospel I can only be open. And I am.'

The team ministry within which he worked also knew. When the Reverend Richard Bentley first interviewed him, Jeremy had said that he lived openly with a homosexual partner and they would expect to do so within the parish. He got the job: but no one told the congregation.

'That's not inconsistent – heaven knows, there are plenty of posts in our society where it is actually not acceptable to ask about a person's sexual orientation. I rather take that approach in interviews for posts within the ministry of the Church.'

On *Heart of the Matter* Jeremy spoke out openly, without any of television's proffered disguises: the head in shadow, the distorted voice, or the actor playing out the interview. For Jeremy the climate of deception was over; the fear had lifted. But then he had already ceased being an officiating minister.

The loss of Jeremy to the ministry may seem to traditionalists a small price to pay for holding the line against change. I think it is a small tragedy – and just one of the many failures of the Church to be generous and understanding, welcoming and open. Jeremy, by his own testimony, was not a great priest: 'I'm not a brilliant priest. I'm not a dreadful priest. I'm just someone trying to exercise a ministry within the Church, something God has called me to and the Church has acknowledged.'

The loss of just such a one – modest, unflamboyant, kind and committed, ready to work hard for little money in an inner city parish – is exactly what the church cannot afford. The only other organizations that systematically hound homosexuals are the Army and the British

National Party. And change is on the way in the Army. Surely that gives the Church pause for thought...

Yet the Church is trapped, divided and unable to heal the divide. The bishops are on the whole liberal thinkers, who believe that the Bible is a human document, written with divine inspiration. They are not required to accept its literal truth and, indeed, more and more ordained priests see large parts of the Bible and the Christian story as symbolic expressions of religious ideas. Congregations, on the other hand, are largely conservative, with a yearning for certainties, a trust in their Sunday School faith, and no time or inclination to read biblical scholars and contemporary theologians who continually challenge those certainties.

At the end of our 1988 programme about gay priests, the Bishop of Ripon said:

'I think it's perfectly possible that our sense of what is actually right and wrong may change... It's possible that in the future there may be some revision of that particular moral rule. But neither I nor the rest of the Church is ready for that change.'

And the Bishop of Chester gave an unwitting clue as to what might occasion our next programme: 'In some ways it's better to be secret about it, I think. It's been the coming out that's caused the problem, hasn't it?'

Almost seven years later, on a Sunday in September 1994, the Right Reverend Michael Turnbull, Bishop of Rochester, woke to a nightmare. The *News of the World* headlined the fact that twenty-six years before, at the age of thirty-two, he had committed an act of gross indecency with another man, in a public toilet. He had pleaded guilty and been given a conditional discharge. He was at that time Domestic Chaplain to the Archbishop of York. But now he was about to be enthroned Bishop of Durham, the fourth most senior post in the Church's hierarchy. The news threw the media and the Church into turmoil. Could the enthronement, a stupendous ceremonial bringing together civil and clerical worthies, go ahead? Once again homosexuality was on the agenda. *Heart of the Matter* went to Durham at the time of the enthronement to ask whether there was hypocrisy at the heart of the Church.

We found that, in the six years since our 1988 programme, attitudes had begun to change. First, the bishops had had a stab at solving the problem. In December 1991 they published a statement: 'Issues in Sexuality', forty-eight pages of closely argued text – 'which we do not pretend to be the last word on the subject' – aimed at 'helping forward a general process'. Clearly this was not an outright condemnation.

The bishops sought 'to promote an educational process as a result of which Christians may both become more informed about, and understanding of, certain human realities'. The realities in question are that homosexuality is legal, and that large numbers of clergy are homosexual. Clearly, the bishops were inclining the Church towards acceptance of homosexuality but, as St Augustine said when praying for chastity, 'not yet'.

For their part the homosexual clergy had become more confident, more forthcoming, and some of them were angry. The Reverend Niall Johnston was ordained in 1992, and in 1994 was running a support group for gay clergy that had some 400 members. He had served in the Army for ten years. While there he rose to the rank of Major and served both in Northern Ireland and the Falklands. While in the Army he had had a nine-year relationship with a soldier he met at Sandhurst. They had been together – defying Army rules against homosexuality – until a car crash in 1990 killed his partner. Niall now spoke openly, defying the Church to sack him:

'I think that if one had been particularly blatant in the Army, then almost certainly one would have been discharged. But those who knew took the view that it was more important that I was efficient at the job I was doing. They colluded in exactly the same way as the Church is doing today. I was told by one bishop that he expected me to behave with exactly the same degree of personal integrity as he would expect from any of his other clergy. I assumed that to mean in a loving and stable relationship rather than promiscuity.'

The bishops' statement of 1991 is the accepted wisdom on the matter at the moment. Its statement that 'homosexual genital acts fall short of the ideal' has, in the event, landed the Church with a two-tier approach to homosexuality. Homosexual couples among the laity, living together and presumably loving together, are not to be turned away from the Church, forbidden its doors or even its sacraments. Churchgoers, after all, 'fall short of the ideal' in all manner of ways. In practice this amounts to lesbians and gays being numbered, without censure, among church congregations.

For the clergy, however, expectations are higher. They must be seen to be actively striving towards the declared ideal. To set up house with a homosexual partner is clearly living in defiance of such an obligation. Thus, practising homosexuality is in reality denied to clergy but permitted to laity.

This double standard is unacceptable to both wings of the argument. Niall finds it 'philosophically impossible to justify'. Tony Higton, with his insistence that a proper discipline be applied within the Church, finds the two-tier morality, 'A diabolical hypocrisy. That's a double standard, and quite wrong.'

In the course of making this programme I was to have an important encounter with a stranger. We wanted to hear the true story of a cleric still too fearful of his church to 'come out'. He was known to me as Chris, and I was told he came from Cumbria. Neither fact was true. His real name and home were, and are, unknown to me. Such was his fear of being uncovered that we not only concealed all facts about him, but agreed to interview him and then recreate the interview with an actor.

It was an electrifying encounter. He arrived at my home, bounding up the stairs, full of energy and adrenalin. I would like to tell you how he looked – tall or squat, bald or blond, slim, bespectacled, shabby or elegant. But such descriptions might be revealing. I feel the impulse to explain his behaviour – was it timid, dogmatic, shy or outraged? – but such characteristics might be recognized. This young man disappeared into the ether the moment the front door slammed behind him. I could not now trace him, or offer any clue as to his whereabouts. He has vanished as though he never existed. And yet those of us who gathered to hear his story will not forget him:

'When you have to admit to yourself that your feelings, which to yourself are about love and friendship and pure things, actually belong in a category that is condemned, from the higher authorities, to the cheapest playground catcalls, you hope it'll go away. And you hope that all the difficulties it posed will be solved, not by great changes in society but by oneself no longer being homosexual. It'll just go away. Somehow you'll grow out of it. And then you can join the happy, content majority and not have to feel different any more.

'Looking back, those are despicable thoughts and hopes. I resent, deeply resent, society and the church for putting me in a position where I felt like that about something which was healthy and good and beautiful and part of me as I believe God created me.

'As a teenager I went away with my youth fellowship to the annual festival known as Spring Harvest. It's such a mixed blessing, evangelical Christianity. So many good things happening. But things go over the top. The leaders get over-excited and full of their own power and self-importance, and they start making it up as they go along.

'They said: "We believe God is saying to us, there are four people in this room who've been suffering a problem with homosexuality." It's a joke. I mean, four people in a room full of 500 teenagers, and Church teenagers at that. You know, gentle, soft people. It's bound to be the case. But I believed in what was happening. I thought this is it. Tonight is the night God has chosen.'

Chris stayed behind after that meeting with dozens of others called to make commitment, to pray for the gifts of the Holy Spirit: 'Bread and butter stuff to evangelical charismatics.' He was the very last one to be counselled.

'I knelt there praying for ten minutes, quarter of an hour, twenty minutes, half an hour, till everyone else had gone. This counselling room in which there had been 100 teenagers, all gone, everyone else gone home to bed and there was me – left.

'Five or six counsellors then began a form of exorcism. I knelt down on the floor, crouched over. They were laying on hands. They asked me to speak some sort of words of renunciation which I did. I had a heavy cold at the time and at that moment coughed heavily, and they thought that was wonderful. That story would have been quoted round the country for months, about the way I coughed it all out.

'It should have been the perfect healing; everything was in place. I knew the categories. I knew the language. I was heavily involved in this stuff. I had been for years, this evangelical charismatic approach. There'd been this great enemy oppressing me all the way through my teens, this great fear, this thing I'd had to keep hidden and now it was driven out and everything was going to be wonderful.'

In the days that followed, Chris came to the realization that nothing had changed. 'That became the turning point: because then I had been through absolutely everything that the evangelical charismatic world could offer.' Nonetheless he was driven by something greater than his sexuality:

'All I ever wanted to be was the best possible Christian that I could be. That's what dictates that now I'm trying to be the best possible priest I can be. It's a far more fundamental part of me than even my sexuality and my relationships with other people.

'From then on I had to begin a new approach to the fact that I was homosexual. I had to accept and acknowledge and name to myself the fact that I was gay. And I began to have new ways of categorizing it. I thought this is a challenge that I've been given and it's a challenge I'll live with. Yes, it's difficult. And yes, I'm going to be celibate. And that's my particular trial. My particular thorn in the flesh. Everyone's got problems and this one's mine. I'm going to live with it and just carry on being the best possible Christian I can be. But, once I named it and acknowledged it, then the process of beginning to value it began. I began to think maybe always being single has an upside in terms of the Christian ministry. Maybe some of the images of being gay have an upside. Maybe being colourful has an upside. Maybe even living in a sort of bohemian flat!

'But the most important part of my life's pilgrimage was about where God would be leading me, and that was about the priesthood. This thing we call vocation, this calling, this whisper of the

Holy Spirit that just won't go away. It keeps wooing you on; it was just pulling me onwards, drawing me onwards, and had been, since I was fourteen.'

Chris first took a degree in humanities at university, then went to theological college.

'By the time I was going to theological college I was reasonably confident that the Church was larger and more accommodating and more spacious and more elastic than it would ever admit in public. That's what makes me very angry. Because that is virtually a definition of hypocrisy. That it says one thing and does another. And that makes me extremely angry.'

Nine years ago Chris met his partner. They were acquaintances, then friends. Six years ago they became a couple. Three years ago they entered into a special relationship in which, at a private ceremony, they made a covenant together, had a special time of prayer and gifts, and entered into a permanent, stable relationship to which they have committed themselves for ever.

'The whole evangelical system I've just described was based on false assumptions about the outside world... And the same is true of the Synod's decisions and the bishops' statement. They're telling themselves lies about the outside world in order to hammer out for themselves a self-serving theology which begins to look respectable, but from the outside is a joke. A lie. A miserable web of hypocrisy.'

Shielded by his anonymity, Chris feels free to give voice to the rage that burns in him. I ask if he feels happy about being a subversive in the Church he loves.

'I am very happy about being subversive. I have some excellent role models, first amongst whom is Thomas Cranmer. He was married before it was legal for a priest to be married. He can't have had that marriage blessed by the Church, so she was not so much a wife as a mistress. And history has proclaimed him a saint, quite rightly. So I'm quite happy to live with that.'

Chris is the sort of person who changes things; who changes those around him. That afternoon he changed those who heard him. Yet he remains 'in the closet', unable yet to speak openly as he has spoken to me. That perhaps explains the tenor of his conversation: garrulous, generous and, at the same time, angry. Some of that anger is for himself.

Once he had left my home, sweeping out on the wing of his own talk – as swiftly and precisely as he had swept in – we all fell back exhausted. It had been like an angelic visitation. Had we really heard what we thought we'd heard? Perhaps he wasn't real; his eloquence simply a materialized form of the case for gay priests. Little of this testimony would find its way into our crowded programme. Television is like that, snatching the most pertinent sound bites away from their context of character and developing conversation. Even on the page, the vigour of his talk is elusive, the power of his presence unremarked. He fled into the early evening. I may never see him again. On the other hand I have a feeling he may one day turn up as the first gay Archbishop of Canterbury ...the first known one, that is.

Within six months of that programme, in March 1995, we had occasion to talk again to the Reverend Niall Johnston who had come out on our programme the previous autumn. *Heart of the Matter* was taking a look at and examining how people's lives had changed since we first interviewed them. For Niall, both his private and public life had been transformed by talking openly about his homosexuality.

'The programme had hardly gone on air before my phone started ringing. I had parishioners at the door just after the programme bringing me a house plant. I've now had almost 500 letters since the programme of which three have taken me to task. The Bishop phoned the next day to say he'd seen the programme and things were OK. The following Sunday, parishioners said they'd seen the programme and wanted to support me. I'm aware some of them felt uncomfortable but sadly they haven't spoken to me directly. So there are still some tensions...'

I was impressed by how thoroughly Niall had changed. It was as though he'd previously been suffering a debilitating illness that made him hesitant and reserved, and had now completed a restorative course of vitamins that had more than renewed a natural vitality and confidence. He clearly wasn't a different man, just the same man released from restrictions and silence into a fuller sense of his own identity – more Niall than before. He bounded down the aisle of the church, greeting us with open pleasure. He talked and moved with more grace and freedom. When I remarked on this he himself was surprised:

'I thought I was pretty together about where I was before the programme. I'm amazed about how much more relaxed I've been since. It's been a great relief to talk in the first person and not in some abstract way about what it might be like to be gay or lesbian.'

Affairs in the Church at large had moved on apace since October 1994. The main engine of this propulsion had been the campaign of outing by the homosexual group OutRage. Peter Tatchell had led the rush of gay protesters who had attempted to disrupt the enthronement of the Bishop of Durham on 23 October 1994. A month later, on 30 November at the Synod in London, OutRage named ten bishops it claimed were homosexual. It also entered into private correspondence with a further five it hoped would come out of their own free will. Two of the five responded. On 8 March the 72-year-old former Bishop of Glasgow and Galloway, Derek Rawcliffe, made a direct admission and a touching tribute to the effect of his homosexual love affair, which occurred when he had a diocese in the Pacific: 'I began to love everyone in a new way and to see that in spite of our failings and sins and so on God loves us and I believe that was the work of the Holy Spirit.'

A week later the Right Reverend David Hope, Bishop of London, called a press conference to reveal his correspondence with OutRage and to describe his sexuality as a 'grey area' and his life as celibate. He spoke with icy distaste for the behaviour of the homosexual lobby, a distaste echoed by most of the media who disliked seeing a good man humiliated and saw in Tatchell the makings of a self-righteous upstart and blackmailer. However the fact remained that within just six months OutRage had revived the Christian debate on homosexuality and moved it forward in leaps and bounds, where the more moderate Lesbian and Gay Christian Movement had been gently but purposefully marginalized. If you want change, then, as the suffragettes showed, a little law-breaking and a few high-profile antics make more impact than hours of talk. Peter Tatchell cast himself as the Emily Davison of gays, flinging himself, as it were, before the King's Derby racehorse and into the limelight.

The bishops had been forced to act. In January 1995 they held unscheduled discussions that produced a strong condemnation of homophobia. The Bishop of Durham had been in talks with gay priests in his diocese. The Bishop of Southwark, the Right Reverend Robert Williamson, when asked on radio whether he would ordain a man having an open homosexual relationship, replied: 'that ...depends on whether that relationship may be stable or not... I simply don't interfere in that kind of thing. A person's sexuality is their own private affair.'

Meanwhile, in March, Cardinal Hume of the Catholic Church had reissued his note of 1993 'concerning homosexual people', with additional paragraphs on friendship and human love. These additions endorsed, almost glorified, Platonic love:

'To love another, whether of the same sex or of a different sex, is to have entered the area of the richest human experience ...'

'Being a homosexual person is neither morally good nor morally bad: it is the homosexual genital acts that are morally wrong.'

And again, confronting the possibility of gay couples living together: 'It is a mistake to say or think or presume that if two persons of the same or different sexes enjoy a deep and lasting friendship, then they must be sexually involved.' This was a confirmation of Vatican policy but expressing a new tenderness for homosexuals, and warning against homophobia.

Then on 17 March, at the bi-annual conference of all thirty-four Primates of the Anglican communion around the world, a statement was issued that declared:

'Within the Church itself there are those whose pattern of sexual expression is at variance with the received Christian moral tradition but whose lives in other respects demonstrate the marks of genuine Christian character. The issues are deep and complex.

They do not always admit of easy answers.'

Clearly the liberal leaders of Christian churches are gradually edging towards acceptance of homosexuality. When the Church of England bishops' statement of 1991 spoke of an education process, it is unlikely that it was referring to a more thorough commitment to the strictures outlined in Leviticus (18:22 and 20:13) and St Paul's Epistle to the Romans (1:24-27). In the autumn of 1995 the Lesbian and Gay Christian Movement began a concerted attempt to get its candidates elected to the Houses of Clergy and Laity. The campaign paid off. In October the Reverend Malcolm Johnson was the first member of the clergy to be elected to the House of Clergy on an openly gay ticket. But, although the liberal wing of the church is on the move, the conservatives are also girding themselves for the struggle. The years ahead will be extremely hard. As with women priests, these changes will lead to some high-profile resignations, the splintering of certain groups and a good deal of bad feeling. The headlines will love it.

Mission Impossible

In the summer of 1992, over a period of six weeks, I was able to follow closer at hand than most the American evangelist Morris Cerullo's extraordinary visit to Britain. News of his 'Mission to London' had been blazoned ahead of his arrival in a series of posters declaring in uncompromising terms that miracles would be happening. No doubt about it. 'Some will hear the message from the Bible clearly for the first time,' ran the caption above a picture of discarded hearing aids. 'Some will see miracles for the first time,' attended a white stick and dark glasses, again discarded. 'Some will be moved by the power of God for the first time', proclaimed the poster showing an abandoned wheelchair.

Before Cerullo's jet had even touched down, the Advertising Standards Authority was being hounded for its feeble attention to such dangerous claims. An ASA spokesman, with the blithe scepticism of the non-believer, explained that they hadn't expected the ads to be taken literally, but, rather, metaphorically. 'They are only invitations to a religious meeting, after all.' So much for the secular world's judgement on religion. It was not a subject a programme within the BBC's Religious Department could be expected to resist. And, indeed, this religious background may have counted in our favour when Morris Cerullo and his henchmen decided to give us access, behind the scenes, throughout the Mission. In the event, it was a decision they probably regretted.

DAY ONE: SATURDAY 20 JUNE
I meet Dr Cerullo and his wife on their arrival at Heathrow, cameras

turning. Plans for the Mission to London have been in the making for over a year and a big part of that preparation is how to deal with the press. So when I step forward to be introduced to Dr Cerullo – the title is honorary – he isn't taken by surprise. Rather he is smiling guardedly, and soon delivering his Mission's message. He talks as we drive to the four-star Metropole Hotel in Central London. Morris Cerullo World Evangelism does a deal there, so he always stays in its four-star luxury. His followers get special rates. It's a style many American evangelists are used to.

Like many people with a powerful stage presence, Morris Cerullo seems subdued and insignificant in daily life. For a start he is physically small, no more than 5 foot 4. I, in my heeled shoes, stand taller. He has flown in overnight from America. Nevertheless he appears immaculate in navy suit, white shirt and silk tie. His hair, which is not thick, has the artificial look of Grecian 2000; its black slick across his head like the crude colours of a children's cartoon. He has large, almost saucer-round brown eyes, which widen in innocent openness when the media fail to take him on his own terms. His jaw has the square line and rounded jowls of good living. He looks, and indeed is, an American businessman at the head of a multi-million dollar enterprise. But he is much more than that.

On the way to the hotel he explains that his mother, an orthodox Jew, died when he was two and his Italian father put him in a Jewish orphanage in New Jersey. He was barmizvahed at thirteen. But at the age of fifteen he had a vision in which God took him out of this world and showed him those suffering in hell. From then on he embraced Christ as his Messiah. I express surprise at this. 'Yes, it wasn't an easy thing for the rabbis. I'd been raised as an orthodox Jew, been going to synagogue every morning. It was uncomfortable for them.' And a formidable start in life for him, lacking a family, to rebel at the age of fifteen against the institution that had given him shelter and schooling, defying all they held dear to proclaim himself a Christian evangelist. Clearly his confidence was manifest early.

Today he is a man of absolute certainty and unwavering single-mindedness. We amble amiably around his sense of the spiritual in the world: 'The churches have failed the people... Every human being has a need... To me this is the most important thing; it's where the church is failing... It's failing to reach out to touch people at the points of their needs.' I sense that you only have to press a button and he will spout on like this for hours. It's what he's good at. But it gets boring after a while. 'Our message is to bring people to know that God can do what he claims to do.' Morris Cerullo consistently avoids taking either responsibility or credit for these promised miracles, alleging always that he is but a man and God works the miracles through him. But miracles he insists they are.

DAY TWO: SUNDAY 21 JUNE

The day of the first service. By 10 a.m. Earls Court is a ferment of final arrangements – lights, microphones, seating. Cerullo, conscious of our cameraman at his elbow, makes a remark to a colleague clearly intended for us: 'These television guys, you know, they think this is a theatrical performance – they don't realize that this is not a show, this is a worship meeting. We're not putting anything on for the cameras. We're here just worshipping God.' He betrays his constant concern about the media. But he has a problem: he wants massive coverage, but he doesn't want criticism. Nor, it emerges, does he want a serious assessment of the medical recoveries he claims as miracles.

However financial considerations, if nothing else, make his cohorts publicity-hungry. The London week is estimated to cost $400 000. Entrance to Earls Court will be free, although a carefully structured series of fundraising appeals is scheduled throughout each evening. More than this, his organization has a bid in for a slice of Britain's cable television: he needs a high and approving profile. So a penned enclosure is made ready for the media, where they can observe without straying. Our cameraman's requirements are met with every appearance of smiling collaboration, while in reality he is given little of the freedom he requests. Only when he is overheard saying to the producer, 'I really wish I could get in among the prayers' does their attitude to him change. They smile large, gratified smiles, believing him to be expressing a religious yearning. But that happens when the show is already in full swing.

First there is the build-up, and even now anxiety is rising: a wall of whispered concern between us, shadow-boxing, his interests against ours. We are permitted backstage, where from about three in the afternoon the 'prayer warriors' are put through their paces. As many as 150 churches across Britain have been recruited to help the Mission, the majority black gospel and Pentecostal churches. From their number come the prayer warriors, who are now urged into an ecstatic state of speaking in tongues; each one gabbling fast and unintelligibly, holding out their arms in passionate appeal. The mingled cacophony rises into the vast echoes of Earls Court. Once the evening meeting begins the prayer warriors will be dispersed among the audience, to prompt, lead – dare one say manipulate – the others. They will also monitor the audience, facing them rather than the stage, watching for those being swept off their feet by emotion, directing those who claim sudden healing to the place where their testimonies – and their addresses – will be noted down.

Morris Cerullo's arrival backstage is inconspicuously important – its only parallel in my experience being Elizabeth Taylor sneaking from a vast limousine into the stage door of the Victoria Theatre. He has already been preparing himself, 'in intense prayer for four hours during the day. I will not have eaten for twenty-four hours before the meeting. This is not a performance. You're dealing with illness, sin, spiritual wickedness. You know, people think you're like Frank Sinatra, and get up and give a performance.' It occurs to me that Frank Sinatra prepares himself too. But it seems an odd comparison to volunteer. His parallel, not ours.

The audience is in place now. Some 7000 people. Many wheelchairs brought to the front. The choir gives voice, a girl in a green silk dress belts out hymns as though they are songs from *Evita*. This goes on, blared through loudspeakers for a headache-inducing hour and a half. And then ... the moment.

Backstage, Cerullo's head is bent in prayer; steadying hands support his slow climb up the stairs – and part the heavy curtains as he reaches the top. As he moves into the blinding lights there is a great roar of welcome. He could well be Frank Sinatra after all. Except Cerullo's hair is still black.

Cerullo's technique is masterly. Slowly he turns up the voltage, charging and recharging his audience, with regular calls to 'Rejoice', 'Give thanks', 'Put up your hands', 'Reach out to the Lord'. He keeps them in a perpetual frenzy of engagement that must certainly change their consciousness of what's happening. Soon the healing will begin. 'We ought to say to the Holy Spirit – you-do-whatever-you-please.' Huge cheers. 'Take it, my brother, take it, my sister. Take it.' The right arm swings into action: 'All kinds of healings are taking place right now.' The crowd are on their feet, reaching out to the stage, palms open, in what looks for a moment like a sunny field of *Zieg Heils*. Some begin to quiver, out of all control; some swoon on the floor. Already they're queuing up to go on stage and give their testimony.

'This is Luanne,' one of the stage cohorts explains. 'Two weeks ago she collapsed and was rushed into hospital; she had no support in her leg. She walked into the meeting tonight with this crutch and is walking out free through the power of God.'

'Come on, darling,' invites Cerullo, 'run, run to the end, run, run. Father I give you praise.'

Luanne, in shirt and leggings, belts round the stage as her crutch is brandished aloft.

'There it flows. That's the power of God. Let it go.' Cerullo has put his hand on her forehead and appears to push her backward. She falls to the ground, but is up in a trice. The same treatment is meted out to all adults lining up to claim their cure. It's called 'being slain in the spirit'. Then Luanne is led offstage – the cohort stage management again – to meet the press. She is a pretty young teenager, happy to pass among us, telling her straightforward tale. Quite clearly she is walking – and running and balancing – normally.

Next a slender Asian woman with cascading dark hair, leads her son forward. 'Last week the optician said he'll need to wear glasses from the moment he wakes up. But today we believe through the power of Jesus his eyesight's been completely restored.' There's no evidence for this at all, but it is numbered unquestioningly as one of the miracles.

Number Three: Janice Butler, a woman who was born with displaced hips, bends to touch her toes with no pain. She is stout and not young so the ease with which she swings around is impressive. We note her case too.

DAY THREE: MONDAY 22 JUNE

We film Morris at his morning exercise, walking miles to nowhere, on the hotel's walking machine. There's a post mortem on last night: his first preoccupation, the media. His cohorts report: 'There were fifty-seven different media people out there. There was some scepticism, but at the same time several of us were bombarded by the press asking "What's happening?" "What are they doing?"'

Today's media agenda is a bomb waiting to go off. Cerullo has agreed to go on ITN at lunchtime, live. There he will come face to face with one of his most dangerous critics. Dr Peter May is both a GP and a devout Christian, a member of the Church of England Synod, no less. He throws out a challenge: 'I cannot find a single case of genuine healing: if there is evidence, then I ask you to produce it.' This is live television and cannot be cut, so Cerullo goes for the big claim: 'We can produce evidence of people being healed of incurable cancer.' It is a claim he is never to substantiate. Dr May gives him the chance: 'I would like you to produce your three best cases this week – then we can see actually what has happened.' Cerullo agrees, without hesitation.

So, is Cerullo a fraud, a showman, a conman, a devout Christian, a genuine healer? Which, if any at all? He is certainly a showman, heading a complex enterprise. Morris Cerullo World Evangelism, worth some thirty million pounds, has headquarters in San Diego and outposts around the world. The UK operation employs ten to twelve people full time. It is a canny fundraiser, asking all those who attend meetings to hand in their names and addresses so they can stay in touch. Requests for money come later.

For over thirty years Cerullo has been evangelizing and has set a target – promised to God – of a billion brought to Christ by the year

2000. I also believe he is, in his own terms, a devout man. He genuinely believes he has been called by God to proclaim his ministry. His huge, unchallenged ego focuses continually on himself as the conduit of God's grace. The world in which he moves centres only around him, organizing, planning, smoothing his progress wherever he goes. It is a self-centred existence.

But between the showman and the Christian there yawns a vast gulf. The Christian prays and preaches and calls down God's healing. Then he moves on. He does not attend to the detail: indeed it is as if he fears the detail. Although he throws out the offer – 'check it out', 'verify it' – it is merely as evidence of his certainty. He doesn't seriously believe anyone will take him at his word. Indeed he ascribes such attempts to the scepticism of the Godless press, rather than any genuine desire they might have to protect vulnerable people from being given false hopes. The businessman Cerullo wants to claim them as proof he's peddling a good product. The devout Cerullo wants to believe God works through him. Serious findings to the contrary might destroy both his bank balance and the faith that has for decades supported the orphaned Jewish boy who invented a gratifying identity for himself.

That night there is an incident. Outside Earls Court, in the gloaming of the early summer night, we come upon a noisy, agitated group huddling round a man in shorts and T-shirt lying on the floor. The man is screaming: 'You bastards, you bastards!' Apparently, when sitting in his wheelchair in the hall, he had begun to protest at what was going on. According to his account, he had been hauled unceremoniously out of the hall and even out of his wheelchair. 'I've got spinal trouble and they dragged me out.' A Cerullo woman – a prayer warrior perhaps – steps forward, showing neither piety nor compassion for the writhing figure: 'We've just had great healing inside and this demonic man would stop what God is doing.' Earls Court Security are summoned on the instant to stop us filming further.

DAY FOUR: TUESDAY 23 JUNE

Cerullo denies all knowledge of last night's troubling events. The wide saucer eyes look pained at my pressing the point. 'I'm not aware of those type of things. I don't get that feedback, but in a situation like this any type of incident is possible, isn't it?' Quite so. It is a well-known political technique for support officers to keep the leader unaware of anything that might be damaging to him. Denial is then not only convincing but true, whether it's arms sales to Iran or crippled people who won't buy the Cerullo line. It is the cohorts' job to keep Cerullo confident.

That night he again gives his all: 'Go, you foul spirit of infirmity. You that have crippled arms and twisted legs, you that have brought strokes into these physical bodies. In the name of Jesus, go.' Cerullo believes that illness is caused by Satan. Those who are sick are possessed by demons, and the spirit of Christ must be invoked to drive them out. Each evening is a knock-out battle between such forces. Perhaps Earls Court is just the place.

But tonight is the most distressing of all. By now I am immune to the endless singing, the swaying hysteria of the crowd, the rabble-rousing exhortations. But not to the frail vulnerability of two small children, both black, both utterly bewildered. A little girl in tears is led on stage by her mother.

Cerullo: Do you feel any pain in your legs?

She: No.

Cerullo: No pain at all?

She: (*sucking at her hankie*) No.

Cerullo: Just run a little bit with me. Come on... (*he pulls her with him and she takes three or four steps*). Oh yes. (*to the audience*) Put your hands up. Cancer of the bone.

Mother:She has cancer in the blood and the bones. It's all over.

Cerullo: (*to the audience)* I want you to raise your hands and say, 'Father, I thank you for the healing of the cancer of the bones.' Go on, praise him. Now get her back to the doctors and come and tell us what they tell you as they verify the healing.

Next a small boy. He is deaf and dumb.

Cerullo: I'm gonna have him look at me just a little bit, and see if we can get him to speak. One –

He holds the boy's attention and mouths at him. The child grunts. The sound, picked up on the microphone, relayed round the hall, could be anything. Our own camera, close up, shows it to be a mere noise.

Cerullo: Two –!

The grunt again. Mounting excitement from the audience.

Cerullo: Three! Four! Five!

Each time a grunt.

'Praise God,' rhapsodizes Cerullo as though he, we and the thousands around had witnessed a miracle. It is altogether a disgusting performance. We include it in our programme.

By the end of the week, 476 healings were being claimed.

We are making two programmes. The first tells of Cerullo's arrival, the evenings at Earls Court and itemizes his claims. The second, seven weeks later, will report on whether his claims have proved medically justified.

By the time of our second, follow-up, programme, there has been a death. Audrey Reynolds, a 25-year-old with a congenital brain abnormality, had been an usher throughout the Earls Court meetings. One evening she'd gone up on stage to testify that her ankle, apparently sprained, had been cured. On the Saturday immediately following, Audrey was found drowned in her bath. She had stopped taking her medication and had had an epileptic fit. She'd been known to give up her medication on previous occasions but nonetheless the Southwark coroner had declared: 'It is a tragedy that she went to that meeting and thought she was cured of everything. Sadly it led to her death.' The media were interested, and Morris Cerullo was back in London on what seemed to be a damage-limitation exercise, regarding both Audrey herself and our first programme, which had ended with a promise to test the claims of miraculous healing.

The Cerullo case, that Audrey had on other occasions stopped taking her tablets, cut no ice with Dr Peter May, the Anglican GP still doggedly tracking down the supposed miracles in search of any medical evidence of genuine healings. I put it to him that Cerullo says, from the stage, and I have heard him, that people should still keep taking their medication. 'Yes,' he replies, 'but that is the small-print message. The large-print message is "have faith and abandon your treatment". The posters proclaim that. It happened on the platform when people cast away their crutches. I'm afraid it is an inevitable consequence. If depressives stop taking their tablets, they're likely to become suicidal; if diabetics stop their insulin, they're likely to go into a coma. An epileptic might well have a fit.' Dr Peter May, a conscientious and devout man, is outraged by what he calls 'the Cerullo circus', and has said so on our programme. It has made him and us *personae non gratae* in the Cerullo camp.

Not surprisingly, then, the *Heart of the Matter* team had a setback. In our first programme we had highlighted five cases claimed as miraculous cures. In the weeks that followed, as we sought to follow them up, four of the five refused to appear on the programme again. Some wouldn't even speak to us. We reported as much and explained what we had been able to find out.

Natalia, the little girl with cancer of the bone, for whose healing Dr Cerullo had thanked God, had since needed several blood transfusions and her prognosis remained unchanged. The parents of the deaf and dumb Elijah Lewis refused to discuss his case. Luanne, who had thrown away her crutches and run around the stage, had been advised, we were told, by her pastor at Gravesend Christian Fellowship, not to speak to us. She refused even to let us check medical records to verify the diagnosis. Not much faith there! Janice Butler also would not allow us access to her records. What had suddenly checked their enthusiasm to bear Christian witness? Medical records are indeed intimate and private, but it was not television that had proclaimed miracles and said they could be proved.

Suddenly, with our game check-mated, the Cerullo organization called a press conference to introduce their own testimonies of healing.

Cerullo was clearly rattled but prepared, despite declaring that he considered our programme had betrayed him, for another encounter. 'Are we at last to see genuine healings?' I asked. 'Oh there'll be dozens! But you see what you guys are doing is twisting the thing around. You're saying give us some testimonies and prove what happened. Well, that's not really our approach. Our approach is we're gonna show you and [with emphasis] *work together with you* to get some testimonies to show what God did at Earls Court.'

Ten people came to the press conference to give testimonies of healing and they made Morris Cerullo feel a whole lot better. He sat, beaming in their midst, for publicity photographs. Then he left us to them, to verify with their permission the changing nature of their illness. They were clearly from among his most devout followers, convinced that Cerullo had brought a miracle of God into their lives. But their accounts are couched in different terms from those of their doctors, clouding the medical detail and exaggerating both the severity of the original ailment and the degree of recovery.

Ann Terry had complained of a lump in her groin and pain in her stomach and right leg. After the Mission, the pain and the lump disappeared. She reported: 'The doctor said "We'd better examine you, young lady." He said, "Oh, I can see where it's been." So that's in the notes. If you want to verify it, you can.'

The doctor who originally saw Ann confirmed to us that she had had a small cyst but he didn't think it worrying enough for treatment. Such cysts can disappear naturally.

Maureen Dawes had X-rays showing a cyst lump in her skull which, pressing forward on her eye, affected her sight and caused great pain. After the Cerullo meeting the pain and the cyst disappeared. She insisted that God had removed it.

Her specialist told us he wasn't at all surprised the cyst had disappeared. Maureen had not been back to the doctor since and refused our request for an X-ray to confirm whether or not the lump in her skull had gone.

Edna Merryman's claim to be cured of diabetes dated back to a Cerullo meeting in Blackpool in 1984, eight years earlier. Clearly the organization was having to search back through the records for plausible cases. Her doctor told us Edna still had diabetes. It cleared up briefly but returned.

Alfred Coombs had cancer of the oesophagus. When he went to the Cerullo meeting he could only swallow liquids, nothing solid.

Now he was eating solids. His doctor revealed he was indeed seriously ill but he was also currently on a course of radiotherapy. God or medicine? Mr Coombs took the shrewd view that it was God through medicine.

From all these testimonies, sincerely and devotedly held, I learned several things, probably about myself as much as others. We don't pay attention or hear with any degree of exactness what doctors say when they are trying to diagnose our illnesses. Also many ailments – aches, pains, even lumps and bumps – do simply go away in the course of the body's own self-healing. That said, I also accept that if we, in the calmness and concentration of prayer, believe God will make us better, then we are probably going to feel in better spirits in consequence.

And then there was the case of Sheila Lambshead. We met Sheila at the press conference but travelled to her home in Barnsley and went with her to see her consultant, Peter Cox. Sheila is a buxom, jolly Lancashire woman, full of energy and bounce. It is the bounce that is remarkable. For years Sheila had been virtually unable to walk – because of crippling back pain. She was on what she called 'a tremendous amount' of strong painkillers. She needed walking sticks to get about; she used a zimmer frame. At weekends her husband Ron pushed her out in a wheelchair. The pain was so great she got very depressed, even sometimes considering suicide: 'take a load of pills, or just get to the kerb when there's a bus coming.'

For two years, she and Ron had been members of an Evangelical gospel church when in 1990 her daughter took her to a Morris Cerullo meeting in Blackpool where she went up to be healed. What happened then was her miracle. 'It was as if I had a hole in my head and the pain that was in all my legs and feet and arms and back just went straight through it. And there was such a beautiful light. It was like Wembley, all lit up.'

That night Sheila ran and danced. The depression and the pain were gone and have not come back. So, what happened? Her consultant showed me two X-rays. One taken in 1989 showed that Sheila had a very degenerate intervertebral disc – what he called a localized arthritic segment – at the base of the spine. The second X-ray, taken at our behest, showed the pathological condition to be unchanged; the damaged bones remain damaged. The strange thing is that the symptoms have entirely cleared up.

Sheila is thrilled with her recovery: she plays with her dog, bending, stretching, running for the camera. A miracle then? Peter Cox is wary: 'I would have called it a miracle if we'd taken X-rays and her lowest lumbar intervertebral disc space had returned entirely to normal. I'm not a religious person and find the definition of miracles very difficult.'

But Sheila is religious and knows it's a miracle. 'God has cancelled the pain: the pain is more important than the bone. If the bone's still wrong, why am I free of pain?' I suggest tentatively – she is a forceful lady and passionate in her conviction – that a psychologist might say the strength of her faith is stopping her feeling the pain. She pours scorn on the suggestion. 'The psychologist can go for miles and miles and miles and say, "Yes, it's marvellous what her brain has done!" But it isn't the brain. It is God and I know it's God. And nothing – hell or high water – would move me from that position.' We leave Sheila bouncing and happy. We have been happy with her and, like her consultant, impressed by her recovery. And if we, like him, regard it not as a physical recovery but a transformed state of mind, who is to say that that is not what a miracle is? Sheila's case stands in the programme.

Most Christians agree that Jesus performed at least thirty-five miracles as reported in the Bible, many of which involved instantaneous healing. After their week-long Mission to London, Morris Cerullo World Evangelism claimed at least 400. What's more, distressed by press criticism and the impact of our two programmes, Cerullo promises to set up a medical symposium of independent doctors in which he will offer irrefutable documentation of case histories. It doesn't happen. Instead, 500 sympathizers are treated to an expenses-paid three-day conference in Birmingham. Dr Martin Soole, a GP from Wanstead and a member of the Christian Medical

Fellowship, went with an open mind but reported later that he found 'no evidence that anything had occurred that is outside the realm of normal clinical experience'.

He touches on an important point. Matters that now come within normal clinical experience would once have been attributed to miracles. As scientific knowledge expands our horizons, logical explanations put the squeeze on the inexplicable. Perhaps that's why the Catholic Church is more rigorous than the evangelist churches in the way it defines and recognizes miracles. The 1993 *Catholic Almanac* defined miracles as:

'Observable events or effects in the physical or moral order of things with reference to salvation which cannot be explained by the ordinary operation of laws of nature and which therefore are attributed to the direct action of God... God who created the laws of nature is their master. Hence, without disturbing the ordinary course of things, he can – and has in the course of history before and after Christ – occasionally set aside these laws and has also produced effects beyond their power of operation.'

Within such definitions, only sixty miracles have been officially recognized at Lourdes since it first became a shrine 130 years ago. Nonetheless, some 50 000 pilgrims go there annually, buoyed up by hope. As human intelligence unlocks more and more of what the church calls 'the laws of nature', belief in miracles will increasingly be associated with members of the Pentecostal and evangelical churches. Their theology puts St Paul's first letter to the Corinthians – with its references to healing, to speaking in tongues, to prophecies – at the centre of their faith. Theirs is the fastest-growing branch of Christianity in Britain today.

Certainly nothing stops Morris Cerullo. He was back in London in 1993, and again in 1994, with less flamboyance but ever more extravagant promises. On offer to those who donated £63, something described as 'His Endtime Financial Anointing' – 'I wouldn't ask if I didn't know God was going to abundantly return it to you, miraculously increased by the release of His Endtime Financial Anointing.' Also on offer 'The Miracle of Debt Cancellation' – this, likely to appeal to those already having money troubles, called for a £30 monthly donation. In 1995 Cerullo was back in the headlines. This time an advertisment had featured a woman from Northampton and the caption: 'I couldn't have a baby. Miracles happen.' Subsequent enquiries revealed she was the mother of three children. Morris Cerullo persists in ignoring, year after year, the dubious tactics of his organization. Why could this be?

Morris Cerullo World Evangelism is now said to be worth £30 million. For a while it took time on Britain's Croydon Cable Television but was ordered off the air for breach of the guidelines. Then it broadcast on the Superchannel network until NBC took over and gave the telly-evangelists three months' notice. The organization currently holds a licence, granted by the Independent Television Commission for its European Christian Family Network, to broadcast in Britain on the condition that it makes capacity available to other religions. So far it has not sought to put that licence into operation. In fact there has been no Morris Cerullo voice on British television since early 1994. There may be many who hope it remains like that.

The Land: The People

At some point earlier this century the number of people actually alive in the world came to outnumber the total of those who had lived and died in all previous ages of human existence. I find something eerie about that fact. It is as though some ghostly landmark – a statistical image – has been glibly passed without our taking notice or warning from what it signifies. I am not even sure exactly what it does signify. But John Ryle, writing in the *Guardian*, caught the essence: 'These facts, if indeed they are facts, seem to add to the existing unease that modernity induces in us: the fear of the runaway power of technological civilization and the consequent loss of a human timescale. In deep ecological vein, one could say that the price we pay for sucking creation dry is this loss of equilibrium.'

The prospect ahead is that each year the living will outnumber the dead by a few million more. The pressure of life on the planet will become ever greater: already the diversity of species and the scale of wildlife has been affected; wildernesses and natural landscapes are threatened. Only some incalculable catastrophe – global war, unstoppable disease, rampant famine, a rash of Chernobyls – might cut numbers back. And who can wish for that? What we are facing, then, is the need to manage exploding numbers in relation to an unexpanding planet.

People everywhere are putting pressure on the land. The institutional response is to attempt to increase control. It is happening piecemeal, in all sorts of ways. Countries are becoming tougher in their immigration controls. Frontiers are policed. Visas are needed. Those who travel must offer evidence of plans to return, means of support, contact through friends or blood relations to legitimize access. Overstaying can carry punishment. The freedom to travel, to wander, to explore, in the sense it was enjoyed even as recently as Victorian times, has been circumscribed with conditions and regulations. Travellers' tales today are more likely to chronicle encounters with bureaucracies than wild beasts.

The political polemic that goes with such policies nurtures a fear of strangers and newcomers. The Turks in Germany, the Algerians in France, the Asians in Britain, all live in dread of being victimized by their host community. In the Balkans things are much worse. Ethnic cleansing is the most vicious means by which an identifiable group establishes control over what it sees as its own land. Loyalty to the group – the tribe, the nation – then takes priority over loyalty to supposed shared and civilized values.

Newcomers everywhere threaten the status quo. New Age travellers who have chosen a wandering life are spurned and spat at by those who've settled for mortgages and tidy front gardens. Gypsies, hounded down the centuries, now have fewer places than ever to set their caravans. In England they still find local pubs closed against them; in Eastern Europe they face far worse.

Within Britain, where people are thicker on the ground than most other countries, individuals act to safeguard their own. Citizen faces down citizen, and battalions of local planning regulations empower us to complain whenever a neighbour plans an alteration to his home we don't like the look of, or a neighbourhood shop applies for change of use. Hostels for the mentally ill or for rehabilitated prisoners run into objections from local communities. A church fête to raise money for roof repairs was abandoned when some of the residents of the estate in whose grounds it was planned objected that things might get out of hand: 'When you advertise these things in the papers, you don't know who'll turn up.' NIMBY – Not In My Back Yard – is virtually a national slogan. The late Tory politician, Nicholas Ridley, condemned those of a NIMBY disposition only for it to be discovered that he himself had objected to farming developments adjacent to his own property. The fear of change, and fear that change can only mean encroachment or loss, is a national neurosis. We are all in the protection racket now, protecting what we can as thoroughly as we can in these tight little islands.

Even in personal terms, our vocabulary expresses our anxiety. We speak of invasion of privacy, and needing our own space. The sense of encroachment is intensified by the information revolution, the proliferation of images, the ubiquity of sound: portable phones, transistors, walkmans. Proposals are already being framed to put further curbs on noisy neighbours. The pressure on land might be manageable if we were all ants, bees or termites, obeying group impulses for the good of the whole. But these increasing demographic pressures coincide with a growing belief in a philosophy of personal fulfilment. And these trends have been encouraged by the fourteen-year reign of a political catechism rooted in self-interest and self-seeking. *Heart of the Matter* has been to places where such pressures have erupted into the social calm and has chronicled the extent to which everyone involved believes themselves to be right.

On 30 April 1993 I took part in the siege of Combe Farm in Warwickshire, where some 250 New Age travellers in around sixty ramshackle vehicles were surrounded and finally evicted by the police. I say 'took part' in the sense that media presence at any such encounter clearly influences what happens. I have often had it whispered to me by confiding protesters, travellers, trespassers that, 'if it weren't for you and the cameras, things would be much worse for us'. Is this a conspiratorial attempt to bond me to their side or to enhance my self-esteem as defender of the dispossessed? Either way, since the miners' strike of 1984 and events at Orgreave Colliery, the first unwritten police rule in such situations must surely be 'never thump someone when a television camera is within focusing length'. Thus, the travellers were pleased to see us. The police were wary.

It hadn't been easy for me to reach the farm at all. First indications that something was happening had come back in March, when a cluster of young people had settled in to the Combe Farm buildings and surrounding fields. The farm was derelict, out of sight and sound of any other habitation, nestling in the luscious countryside south-west of Stratford-upon-Avon. The young Shakespeare, one imagines, might have joined them for a pot of ale as he travelled towards London to join the winter's season of plays at the Globe: the old Shakespeare – Stratford burgher and owner of New Place – might have rounded them up and set them before Justice Shallow. The young people travelled and lived in a motley set of vehicles – buses mostly, the occasional double-decker, lorries, trailers, even the odd old-fashioned horse-drawn caravan. Some created 'bender homes' for themselves – planting long willows, bending them and covering them over to create a shelter. Each vehicle, I was told, carried a spade for the purpose of digging and then covering a latrine hole.

For days stretching into weeks things were peaceable enough. The actual owner of the land, the man in whose name subsequent events were about to unfold, was absent, rumoured to be in London. His ownership of this place, his absolute right over its disposal and the expenditure of £25 000 of public money and the resources of 700 police from five forces to get it back for him, was never questioned or even mentioned. Englishmen who own property have such rights.

Each summer in Britain some 30 000 young people move between the many free festivals that dot the countryside. Some 10 000 of them are year-round travellers, largely working-class young people, preferring an open-air nomadic existence, even with all the harassment that goes with it, to isolation in a city tower block, or the drab uneventfulness of an inner-city squat. They recognize each other wherever they go. 'I suppose every subculture ends up having their distinguishing marks: the Beats wore polo-necks and dark shades. I'm sure if I went to the BBC I'd find a lot of women dressed similarly.' Chris is right about that. But, unlike the sassy women of the BBC, the travellers' appearance strikes disgust, if not terror, into the hearts of Middle England. Perhaps it's meant to. A sort of defiance in the face of so much hatred. Chris explains to me how he cultivated his own dreadlocks without even the head start of African hair or Rastafarianism:

'You wash it, you keep it clean, but you stop brushing it. You can put oil on it – some people use jasmine oil – and maybe rub it together in strands to help it matt up. Anywhere we go, if we're walking through a town centre somewhere, we see someone with this hairstyle – or maybe they have a dog, combat boots – we know we can go up to them at once and engage in conversation. That's one of the brilliant things between travellers. There's no ice to break.'

So the young people at Combe Farm are a loosely knit group, perhaps some familiar to each other from earlier encounters; others, strangers on meeting, become, as kindred spirits, instant friends. There are a number of mothers with small children. Plenty of dogs. And it is the dogs that started the trouble.

Tom Dancer farms 215 hectares not far from Combe Farm. He keeps some 700 ewes, many at this time of year with small lambs. On 19 March two dogs attacked his sheep. Tom, alerted by strange barking, moved fast, but too late. He came upon a scene of carnage:

'The two dogs had all the sheep in a heap in the corner of the field where there's a big ditch. We managed to cut one dog off and got near enough to shoot and kill him. Instead we followed him back to the camp at Red Hill site, another empty local farm where travellers were camped. There's no ifs and buts or doubts. That's where he came from. When we came back there was a ditch of dead and dying sheep.'

Six sheep were killed outright, five more had to be shot. Twenty-nine lambs were left motherless and had to be hand-reared. Mr Dancer went at once to confront the travellers. No sooner had he opened the doors of his van than he was surrounded by thirty or so young people who flatly denied all he claimed. 'Never seen a dog like that, sir.'

Tom Dancer was covered by insurance for his loss, but next time round, he feels, the insurers won't be so willing. He voices the outrage of the farming community, who feel they work long and hard to sustain their way of life only to see it threatened by strangers who have no right to be there. 'The travellers have got the right to opt out if they wish. But not to opt out and cause trouble for others.' His fury is contained but fierce. How can he, with his attention concentrated on his land, his animals, his modest yields, understand the rootless drifters who have straggled across his path? To him they're creatures from another planet. Farmers, after all, are having a rough enough time of things as it is, with falling demand and prices for what they produce.

Yet, ironically, farmers are one group of people who have more land at their disposal than the market can support. Many of them are paid by the Government to set some of it aside and leave it uncultivated. How if, I suggest, a farmer was to make such a field available for just a few travellers and attempt to live in harmony with them, with both sides making an effort? Tom Dancer, stiff-jawed, unrelenting, rules the idea out: 'A man'd be shunned by the rest of the farming community – he just wouldn't be accepted.'

The solidarity of the farming community had already begun showing its muscle. When word of the travellers' arrival spread, the locals began talking, anxiety mounted, murmurs turned to a call for the police to act. A public meeting was convened to explain what was being done about the problem. By mid-April the police had located and alerted the absentee owner, who then went to court to gain a possession order to have the young people evicted. But the travellers trumped that move by obtaining a fourteen-day postponement of the possession order. This was too much for the farmers at the meeting. Mr Dancer, among others, declared then and there that something must be done. Next day a number of them decided to ensure that the Red Hill site should be made uninhabitable. They went over with their ploughs and simply ploughed up all the fields, rendering it physically impossible for the travellers to park their vehicles. At the same time, throughout the area, lanes and turnings, field gateways, even the drives of some houses, suddenly sprouted mounds of rubble, debris, gravel, every manner of obstruction, enough to slow an invading army. For that is how they saw the travellers. And in truth they weren't far wrong.

For already, as April advanced, a new phenomenon was being noticed across the country. Slowly and discreetly, like the rousing of a sleeping creature, groups of young people were packing their vans and buses and taking to the roads. The travellers' grapevine – in reality a network of high-tech mobile phones – had spread the word that on the Bank Holiday of 3 May a great Beltane festival would be held at Combe Farm. Beltane is an ancient Celtic festival. Tom Dancer would not be pleased to know it once involved driving sheep through hilltop fires.

The police themselves were soon on to the grapevine. Chris Fox, Assistant Chief Constable of the Warwickshire Police, is one of the bright, thoughtful new generation of policemen who know that dogmatic confrontation is the last resort. I put it to him that I am surprised at what extensive powers the police have to act when no offence, civil or criminal, has been committed, but merely in anticipation of a breach of the peace:

'It does look repressive, but we're not talking about individuals. We're talking about lots of people coming together. And if those numbers are getting to the stage where local people are frightened, we have to make a decision. Smaller groups are not a problem. It's when there's a mismatch of expectations. The travellers are expecting to have a big, joyful party; the farmers are expecting to be under siege, and the shopkeepers are expecting to have to put up the barricades. The travellers will say it will not happen. Experience says that at a certain level at a certain time it does happen. That's the point we have to try and stop it. When do you act? We walk a very fine line.'

The police in fact have powers, under the Public Order Act of 1986, to block roads to certain people. Police throughout Warwickshire now closed many roads in the county to New Age travellers. Help had been summoned from five other county forces. At Combe Farm there was a sense of febrile excitement in the air. One or two travellers' vans and cars came tearing in at the last minute, having evaded road blocks and made it before the siege was laid. And that was it. Nothing to do but wait. Kettles were boiled on open fires, a few cans of lager shared, a bid to fetch diesel turned back by the police.

I had arrived at about 10 a.m. on the morning of 30 April. Police attending road blocks had been diverting all media enquiries to await a full briefing in a particular field. A number of us stood around in city shoes feeling helpless and remembering deadlines. I knew my camera crew, taking no risks with police delays, were at that moment hacking their way through bramble undergrowth towards the farm. As the minutes ticked by, I became uneasy about the police being so helpful to the media in this way. A shrewd move to contain us, I realized. These operations are all about control. Eventually I made a polite enquiry: 'Am I as a reporter actually being forbidden access to Combe Farm?' The question was registered and relayed on the police car phone for an authoritative answer. It was a while in coming. When it did, it managed to convey by its formal language and warning that I was about to enter a war zone: 'Miss Bakewell, you are not being forbidden. You are being advised for your own good. If you decide to proceed it must be understood it will be entirely at your own risk.'

And so, as the mist lifted over Combe Farm, I strode down the lane towards them: young men in big boots with shaved heads, women in rainbow sweaters and gypsy skirts, children riding bareback on horses. Everyone uneasy, bewildered, gentle. Two questions greeted me: 'Would you like a cup of coffee?' and 'You aren't a lawyer come to help us, are you?'

A siege is already a confrontation: the outer ring of the community vaguely aware of what is proceeding; the inner ring of police, more and more buses of them parking along the perimeter roads; and within, the besieged; drawn closer by the net closing in, chatty, defiant, expectant. There was a sense of cosy camaraderie. All right as long as it wasn't Bosnia. But Bosnia is also about claims to land. Some of the young people muttered darkly about ethnic cleansing having come to Britain. Because travellers are an open society and turn no one away, they attract a fair share of loners and eccentrics. One or two of these were getting wound up: swearing, slamming around, dangerously volatile. The mood of the company was to soothe and contain them.

And there they came, the men in blue. In double-file, marching down the lane, the sunlight catching the silver knobs on their policemen's helmets. Behind them, the armoured division – the heavier head-protection helmets, the riot shields, and rolled packs on their backs that, so the word went round, contained CS gas. For a fleeting moment of historical romanticism it felt like Peterloo, Tolpuddle – the people under attack for demanding their rights. Except that these harmless young people had no right to be there, no right to be anywhere in fact. This farm belonged to a man in London who could get the County Court Bailiff from Stratford County Court to turn up for him.

Assistant Chief Constable Fox is caught in the middle:

'The first question a traveller will ask is where can we go? And I don't know the answer. I just have to say, "You'll have to move on. If you stay here in such numbers that people are living in fear, we can't have that." So we move them on. Society doesn't seem to know what to do with a number of people who've chosen the travelling life at the moment.'

More than that, many positively rejoice in their discomfiture. Mrs Thatcher in 1986 declared: 'I'm only too delighted to do anything we can to make life difficult for such things as hippy convoys.' And Peter Lilley at the 1992 Conservative Party Conference: 'This summer I announced tougher rules affecting so-called New Age travellers. Most people were as sickened as I was by the sight of these spongers.' Six months later, here were his rules being put into practice.

At the head of the column, the County Court Bailiff advanced, the only one in mufti among the dark blue uniforms – grey slacks, white shirt and tie, no jacket. The day was hot. He read his lines: 'I'm here from Stratford County Court and I have a warrant for repossession of this...' At that moment a slab of muddy turf landed full on his chin and stuck there. A horrified silence. No one moved or jeered or laughed. With great dignity and a single gesture he removed the glutinous mass from his face and continued: '...repossession of this land. Could you please vacate it at once.' He still showed no anger, no emotion at all.

A line of travellers pressed forward. 'Are you telling us to move, then?'

'Yes.'

'You're telling us to move?'

'Yes.'

Scuffles broke out. A young man with a shaven head, carrying a toddler deliberately close to the confrontation, complained that children were under attack. Within two minutes there were a couple of arrests, some shouting. Nothing much, merely token gestures of defiance, enough to salve the sense of powerlessness among teenage males. It was a summer ritual they were used to. Slowly and without too much ill-humour they began loading up the vehicles: pots and pans scooped from dying fires, a broken sofa with a flowered cover heaved onto a bus. Children collected, dogs on board, and the whole ramshackle armada made for the roads of Warwickshire.

And so a new nightmare began: sixty-two vehicles, released six at a time, with no destination and many roads blocked to them, looking for somewhere to spend the night. I clambered into the cab of an old bus which swayed and creaked along, stopping occasionally to consult vehicles fore and aft. Passing motorists frowned and hooted. One learnt to avoid eye contact with scowling suburbanites who stared from roadside gardens bright with confident colours. A police helicopter overhead monitored progress. The lanes got narrower, the route more purposeless. Towards evening one group pitched up in a lay-by just six miles from where we had set out that morning. It had taken us all day to get there, a circuit of some 30 miles. In the lay-by a police car quietly checked out numbers and intent.

The episode was over: young people diffused, the party avoided. As I headed for home in the warm summer air, the hedges heavy with blossom showing suddenly bright against the dusk, I reflected on what an English day it had been: inconclusive, but without rancour. For the police a sense of purpose achieved, yet a purpose that was only short-term and pragmatic: to stop a party, to protect the farmers, reassure locals, move young people along already congested roads. No great social solution conceived or expedited; just an operation carried through that left no one hurt. The travellers, disappointed but not surprised, travelled towards another dawn. The locals, their hatred dissipated, began to sweep the rubble from their driveways. The caravans moved on.

Within two weeks I was to meet up with a number of them again. This was at the annual Forest Fair in the forest of Dean: a three-day event with car parks and toilets as well as stalls and entertainments. The travellers' stay here was legal and licensed. The farmer who owns the land had given his permission. Here came Chris, with his blond dreadlocks still matted, meeting up with his own kind. Here, too, I found on a grassy plateau a wide circle of tall white wigwams, their white canvas silhouetted against a clear blue sky. How strange to find in rural England young people trying to recapture the respect for the land I had encountered amongst the Cree Indians in northern Canada.

Their belief that the land does not belong to them but they belong to the land also characterized the Plains Indians of North America and the Aborigines of Australia. We look back at what history did to them with shame and regret. Yet Britain now is in the iron grip of absolute property rights; land ownership is more exact than anywhere else in Europe, and rigorously honoured. So-called common land is no longer everybody's. Much of it is in private ownership or subject to the rights of grazers or tenant farmers. And Britain's laws of trespass make little allowance for shared use. As one of the travellers put it: 'Society as a whole was greedy enough to take all the common land away, to swallow all the waste land. The only reason we're stepping on people's feet is because there's no land left.' Just over a year later I was stepping on people's feet again.

Anyone who saw Twyford Down when the new M3 extension was being cut through it shuddered. The sense of injury to the landscape caught the breath. Even local people benefiting from the bypass had the honesty to admit the damage was extensive. In France or Italy such a road would have gone through a tunnel, preserving the Down and easing the traffic. In 1992 Twyford Down had been the scene of a famous and sustained protest by anti-road direct action groups. But in July 1994 it attracted another, much broader protest, and I joined it.

The people who gathered for an act of civil trespass onto Ministry of Transport land did so to draw attention to the fact that within months the Criminal Justice Bill would transform their civil crime into a criminal offence. The Government was putting the squeeze on protest groups who caused a nuisance, caused damage, caused intrusion into other people's space and lives. Protesting as an activity was to be so circumscribed that it would not in any way infringe the rights of others. This is a tricky balancing act and *Heart of the Matter* set out to demonstrate its trickiness. How far, we asked, should people of conviction go, faced with a law that offends their conscience? Many are prepared to break the law and take the consequences. But, as the laws controlling protest are strengthened, the numbers likely to find themselves on the wrong side of the legislation increase accordingly.

Here, at Twyford Down, hundreds of people came together to protest at a law that would criminalize so many. We foregathered in a lush meadow lying between rolling green hills. A mile or so further on, the slashed hillsides gaped wide and naked, their freshly uncovered chalk as dazzlingly white in the sun as a ski-slope. A lean-to building, not much more than a strip of canvas over poles, masqueraded as a press centre. Helpful young people were being helpful in a number of directions. The forces of law and order, with their glossy PR advisers and their slick sound bites, had little to fear from this wholesomely well-intentioned but chaotic attempt to tell the media what was going on. Eventually, strewn across the tussocky grass, a scattering of people with notebooks waited to hear their case. They heard many. And many cases begat many words.

First came Bernie, veteran of the Kinder Scout trespass of 1932 when, as Secretary of the Young Workers Sports Association, he'd led some 500 members onto this Derbyshire beauty spot in defiance of a third of the county force. Sixty years later he was still speaking up for walkers and pausing for laughter with cheeky references to 'the nice, peaceful activity of slaughtering grouse'. Bernie held his ground as he must have been doing through a lifetime of 'struggles'. His hands clasped through his braces over his washed-out tartan shirt, he had the red cheeks and wispy white hair of one of the seven dwarfs.

Following him, the woman from Liberty spoke of the great radical tradition of Britain, and pressed the case for a Bill of Rights. Michelle from the Advance Party explained that they were the relatively recent voice of travelling people. Helen from Road Alert told us that even where we were sitting there were ten different types of plants at our feet: 'We may have lost the Down, but it's now a symbol that direct action is part of our democracy.' Anna from the Freedom Network spoke up for squatters: 'I'm called criminal but I don't feel like one.' Anna didn't look particularly threatening but her cry of innocence ignores the fact that too many serious criminals feel as she does.

The meeting was drifting heavily now in a tide of self-justification. Adrian: 'I'm a road campaigner but I want to speak up for squats.' Someone heavy arrived from Greenpeace: 'I'm from Greenpeace,' he declared, striding in and taking over. Suddenly the talk was of activists against whaling being thrown into the sea by the Norwegian Navy. It was becoming hard to get a purchase on what we were here for. The right to protest, yes? Then let's get on with it.

But anyone who's ever been on a protest knows it never happens like that. Political dissent in this country would die of boredom, and long before the police put the boot in, if it weren't for the almost heroic persistence of its leaders in the face of the sheer animal incapacity of large groups of people to organize themselves into a seemly procession. Indeed when any demonstration, late in the day and long in coming, reaches its destination, the provocative behaviour that often breaks out could as well be due to the pent-up frustration of so many hours spent doing virtually nothing in the hope of achieving much.

Several hours and squashed sandwiches later, the marchers set out, and I lined up with one of that new band of protesters that is suddenly making itself heard: the formerly law-abiding middle classes. It isn't their behaviour that has changed: the law has moved the goalposts so they're now off-side. Amanda Martin was once among that rare breed: a Tory voter in South Wales. No longer:

'I used to spend my days sewing and gardening and looking after my children. Now I spend it going over ten-foot barbed wire fences and being manhandled off construction sites by large men with no scruples. But it's much less frustrating than biting your nails on the periphery.'

As we stride off along the dusty track, I notice some of the banners. One of them reads, 'Forgive us our trespasses', unaware perhaps that in the latest update of the Lord's Prayer the supposedly arcane word has given way to 'sins'. Still, the older phrase lends a certain wry wit. God on our side, perhaps. Or even an acknowledgement that, by today's values, stepping on someone else's land is now elevated to a cardinal sin. And yet the Department of Transport are doing it all the time.

Amanda Martin is angry about plans to build fifteen miles of six-lane relief road south of Newport. In 1994 the Welsh Office designated a grey corridor on the map that swept right across the Gwent Levels, and close to the small village of Magor where Amanda lives with her husband, her parents and two children. The case of the Gwent Levels is likely to become Wales' own Twyford Down. Graham Wynne of the Royal Society for the Protection of Birds has called the route one of the UK's most environmentally damaging road proposals. It will destroy ancient ditch systems that support unique plant and insect life and provide extensive bird-breeding areas. The numbers of people there are not great: two cottages will be demolished as well as an established caravan park where twenty-eight families have settled. It is an irony of the global land grab that one of the resistances to it is not in the name of other would-be occupiers but in the interests of keeping people out altogether. Amanda and her colleagues in the National Transport Reform Movement find allies among all the conservation and ecology groups.

I went down to Magor to meet Amanda in her natural habitat. She is slight in build, delicately boned and graceful. Unruly dark hair either breaks round her shoulders or is held back in a thick rope-like plait. Her large brown eyes express thoughtfulness at my questions; she takes my allegation that she is defying the wishes of most people – who want bypasses to ease congestion and roads to save time – with a gentle seriousness. Clearly she believes in reasoned argument. Anyone looking less like a ranting fanatic it would be hard to imagine. Nor is the little village of Magor a place where one would look for troublemakers.

At its heart is Magor Square, actually a three-sided space with a pathway leading towards the church of St Mary the Virgin. The Vicar, who I find mounting his bicycle, explains that it was founded in the fifteenth century by the monks of Tintern Abbey. In the porch a swallow flies in to feed her four fledglings, noisily making their hunger heard from the nest. Hunger features again on the war memorial, reminding us to 'Remember also David Alfred Thomas, 1st Viscount Rhondda. He too died serving the nation, as Food Controller.'

Along one side of the square is one of the oldest houses in the village. Double-fronted and covered in ivy, it might well feature in magazine articles about country homes. Inside is a cool white hall with glimpses of glass and plants beyond. Rooms have comfortable armchairs in flowered loose covers; family photographs – a wedding, a naked baby – line the bookcase. A poster in the front window is the give-away: 'For your children's sake, save the Gwent Levels.' This, Amanda Martin's home, offers her the safe haven of three generations living together from which to campaign. Another poster declares: 'We don't want asthma.' The safety of her children's future is a continuing thread of her cause:

'We all know the consequences of unbridled traffic growth, and I think as a mother of two children it really makes my hair stand on end to think of there being twice the volume in twenty-five years. This is inconceivable and any politician who doesn't acknowledge that is being grossly irresponsible in my view. The answer is not to build more roads, but to look for other ways of solving our long-term transport problems.'

We visit the Gwent Levels – the broad acres of wetland where some 115 nationally and internationally rare species of flora and fauna thrive. Some of it is in the care of the Gwent Wildlife Trust. The ditches are deep with flowers, showing a variety of colour rare in English hedgerows now tyrannized by the ubiquitous cow parsley. Hawks rise in the air, bees and insects provide the kind of background noise radio producers die for. This is fecund, unspoilt countryside, heaving with small animal life that is beginning to be valued by humans for its own sake.

Again Amanda speaks of her children: 'Countryside is a tremendously important part of our children's natural heritage and once it's gone, it's gone forever and our children are going to be deprived of it.' She has tried to explain to her son why she is so often at public meetings or waving banners and risking prison rather than spending time at home. 'He has that instinct, which a lot of children have, that nature has an intrinsic value of its own, irrespective of its usefulness or economic potential to man. It is wrong to destroy it. We must try to act as guardians for future generations.' And finally, when I ask whether she would give up her road campaign, were a referendum to show that the majority supported the road-building programme, she pauses, cautiously, seeing this as a challenge to her democratic principles – frowns, then grins:

'It's very difficult to answer such an academic question... But I think the health argument is probably going to be the most potent force for change. The reason I hesitated in answering the question is that I really couldn't imagine myself sitting by, while increasing numbers of children were becoming asthmatic. We now have one in ten of our children suffering from what mainstream medical opinion accepts as pollution-related asthma.'

Amanda's point of view has the logic of a committed conscience. It also follows a very ordinary but honourable course. These days we hear much about the collapse of moral values, the lack of common purpose and dedication to a consensus of moral principles. Recent studies by the European Values Group – an informal network of social scientists, theologians, philosophers, opinion researchers – revealed not a moral vacuum but a multiplicity of overlapping ethical systems operating in a context of tolerance one for another, with distinct clusters of values gathered round certain aspects of life. The overwhelming moral commitment for most Europeans is to the family, the second area of commitment is to friends.

Thus Amanda Martin speaks for the majority in claiming her actions are driven by concern for her children, their health and welfare, within a context of family life. Which of us would not claim as much? But it is here that noble motive clashes with popular sneer. The phrase NIMBY – Not In My Back Yard – is used as an easy dismissal, a contemptuous put-down of those who act from rampant self-interest. It is a way of minimizing people's feelings and thus disregarding their claim on our attention. But NIMBY is where all human concerns begin, close to home. Amanda Martin may have been initially roused to action by her own home being threatened. But she is now taking a broader view of British transport policy and seeking to influence it. However in choosing direct action she takes a risk. There is a mood of surly resentment in the community at large, often abetted by daily newspapers, that marginalizes the arguments of protesters while headlining their antics and giving big-picture coverage to any who break ranks and get violent.

Back at Twyford Down the long dusty march reaches its climax when the summer afternoon is at its hottest. The frail fencing yields easily as hundreds of hands wrench it aloft and protesters surge down to where the broad new tarmac is already laid. A young man sits cross-legged, playing a tin whistle. There are funny hats, coloured hair. A girl strums a painted guitar. A small, serious person with white hair carries a dark umbrella against the sun. The camera crew have plenty to film, to catch the atmosphere. Then in one sector the atmosphere changes. A group suddenly begin pulling at the metal barriers already erected along the roadside. They tear them from their foundations. The sudden noise and dust and destruction attracts a few others – the impulse spreads. The camera is filming it all.

Our cameraman addresses one of the vandals: 'I think it's bad to see this on television. It won't do your cause any good.'

Reply: 'Why are you filming it, then?'

Cameraman: 'Because it's happening.'

That night on the local news the images are of mainly young people aggressively manhandling a van. Our programme, with more time at its disposal, balances such shots with young people disclaiming the violence. But what will the public remember?

Amanda expresses her protest at all levels. In South Wales she is a founder and leader of Save Our Severnside. She distributes leaflets and addresses public meetings. But she is also part of the National Transport Reform Movement, and has attended road protests at Bath and Wanstead. Now she holds herself in readiness to go to prison for her defiance of the law. Is she right to take direct action?

'In the early years of the century a group of women went round chaining themselves to railings and setting fire to letter-boxes. They were regarded as terrorists by the government of the day. Now the suffragettes are seen as heroines. I think if you're going to have a free society, then the right to demonstrate, to express your views publicly, is crucial. Democracy is not just about electing a government every four years, then turning your back on what they do in the meantime.

'The people out protesting are the thin end of the wedge. The greater the numbers on the streets, the greater the numbers at home nodding their heads in agreement. A lot of people support campaigns passively. At the back of our minds is the thought that we have an enormous amount of public support behind us, that people are crying out for change.'

Others, however, are groaning behind their steering wheels, with a carload of disgruntled children on a hot Saturday afternoon. The protest has ground traffic to a halt. Amanda is sanguine: 'Most people who know anything about this issue would feel minor passing disruption is a price worth paying.'

According to Dr Rodney Baker, of the London School of Economics, Amanda's law-breaking remains *within* democracy rather than threatening it:

'There's a distinction between crimes – that is, breaking the law for your own personal advantage and seeking to avoid being caught and punished; and protest, where you say "Here I am breaking the law. Use the force of the Government against me." They may be breaking the law, but they are not challenging the law. They accept, even welcome, the consequences as a means of drawing attention to what they believe. Democracy accepting civil disobedience is not turning a blind eye to it, because that would be an end to the rule of law.'

She knows her cause may land her in prison, but Amanda Martin nonetheless believes in the rule of law:

'I'm not getting this issue out of perspective. By and large we live in a reasonably stable, egalitarian society. My concern is that in the absence of a written constitution and a bill of rights the Government is able to nibble away at our freedom of speech, at our civil liberties, in a very insidious manner, in a way people don't readily recognize until they need to use that freedom of speech.'

Amanda is in a long line of free speakers to defy the law – from John Lilburne, John Milton and William Blake. It is when such people fail to come forward and make a stand, or are cowed into silence and conformity, that we should really worry.

On 14 July 1995, William Hague, the newly appointed 34-year-old Welsh Secretary, gave approval for the M4 relief road to go ahead and designated the preferred route. It will cost £330 million.

Two weeks later, under pressure from several lobbies, he agreed to a future meeting with their representatives. Amanda Martin will be one of them. She's convinced there will have to be a public inquiry. The matter is too serious to steamroller through. Amanda and her kind will be standing in its path if they even try. Meanwhile Amanda is back at university, planning to take a Masters degree in urban and regional transport. The bureaucrats had better watch out.

Conflicts of interest over land and space are now arising everywhere. Look up from this book and there will be some such issue within the not-too-distant horizon. Following my initial question – who has the right to roam the countryside? – I had already found that travellers did it with difficulty and protesters only at the risk of criminal prosecution. But it was in the Lake District that *Heart of the Matter* found people actively seeking answers to these dilemmas.

In this part of northern England a whole clutch of different interest groups are now able to enjoy the countryside within carefully proscribed limits. Here is a paradigm for our crowded world: everyone enjoying some freedom, none enjoying total freedom and a few denied specific freedoms. Nor have the rules been set in stone: at any moment things are in a state of flux, with pressures being put to make adjustments by which some lose, some gain.

The Lake District, in Cumbria, is a special case. It is the largest of the country's eleven National Parks, set up in the post-war years by legislation intended to give the public access to areas of great natural beauty. It covers some 885 square miles, of which the National Trust owns almost a quarter. Its population of some 42 000, rarely for a rural area, is actually increasing. The infrastructure of lakes and roads, small towns and settlements, sustains an annual invasion of over fourteen million visitors. Tourism long ago overtook farming as the area's main economic activity. Alongside the come-and-go visitors is the more sustained invasion of weekenders and second-homers: 40 per cent of homes are so owned. Nowhere is there such a convergence of different interests jostling for the right to be there.

At one extreme, both in Cumbria and elsewhere, are the landowners, who feel theirs is the more absolute claim by virtue of antiquity and possession. Martin Gillibrand, himself a landowner and Secretary of the Moorland Association, speaks for the fundamental and basic right of ownership as it has been enacted down the centuries:

'We start from the basic premise that this land is our land. Many people in the access lobby wish it wasn't. But morally it's owned land. If you have a front door to your house, when you shut that door you regard it as your house. My members view their land in exactly the same way. We recognize its importance to other people and we're very happy to share it, provided it can be done in a way that doesn't put at risk the well-being of the land itself. Those who ask for our land for their use provide nothing. They take. We are prepared to share it with them but we can't abandon control.'

Marion Shoard, who lectures on countryside matters at University College, London, holds views at the other extreme, her book *The Theft of the Countryside* being infected with what Martin Gillibrand thinks of as socialist notions. She wants to see a 'right to roam' enacted in law and an easing of British landlords' rights of absolute control. It's a right the Labour Party has plans to introduce if it is returned to power. Increasingly, people are challenging the idea that ownership of land should be equated with an exclusive right to enjoy it. For 'countryside' read 'environment' and you get the right perspective.

'There's a general increase in interest in the environment and a general feeling that we have some responsibility for it. Now if people are to feel responsible for it, surely they have some kinds of rights in it, or at least a right to see it and be in it? You don't get the exclusive possessive attitude to land you have here in other European countries. I'd like to see some redefinition of ownership in this country so that landowners can no longer stop people moving around over what is essentially part of the environment.'

Gillibrand and Shoard agree about one thing, that the present landowning patterns were originally created in England by William the Conqueror, who seized it by conquest and parcelled it out to his friends and supporters. It has been subdivided and passed on ever since. Seven hundred years later, Thomas Paine, writing in support of the independence of the American colonies, called even William's inheritance into question: 'A French bastard landing with armed bandits and establishing himself King of England against the consent of the natives, is in plain terms a very paltry, rascally original.'

However, in the absence of any major land-reforming revolution such as Paine welcomed in France, the pattern of large estates has survived. (Most of the leaders of Cromwell's revolution were, after all, landowners themselves, with a stake in the existing order.) What's more, it was established early on that the King and his courtiers had the right to designate much of the countryside for sport, and ordinary people were excluded from hunting forests across England. The link between countryside and the sporting pursuits of its owners remains today. When landowners, fearful of hikers wandering at random, speak of land management, they refer not only to crops and farming, for which there is a declining demand, but to the sustaining of grouse and deer moors for which there is a flourishing demand.

Eighteenth-century enclosures in England and Highland clearances in Scotland concentrated yet more acres in fewer hands (what Marion Shoard calls 'the privatization of the land'). But in the 1930s the hollow eyes of millions living in the blighted industrial cities began to turn to the countryside. Cycling clubs, ramblers, hikers, and youth hostellers began the great spilling back of people into the countryside their ancestors had left. Leisure, affluence and sheer individuality of spirit have accelerated this move. The Lake District epitomizes its problems.

Arnold Lancaster is a farmer of the old school; his family have farmed sheep on the fells round Coniston for hundreds of years. He farms some 33 hectares with 320 breeding ewes at Torver. Red of face, with sinewy hands and neck, he tempers his sad tale with a kind of disparaging wit, as though keen that the people from television should not mark him down as a whinger. Where once his family walked the fells and farmed as they thought best, today a host of regulations impose someone else's judgements, striking at his dignity and cutting down his pride. He remains a proud man: a joking belligerence towards us warns he is not to be trifled with, but I sense behind this joviality not a mere transitory irritation but a deep resignation and grief for a lost way of life.

'They're not breeding, are they? They're only visiting. They're not breeding in this area. Local people seem to be getting less. The local way of life's gone.' As a sheep farmer he's caught between the forces of tourism and conservation. Tourism sends walkers with dogs and parties of schoolchildren across his land. 'These fells have been made open access. The Lake District Planning Board have the authority to do that. And don't get me wrong – we welcome dogs if they're wormed, if they're injected, if they're under control.' He lost thirteen sheep in one episode. 'Once a dog's got the taste for blood they're usually hard to stop. I ended up shooting that one in front of the family. They'll never forget it, won't that family. And I didn't like it.' He'd recently lost a litter of puppies – all dead in a fortnight – to an infection introduced by a tourist's dog. He speaks with amazed exasperation of how little city dog owners understand what happens in the country:

'You can't work a dog on a farm, gathering sheep, if some daft devil walks a bitch through in season. We must get the tourists educated.

You know, you're working a packet of sheep, you've two or three dogs and you whistle at your dogs to give the command. And a party of school kids go by. I'll guarantee there'll be half a dozen start mimicking your whistling. Your dogs don't know whether they're coming left, right, backwards or forwards. At the time, if you could get your hands on them, you'd wring their necks.'

From the other direction come the conservationists, worried about overgrazing the fells and seeking to limit the farmers' flocks. 'Ours is an Environmentally Sensitive Area. So we should farm this way with six sheep per hectare. Now they're wanting it down to two sheep per hectare.'

Being designated such an area brings farmers like Arnold Lancaster considerable subsidies. In exchange, it requires obedience to a whole set of restrictions imposed from outside: which fertilizers to use, the upkeep of traditional stone walls, farming in the traditional way. 'They're asking us to be caretakers. They seem to forget we've had the farms all these years.' In policing his farming methods, conservation interests have curtailed his freedom and damaged his gnarled spirit. There must be many like him.

Now meet the latest comers to the Lake District: the mountain bikers and the water-skiers. It is characteristic of both groups that they move with terrific speed, and in the case of the latter sudden gusts of perturbing noise across the surface of the landscape. They can scarcely be seen as existing within the landscape for they are no sooner there than gone. Despite the brevity of their intrusion, those who seek contemplation and serenity in the mountains legitimately complain that sudden eruptions of noise and colour that are gone in moments destroy their sense of peace for the day.

John Stevenson, a passionate biker, Editor of *Mountain Biking UK* and a fervent proselytizer for the sport, will have none of such criticism:

'Any gaggle of mountain bikers is through and away fairly swiftly. It's a very short time-frame in which they impinge on your experience. You have the rest of the day, the rest of the week to enjoy the countryside. We're a very minor countryside group in that respect.

But because we're a new user group in areas massively over-trafficked already, some people, not many, would like it to be last in, first out. Their deep-seated feeling is, "Oh God, here's another bunch of country users", whereas the landowners in some cases would really prefer not to have any countryside users at all.'

I met up with John and his friends on a bridle path rough with shale and stones that bounced the bikes inches off the ground as they sped past them, then braked with force as the route met the road. They certainly made no effort to be inconspicuous. Not for them any discreet attempts to camouflage themselves against the trees. Both bikes and clothing screamed raw colours: glowing purples, acid greens, sharp pinks testified to the eye-bruising capacities of chemical rather than natural dyes. The garish juxtaposing of outlandish colours challenged the tolerance of barbours and country tweeds they met along the way. John, who himself sports a blond ponytail and displays plenty of likeable attitude and style, grins when I mention how they look. 'It's really a carry-over from the fact that cyclists tend to wear bright clothing so that we're visible on the roads. That said, there's some fairly garish walking gear out there as well!'

Although the bikers make common cause with hikers in their claim to have open access to the countryside, the bikers have an issue specific to themselves to fight. A code created by the National Parks asks that cyclists ride on bridle paths and not on footpaths. John explains why the code is often broken:

'The law as it stands doesn't actually make a great deal of sense because the legal status of a particular trail usually bears no relevance to what it's like on the ground. The problem stems from the fact that at the end of the Second World War, when the maintenance of bridle paths and footpaths was allocated to parish councils, many bridle paths were downgraded to footpaths because their upkeep was cheaper. The standard was lowered. So there's a lot of stuff out there that is of good enough quality to be a bridle path, but is merely designated a footpath, where we don't have the right to ride.'

He indicates the very path on which we stand. It is about 2 metres wide, rocky-surfaced, quite adequate to take a Land Rover, yet it's designated a footpath. There is a potential conflict here with walkers, and, as with many conflicts in the Lakes, the National Trust is looked to for a solution.

Oliver Maurice, the regional director of the National Trust in the North-West, is keen to provide low-level cycle routes. At the moment a cycle route from Kendal to Keswick is proposed and there are more in the offing:

'As part of our centenary we're hoping to put a route round Derwent Water, provided we can get consent from neighbouring landowners. It's a shame they're called "mountain bikes". I believe if they were called "all-terrain bikes" then people wouldn't feel the need to go straight out on a mountain.'

Oliver Maurice diplomatically negotiates between bikers, hikers and landowners. Water-skiers get a rougher deal. Our television team was up early and down to the shores of Lake Windermere to meet Mark Boon and film him executing flips and turns, cross-overs and turn-arounds – not explicit terms, these, but my description of his impressive skills. And he clearly loves being there:

'As we look around, the surroundings this morning are beautiful. It's a beautiful place to ski. My children come skiing with me. We all go out in the boat together for the morning. We all ski together. We ski with friends. It's a sociable sport, a good family sport. We are privileged to be able to ski here, and I am quite upset that it might all come to an end.'

At the time we spoke, the future of water-skiing on Lake Windermere hung in the balance. The Countryside Commission's report of March 1991 had many recommendations, several of which the Government had decided to support, endorsing the National Parks' remit to provide 'quiet enjoyment and understanding of the countryside'. The water-skiers know they are the target. A National Park Authority-proposed bye-law would prevent water-skiing on Windermere – the only lake on which it has been allowed. Water-skiers feel aggrieved that, having willingly agreed to leave Coniston and other lakes free of noise and concentrate all their sport and noise on Windermere, they have unwittingly collaborated in their own downfall.

The National Trust will support the new bye-law.

Oliver Maurice again: 'The noise is the key, from the Trust's point of view. I don't think the noise of speedboats on the shores of Lake Windermere, where so many people come to enjoy quietness and solitude, is appropriate.'

Solitude? With fourteen million visitors a year? Well, an interesting fact is emerging from all the enquiries into and about this great National Park. People are attracted in large numbers only to certain places, honeypot areas, leaving very large tracts of land uncrowded and unspoilt. Although, in high summer, coaches and cars jam the roads from Kendal to Ambleside, and crowds jostle round the tea shops and souvenir stalls, there remain large areas where neither hikers nor bikers, climbers, abseilers, school parties or office outings come at all.

The human race wants to congregate as much as it wants to be solitary. Where there is a clash between divergent claims to the land, the antagonisms are rarely about the actual amount of space but about opposing lifestyles laying claim to it. Even though the living now outnumber the dead, there is plenty of planet to accommodate us all. Conflict and confrontation are not about land itself, but often about self-generated group antagonisms. In the Lake District, barbours versus wetsuits; in the Home Counties, hippies versus conformists. Throughout it all the land remains.

Birth Rights

More and more moral dilemmas have come to focus around the mysteries of birth and death. Once, such events were accepted as arbitrary, wayward Fate lurking at either end of the lottery of life. Not any more. The haphazardness of nature has given way to increasing control exercised by individuals in pursuit of their own fulfilment and happiness. The results haven't always been happy for others, and it is when a conflict of interests arises about how a child is born and brought up that moral choices have to be made. But individuals in pursuit of happiness rarely find time to debate moral choices, and when they do, they have a tendency to favour the moral option that most nearly coincides with their personal wishes. It is, after all, hard for anyone to be totally selfless. At that point other agencies voice their opinions and seek to make them effective: moralists, doctors, the media, citizens, lawmakers. We almost all have our own view of how children should be born and to what degree patterns that diverge from the norm should be tolerated or even allowed.

Over the years *Heart of the Matter* has unfolded some of those diverging patterns: babies borne by surrogate mothers, babies born by insemination from a sperm donor, babies sought for adoption and fostering by gay and lesbian couples. All had in common the yearning for a baby and, in all but the last case, the couples' sincere wish to bear their own child was frustrated by infertility. Infertility is on the increase in the developed world. Humans are already the least fecund of animal species. Women having babies at an older age reduce their chances of conception. Also pollution in the environment – especially oestrogens in the water – are suspected of affecting male fertility. In Britain one in six people experience difficulty with fertility at some point in their lives. The sperm count of the average white European male has fallen 25 per cent in twenty-five years. And where once couples accepted with resignation news of their infertility, today great numbers of them seek to defy the medical findings. Being resigned to your lot, a mainstay of Victorian morality, has been superseded by a resolute determination to get what you want, even against seemingly insurmountable odds. And nowhere is the dedication to fulfilling personal goals better exemplified than by the degree to which the infertile seek out methods of having babies. There is much heartbreak on the way, and later.

Surrogacy is one such method. It involves a woman agreeing to bear a child for a childless couple, and then at birth handing it over to them. There are two types of surrogacy. By the first, the male partner's sperm fertilizes the egg of the surrogate woman. This is usually done, for reasons of personal delicacy, not by the more natural way of his making love to her but by mechanical and thus emotionally neutral means, involving the use, I'm told, of equipment as easily available in the home where it usually happens, as jam jars and meat basters. Thus it is possible for such arrangements to be informally organized, often through private agencies. It is also impossible to monitor or control such activities by law.

The second form of surrogacy is known as in vitro fertilization (IVF) surrogacy and takes place within IVF and fertility clinics. This is possible when, despite not being able to bear a child, the couple can produce their own egg and sperm which are then brought together and implanted in the womb of the surrogate mother. In this case the surrogate is merely providing the growing and nourishing process for the embryo. By this type of surrogacy the child that results has the genetic make-up of the couple who will bring it up. It is genuinely their offspring.

Alexandra Calder is now thirty-two, a single parent living in Newcastle with her three children. Danny and Nicki, who are ten and seven, make up her original family. But since their births Alex has borne three subsequent children. At the age of twenty-seven she embarked on a career of surrogate motherhood, having three children in three years, each of them conceived and intended to be handed over to childless couples. I went to visit Alex and spent the day with her, trying to understand her behaviour and why it had led to tragedy.

The motives of women who offer to be surrogates are diverse. Pregnancy certainly gives a woman status, and it may be that certain women, alert to their own needs but with no immediate chance of fulfilling them, find in surrogate pregnancy a sense of purpose for their lives. That seems to have been the case for Alex Calder. Neither of the fathers of her two children has lived with her. She speaks with some pain, eyes averted, of her relationships with them. She refers, in passing, to periods of bad depression, of trying to make some plans for the future. Her emotions may have been chaotic and tumultuous, but she was trying to get her life on track with few resources except her native intelligence and her own body:

'I'd watched something about surrogacy on television and I thought, well, that's ideal in a way. I didn't want more children of my own, but I found comfort in pregnancy in the same way as I did in being overweight. Pregnancy makes you feel really safe and it gives your life some sort of structure. It's something to work towards. And what can be more useful than having a baby either for yourself or for somebody else? It's very special.'

Alex's reasons for choosing straight surrogacy in preference to IVF are even more revealing:

'IVF would be out of my control. The hospital has control of everything: your appointments, your cycle. You have to go through committees – it would be very long and drawn out, and just too much out of my control.' Here was Alex, a working-class girl with no job prospects, no close relationships with men, two children to care for, trying to give her life and her emotions some direction and remain responsibly in control of how she lived. Surrogacy was something that would use the skills she had: she enjoyed being pregnant and having babies. After seeing the television programme, she contacted an agency.

COTS, Childlessness Overcome Through Surrogacy, is just such an informal agency run by another surrogate mother, Kim Cotton, whose own story caused a tabloid scandal in 1985, when she revealed that she had borne a child for an American couple who had paid her £6500 to do so. The British government had responded immediately, outlawing surrogacy for payment, but allowing so-called 'expenses' of an indeterminate amount. By their fifth year, in 1993, there had been sixty-four surrogate births among COTS members. In 1994 it cost £50 to join, £25 annual membership. It claimed some 500 members, and 140 surrogates willing to bear children.

COTS put Alex in touch with her first couple. 'When I did finally choose a couple it was because they just accepted me. They weren't worried that I was on my own, that I was a bit unconventional. They were very easy-going and that was why I liked them.' But then, once pregnant, Alex's attitude towards them changed:

'I was scared I would very much dislike them, and maybe not want to hand the baby over to them. So I decided I would keep them at a distance. I kept them informed the whole way through and told them what was going on, and rang them as soon as I went into labour, and they were at the hospital for the birth; not actually in the room but outside.'

Throughout her pregnancy Alex battled with herself as to what view to take of the child:

'I think some women are encouraged to think, "It's not your baby, it's their baby; you've got to remember that." And it's not. But I try to think, "It's your baby, but you went into this with your eyes open and maybe you're going to be upset but you'll get over it." I tried to work it out that way.'

And she did. But discretion was required. 'It was recommended that nobody knew, that nobody was told. So the doctors and nurses in the maternity hospital weren't told. Only really close friends and family.' This proved slightly awkward at the birth – 'A close friend of mine went with me, and I just said to the midwife, "Can you give the baby to her." I thought it was better than holding her myself.'

The stay in hospital, caring for her new daughter, became increasingly difficult. Surrounded by mothers delighted with their newborn babies, Alex was made even more anxious about what she was doing.

She insisted on leaving the second day. 'If I'd stayed in the hospital with her another day it would have been very difficult to part with her.' Back at home, over cups of coffee, the little girl was handed to the commissioning couple, the agreed arrangement complete. 'All the time I was thinking, "Please go, please go." I just didn't want to cry in front of them; while they were there. It was awful waiting until they had gone.' The first few days after the birth were hard for Alex but within weeks she was 'pretty much on top of it'. So much so that a mere ten weeks later she was in discussion with COTS about being a surrogate again. This time was to prove tragic for the couple she chose: Erik and Patricia Cliffe.

Erik and Patricia had been married eighteen years and had been trying for most of those years to have a baby. They both had full-time jobs: he as manager of a dry ski-slope; she as a junior school teacher surrounded daily by the tormenting sight of bustling, busy families, taking for granted what for her was so painfully unattainable. They lived comfortably in Rochdale, some 135 miles from Alex's Newcastle home. The actual distance between them was to be one of the more tangible difficulties that would arise. Others – private, emotional, enigmatic – would never be fully explained.

Medical tests had shown no physical reason why they couldn't conceive, so they persisted with treatment. Ironically it was fertility drugs themselves that ended their hopes, causing Patricia an early menopause. She was devastated. They tried for adoption but by this time were judged too old. When they made contact with Alex, Erik was forty-eight, Patricia forty-two.

Erik was totally supportive of Patricia's needs:

'I think she's a natural mother, and when you see someone like that getting so upset every month because she's not having children, and all around you life is just family-orientated: all our friends having children, and wherever you go – shopping centres, parks – everyone has a family. It's draining – just so very draining.'

These were people with a desperate longing for a child. Their joy when Alex became pregnant at once, with Erik's sperm, was overwhelming.

It was July 1991. But the pregnancy slowly opened up a gulf between them and Alex. With hindsight it's not difficult to see that a woman who only a few months before had given away her daughter would have complex reactions to another pregnancy with the same intended outcome. Alex feels her needs weren't met:

'I wanted a lot of visiting and a lot of pampering. I wanted a lot of concern and a lot of fuss. Nothing seemed to get through to them. I was saying please, I need more support, I need you to visit more often. I felt totally rejected.'

Such is Alex's account. The Cliffes' version doesn't tally:

'We tried to give as much support as we could. We would go to see them and get on so well. We'd make models for the children and play. On one occasion we all went up to Hadrian's Wall. It was great. Other times, we'd visit and Alex's face would be like thunder.'

Then, in December, they received what they call a dreadful letter from Alex. It seems they had fallen behind in their agreed payments and driven Alex's bank balance into the red. Money has to come into these arrangements at some point and can trigger trouble. Alex had refused to tell us how much in expenses the first couple had paid, but it was enough for her to remark: 'It helped us a lot. It didn't pay for the baby – people say you sold your baby, and I didn't. But it's made life so much easier for me and the other two.' And indeed the comfort is palpable. Her modest house has soft velvet-covered sofas and armchairs and shag-pile carpets. It feels comfy in a motherly kind of way. Alex is nothing if not motherly. The Cliffes paid Alex £7000 in so-called expenses for being their surrogate. Such a transaction doesn't horrify me as much as it does many. I do not believe children should be bought and sold. However, while I think the sum Alex asked was excessive for expenses, I am aware that she put it to wholesome domestic use for the well-being of her family. And that at least is an honourable thing to do with money you may have acquired from less than honourable transactions. In the event – dishonourably this time – Alex was to keep not only the daughter she bore Erik but, in the short term at least, the money as well.

As her pregnancy proceeded, Alex says she became increasingly fraught and wound up. She was beginning to feel the Cliffes would not make good parents. She grew curious. She knew they'd been turned down for adoption and contacted Rochdale Social Services to find out why. She maintains they expressed reservations to her about 'the emotional well-being' of a child adoped by the Cliffes. Rochdale Social Services refuse to confirm Alex Calder's account of their conversation, but have since told the Cliffes they will not do anything to prejudice any adoption applications they might make to other local authorities.

By now, in the eighth month of her pregnancy, Alex was hugely distressed. By the time her daughter – she called her Sophie – was born, she could find nothing but fault in Patricia's handling of the baby. The day after the birth, in April 1992, they came together at Alex's home.

The moment she refused to hand over Sophie – a small bundle with a shock of bright red hair, an inheritance from Erik – must have been worthy of Greek tragedy. Both their accounts – rambling, painful, disjointed, distraught – focus on particular moments: Alex, upstairs with the baby, letting out a sudden scream of grief; her friend coming down on her behalf to explain that Alex had decided not to give up the child; Erik collapsing in physical pain at the shock; Patricia, stunned by loss at this point where her dreams seemed about to be fulfilled. The furies unleashed, destroying hopes and plans, driven by God knows what impulses of need, suffering, yearning and loss.

The Cliffes, devastated by what had happened, took legal action and gained some rights to visit Sophie, who is, after all, Erik's daughter. But commissioning couples have no legally enforceable rights, so they eventually dropped the case. Nor did they seek the return of the £7000. In August 1994, three months after the birth, the Child Support Agency indicated they would require Erik to pay maintenance to Alex for the child.

How does any of this have anything to do with the rest of us? We can tut-tut as much as we like, and the tabloids can roar 'The Buying of Baby Sophie', but no one can legislate against poor judgement. Looking back, it's easy to say that Alex, possibly still grieving for her last surrogate child, should not have embarked on another surrogate pregnancy so soon. Who could have advised her – friends, the surrogacy agency? But Alex emerges as stubbornly individual in seeking her own solutions to life's problems. It is, after all, a contemporary outlook. What's more, in odd ways she expresses a strict morality of her own. Speaking with her of how babies were once treated – strict regimes of four-hourly feeds, not being picked up when they cried – she responds with outrage: 'To do that to children is wicked, absolutely wicked.' Clearly she has decided views on childcare, and her children – lively and bright – bear witness to her qualities as a mother. What happened next is perhaps most surprising of all. The following year Alex went on to bear another surrogate baby for the couple with whom she'd made the first arrangement. This time the handover went ahead without dispute or heartbreak.

As for the Cliffes, one can say easily enough that they might have exercised more thought and judgement in choosing a surrogate (initially such selections tend to proceed largely by phone). And they might have followed through Alex's pregnancy more assiduously. But Erik and Patricia were driven by their own passion to have a child. Their continuing grief is a heavy judgement to bear. Besides, out of this unhappy mayhem has emerged a new life – now a three-year-old, white-skinned little girl with tumbling red curls: Sophie.

Since the programme went out and the newspaper fuss died down, Alex Calder has calmly been putting her life in order. She took and passed a GCSE in law. She is now studying for her 'A' level and would like to work in trading standards. Her behaviour towards the Cliffes still grieves her. In April 1995 she quietly began repaying some of the £7000. 'Keeping the money was the one thing I shouldn't have done.' Her monthly cheques are cashed but never acknowledged.

Should surrogacy be allowed? Obviously informal surrogacy cannot be controlled. Where IVF surrogacy is concerned, it already occurs within the medical world which is governed by the Human Fertilization and Embryology Act 1990. At the time our programme was transmitted, October 1994, Section 30 of that Act was about to come into effect, making certain aspects of surrogacy easier. Formerly, after a surrogate birth, the child's birth certificate carried the name of the surrogate mother and her husband. As he clearly had no part in the affair, the situation called for remedy. Also, once the child had been handed over to the commissioning couple, they were required to go through the whole protracted process of formal adoption, which can take up to two years. This has been changed to hurry matters along. They can now apply for a parental order entitling them to be treated in law as the true parents of the child, giving the birth mother the right to change her mind for only six weeks. Thus the state is sanctioning surrogacy and treating it with a light touch. But anxieties remain.

Surrogacy points up one of the paradoxes of family life in the 1990s, a major shift away from the traditional pattern of historical generation to generation. On the one hand, genetics and DNA research is revealing just how crucial is the legacy of biological parents, their genes influencing not only the health but the character and personality of the child. At the same time, those concerned with the welfare of children, the Social Services, argue ever more insistently that biology is not the only form of parenting (their word), and that adoptive or foster parents, IVF parents, step-parents, those who care for and nurture the child through its formative years, are as 'real' parents as any other.

In little more than a decade the human genome project will have mapped the entire spread of human genes. The genetic recipe that has gone into our making will be on record, if we choose to access it. At the same time infertility treatments are transferring eggs – sperm and ova – from body to body and cutting across the natural heredity of families. If children are experiencing a crisis of identity today, these techniques could well exacerbate it. Surrogate children need to know, as much as adopted children need to know, where they came from. There are clearly grounds for requiring surrogacy agencies to be licensed, so that all such records are formally available. And surrogacy is not the only case where this applies.

In the summer of 1990 *Heart of the Matter* asked: should a sperm donor's right to anonymity transcend the right of children to know their biological parentage? In Britain there are some 1500 babies born each year by donor insemination. Many parents are determined to see this merely as a medical procedure about which they have no obligation to tell their child. They pledge themselves to keep a family secret. At the same time, many doctors feel that if the identity of the donor is to be on record, the supply of donors will dry up. Young men – they have in the past tended to be students or young soldiers – might be willing to donate sperm but would not welcome a teenager tracing them fifteen years later, turning up on the doorstep and greeting them as father.

The case for secrecy was exemplified by a young mother who was so anxious to retain her anonymity that she refused to be filmed even in the shadows, even in silhouette. I recorded the interview with her and then an actress acted out the part. Her attitude to artificial insemination was that the donor giving sperm was like a blood donor giving blood; there was no need for any identification, no sense of anything more serious taking place. Indeed, she and her husband deliberately sought to confuse the issue, coming to believe the donor hardly existed:

'Whenever I'd had a treatment I'd go home and we'd make love, so that it was his baby. We treated it as my husband's sperm. I just treated it as I do a cervical smear. The donor played no role. None. It was there for our convenience. It was just one of those things we had to go through. Like taking tablets. So each month it could have been my husband's child, only it just happened that we needed a bit of a boost with something else. I would never tell my children. I don't think they need to know. I think it could confuse their identity, and lead to unnecessary problems. Our children are our children. My husband is their father and unless they actually have blood tests to prove differently, there is no difference. They are his children – and that is not a lie.'

Here is a mother being more honest with me than she is prepared to be with her children. Certainly the line she takes is not dissimilar to that suggested by the medical profession when insemination by donor was first practised early this century, basically not only recommending secrecy but self-deception. The argument went that if you are continuing to have sexual intercourse with your wife during the period she is receiving donor insemination, no one's ever going to know it's not your sperm. No one will ever be able to prove one way or another that one particular occasion produced that child. That situation is perpetuated in law, by which the donor remains totally concealed.

But times have changed. Biology and genetics are now looking into the microcosm of human identity. DNA testing for inherited illness, for faulty genes, is becoming common. Blood tests do get done. And while anonymity might suit the parents and the donor, there is someone else involved: the child.

Candace Turner is a 47-year-old American, happily married, the mother of four children. She was born from donor sperm, a fact her parents kept secret until the news tumbled out in the chaotic way such secrets do. Candace's father already had his own daughter, Joyce, from an earlier marriage. Candace and her brother were then born by donor insemination. The couple parted when Candace was five, and her mother remarried. Their new stepfather was violent and drunk. One day during a family row he let out the family secret. Candace was twelve years old at the time, about to visit the man she believed was her true father. 'My stepfather was drunk, and suddenly said, "Why is she planning to go and see him because he's not even her father?"' Candace pauses. The story has clearly been told many times, but each time she relives the shock.

'So after things calmed down again, that night my brother and I went and asked Mother what did this mean? Tearfully she told us about the donor insemination and that she had requested the same donor for us both. I felt odd. I felt like I was from Mars. I had never in my life met anybody else from a spermbank except my kid brother. It's not fun feeling that odd. We are not test tubes from a brave new world. We are real. We have real pain.'

Candace is immensely real. The air around her quivers with her sensibility. She has the intensity of a greyhound: alert and vulnerable. As an adult, she has founded 'Donors' Offspring', to speak for those she calls 'spermbank children'. For her the knowledge has been traumatic. It has also made certain things clear. 'I was in a way relieved to find out because there was this distance between my father and me. I've known others say this too – that they've felt something different.' Candace's brother couldn't deal with the situation and refused to see his father again. Candace went to see him that summer:

'I blurted it out and was all very excited about it and had lots of questions. I guess I wanted reassurance that he loved me as much as his own daughter. He didn't want to say too much about it. He's refrained from ever talking about it again. I'm sure now he loved me as much as he could, but I don't think men who agree to this realize they're making a lifelong commitment to be a pretend father and a pretend grandfather.'

In every culture the identity of a child's father has been of the greatest significance. Paternity commands the loyalties of tribes. It governs the inheritance laws of societies. It is at the root of complex intermarriage taboos. Now it is seen as part and parcel of an individual's identity. It is also personal information that we may wish, for emotional or psychological reasons, to keep confidential. But the risks of keeping such a secret are great, not just because secrets leak out but because medical and legal procedures are penetrating ever further into the very essence of our being. Not only are our external characteristics catalogued, our buying habits and social lives held in data banks and civic records; increasingly our inner selves are being tabulated too: blood group details, DNA fingerprinting, ID cards with identifying photographs. In April 1995 police investigating the rape and murder of a schoolgirl in South Wales asked everyone within a certain area at a certain time to come forward for DNA fingerprinting 'for the purposes of elimination' – adding, ominously, 'We shall take particular interest in those who refuse.'

So the case against secrecy is gaining strength: not simply that it is ill-advised but that it is impossible to sustain. Those who counsel couples seeking artificial insemination therefore have to confront their fears. Robert Snowdon is just such a counsellor:

'I am of the view that the man there from the beginning, the man who is part of the planning of the baby – they're always much-wanted children – and then bringing it up once it breathes air is the father. We have to educate such social fathers to understand they're the fathers, they're the strong ones – but that to deny the biological link that they have helped to plan is in some respect doing themselves a disservice. We work to convince them they have nothing to lose by this procedure. Psychologically they would be stronger, more powerful if they were to accept the biological paternity but recognize they really are the father. All the children of such procedures I've talked to – they're in their twenties and thirties now – have said that when they were told by their parents that they were children conceived in this way, they felt, as one put it, "as if a cloud were lifted off our shoulders". They knew something was strange. They knew all those years there was something funny. And these children end up saying things like, "You know, he must have really loved me – he must have gone through an awful lot for me." And in fact the bonds between the child and the father they've always regarded as father have been made stronger. People are afraid of the uncertainty rather than dealing with the problems being open about it might create.'

No one is suggesting that any authority – governmental or medical – should insist that all donor insemination (DI) children are told. The matter was debated in Parliament at the time of the Human Fertilization and Embryology Act. The law now requires information on donors to be held by the new statutory licensing authority, but not to be available to the child. Nowadays couples having IV treatment are counselled as to whether to tell or not, the final decision being left to them. If they do decide to tell, then the matter of how and to whom to disclose the truth is also discussed. However, at the age of eighteen, children can, if they wish, ask whether they were born of donor insemination. If the answer is 'yes' and their proposed partner is also DI they can both ask: was it the same donor? They must be given a correct answer and can also be given certain non-identifiable information – eye and hair colour, height of their parent. Such children cannot at the present time find out the identity of their genetic father. One day they may have that right.

In the scramble for eggs – an unhappy phrase but accurate – to make infertile couples pregnant, it's physically easier to get donor sperm than to acquire eggs from healthy females. Women who volunteer to give eggs are subject to a course of hormones and must then have the eggs extracted by minor surgical intervention. In Britain they don't get paid. In America things are more commercial. Such women are heroic in their generosity, but there aren't enough of them. The search for female eggs is pushing the ethical debate to the limit of what society will tolerate. There has been talk of taking eggs from aborted female foetuses, or from dead women. The response has been one of public horror, as though such a move would finally tip us over the brink into an abhorrent brave new world. But there *is* no brink, no cliff, no sudden fall. New procedures are accepted piecemeal. The shifting pattern of what slowly becomes tolerable can be charted from the shock that greeted the first test tube baby in 1978. Today IVF is no longer a shocking procedure.

I believe morality will one day accept that, just as at present someone who dies can leave their organs for transplant, so women could similarly donate their eggs. The brave new world of medicine and genetics is already here. The task is to manage it by social, political and legal means agreed by the community. Currently in Britain that is expressed through the Human Fertilization and Embryology Authority which has the task of drawing the line at each particular moment. The question of whether women who are past the menopause should be enabled to bear children comes within their remit.

In the summer of 1992 a *Heart of the Matter* team flew to Italy. It's ironic that Rome, home of the Papal See, the moral arbiter for the Catholic world and implacably opposed to all IVF treatment, was also at that time the world leader in creating late pregnancies. This was all down to one doctor, Severino Antinori, who was running his own Human Reproduction and Fertility Clinic in Rome. Would-be mothers were arriving there in droves. As many as 500 over fifty-year-olds had applied within the previous three years. Eighty-five had been treated. There had been twenty-eight healthy babies born. He had a waiting list of a year.

Guiseppina Maganuco was one of those he treated. Now, at fifty-five, she was the mother of six-month-old Anna Maria. I went to visit her and her husband Angelo at their family home in Sicily. It was a family home in a typically Italian sense, with Guiseppina and Angelo's flat on one floor, and Angelo's other brothers on other floors, of a tall terrace house in a narrow dusty back street in the industrial city of Gela. It was a street where white-haired women in black stop to talk, where vegetable sellers cry their wares from hooting vans. The stairs – an echoing marble flight rising through the middle of their home – clattered with cousins and children coming and going. Anna Maria was surrounded by an extended family overjoyed that, after thirty-two years of marriage Guiseppina and Angelo had finally had a child.

Within the Maganuco household there is a sense of two miracles converging. Guiseppina is a devout Catholic, one of five children, and when she married Angelo, himself one of fourteen children, they simply took it for granted that children would follow. It wasn't their way to worry about ovulation dates or the right moment for intercourse. But when babies didn't come they began to seek help. As their search and their prayers persisted, their longing increased. They sold family land to raise the money they needed. They travelled to a Swiss clinic for treatment. Still no baby. And still Guiseppina prayed to God for a child, claiming to see a vision of the Virgin holding out the infant Jesus towards her. As far as she is concerned, God answered those prayers, so arranging things that she and Angelo saw on television the renowned Dr Antinori discoursing on how old women can have children. Dr Antinori, too, claims to be a devout Catholic. Soon they were in touch and Guiseppina embarked on four years of treatment. It would cost them £45 000 and bring them a daughter.

The proud parents take us to see the little girl cradled in an enormous cot sumptuously draped with fine white muslin and looking like the theatrical cradle in *The Sleeping Beauty* where the newborn princess receives the blessings of all the guests and the curse of the fairy who was not invited. Anna Maria holds a similar place within the family, but without the wicked fairy. Treasured, cooed over, adored, she is their little princess. It is clear the Maganucos are not rich. Angelo, now fifty-eight, has a job as a junior manager in the local oil company. Soon he will retire, he tells me, without regret. It will allow him more time with his daughter.

Their home is furnished in what can only be called peasant baroque: heavy wooden veneered furniture polished to a dazzling gloss; long bevelled mirrors on a wall-length run of wardrobe; tiled floor, crystal chandelier. Homes such as this, I realize, are the repositories of all that elaborate timeless furniture glimpsed in showroom windows along the main streets of minor Italian towns. It is all brand new – and has a sense of being destined never to get old. The Maganucos are comfortably off.

As we film – in the bedroom, the roomy kitchen, on the narrow pavements outside – Anna Maria's cousins come and go. With them two of the widely expressed anxieties concerning late births find a satisfactory answer. Both such worries focus on the emotional well-being of the growing child. Will he or she be victimized by other children for being different, teased and taunted when sixty-year-olds come along with younger parents to school occasions, local festivals and the like? And what will happen in the event of the parents' death? It is clear that Anna Maria will not grow up as the isolated child of older parents, but will mix happily with the many different generations of Maganucos.

Dr Antinori insists that he only gives his treatment to women who have undergone stringent medical tests that prove them outstandingly fit. He also looks into the record of longevity in their families. Angelo and Guiseppina respond to my questions with comfortable confidence. Their large and loving family will certainly cope with all eventualities. The glow of Anna Maria's birth is still upon them, and its joy swamps any anxieties a probing world sets before them. Guiseppina is a small, ample figure, dressed in black. The hormone treatment she's been receiving may be responsible for her clear, unwrinkled skin and bright eyes. But then happiness might do as much. Her large mouth smiles often, revealing strong white teeth, and hinting at the beginning of a double chin. It is only when I turn the questioning to the nature of the treatment that Angelo steps in to protect her from too much truth.

We are communicating, for Guiseppina's sake, through an interpreter. Angelo has enough English to understand, but answers in Italian. When I put it to them both that Dr Antinori's treatment involves the fertilizing of an egg from a younger woman with Angelo's sperm and implanting the embryo in Guiseppina's womb, it is clearly a question he does not wish to have translated, a subject he does not wish to have discussed. As far as Guiseppina is concerned, she has had a series of treatments that have resulted in a baby, her own and Angelo's baby. It is both a medical and a religious miracle. She remains in ignorance of the fact that Anna Maria's genetic make-up is not her own, that in genetic terms at least their miracle baby has another mother. Hers is a rejection of what has happened technically and a refusal to countenance the significance of such treatment. In Guiseppina's case it leaves her free to praise God and thank him for what has occurred, to believe her prayers have been answered.

We accompany them, bearing flowers, to a roadside shrine of the Virgin Mary. Guiseppina kneels in prayer before the familiar bluc and white robed figure. Perhaps the Virgin Mary, after all a surrogate mother of a kind herself, might be more understanding of Guiseppina than her church. Pope John Paul II has often reiterated that the Catholic Church is resolutely opposed to all IVF procedures. Guiseppina and Angelo, desperate for a child, have by a mental sleight of hand let such religious dictates move out of focus. Instead they deal directly through prayer with God and the Virgin. Guiseppina, as I left, was planning to go on a pilgrimage in thanks for her child. In such ways does the force of human passion and longing subvert the institutions which set out rules telling us how we must behave.

Since our visit to Italy, Dr Antinori's public profile has soared even higher. Happy to collude with such publicity in the interests of women who could find help nowhere else, and of course in the furtherance of his career, he was to find that it also drew the attention of others less enthusiastic. In April 1995 the Association of Italian Medical and Dental Surgeons set out guidelines stating that artificial insemination should only be made available to 'normal couples', and that did not include women considered too old and homosexual couples. The ban, voted on by the Association's National Council, is binding on its 300 000 members. Those who disobey risk disciplinary action. The Council has also called on the Italian government to enshrine the ruling in law.

In Britain, too, it is largely the medical profession that governs the matter. Many doctors have strong medical and ethical objections. Professor Winston, head of Britain's largest National Health infertility clinic at Hammersmith Hospital, puts their case:

'A woman in her fifties who's pregnant risks a number of very serious medical conditions: high blood pressure, toxaemia, renal problems; she's more likely to miscarry, and you would then have to deal with emotional problems. To lose such a pregnancy would seem to be emotionally and psychologically disastrous. But there are no absolutes in this sort of argument. What counts as an older woman – thirty-eight? No. Forty-two? No. But forty-four? Well, no. There can't be an arbitrary dividing line. But when you get to higher ages you are running risks I think are medically unacceptable and which often desperate people may not actually be prepared to recognize.'

This controversial treatment is easier to get in the private sector. Professor Craft of the London Fertility and Gynaecology Centre takes a less stringent view of the risks:

'Natural conception does occur in women at the age of fifty, albeit very infrequently. To my knowledge the oldest person to have a child in this country was fifty-five. I wouldn't wish to be treating people over the age at which pregnancy has occurred naturally. But I don't think it's such a horrendous thing as some fertility specialists would lead you to believe. And I think we're at risk as doctors of moralizing about people's predicaments and passing our judgements on to those patients.'

These are times of continuing change for women. They want careers, not just jobs. They want to control and plan their own lives.

Many want to delay having a family until well up their particular career ladder. Women are living longer, with medication such as hormone replacement therapy sustaining their energy and well-being into years once considered sear and yellow. The demand for treatment to enable late pregnancy will increase. Medically it might well become safer. In which case it will be time to reconsider.

The case against late pregnancies appears to stack up a formidable list of objections: children may feel awkwardly different among their contemporaries; their parents may lack the patience and energy to deal with childish antics; teenagers will find older parents even less sympathetic to the tenor of their times than is customarily the case; early bereavement might inflict traumatic suffering at a time of particular emotional vulnerability. Of all these, I find only the last one rooted in fundamental reality. The loss of parents in death is a major and actual emotional wound. The other objections focus on attitude – awkwardness, patience, sympathy – and can change with changing times.

I believe the day will come when it is more acceptable for older women to have children. There are certain things actually in their favour: more emotional security, a maturity of judgement, a proper sense of priorities; not to mention more money, a more settled lifestyle and the time to spend on bringing up a child. Having said that, I do not think the numbers rushing to have a post-menopausal child will ever be very great. That is why the current disapproval is out of all proportion. It also reflects a knee-jerk reaction in our culture whose ideal woman is young and beautiful, and in whose eyes older women have little status except to be patronized and who remain virtually invisible in the decision-making arenas of society. As the liberated women who shouldered the burdens and hopes of the feminist movement in the 1970s grow older, they will insist that attitudes surrounding late pregnancies are revised. And they will succeed, because both medicine and ideology are moving that way.

Fostering Prejudice

Of all the dilemmas proposed by *Heart of the Matter*, the next is the one which completely changed my mind. I went into it with an almost complete conviction that one view of the situation was right. I emerged, having encountered particular individuals at the heart of such dilemmas, knowing that my judgement had been premature and too dogmatic. As with most issues involving social behaviour and how we live together, it is easiest to keep your opinions crisp and uncluttered by staying away from the evidence. But humanity is rich and various and comes to its own solutions by a variety of thought processes and deductions that have less to do with prevailing moral absolutes than with instinctive common sense. Over and over I find that the so-called ordinary people I meet turn out to be extraordinary and that limits and obligations set down by society are only effective in so far as they respect the diversity of individuals and allow them enough freedom to be intelligently responsible for their actions. Such, I believe, is the case for lesbian and gay couples who want to adopt children.

When I met them, in the spring of 1993, Susan and Jane had lived together for nine years. Jane had been married for five years before that and her two children lived with her. Throughout the filming we made strenuous efforts on their behalf not to reveal their identities. One of the consistently distressing aspects of making *Heart of the Matter* programmes is how people who are willing to share their problems with me, and thus the public, wish to remain in the shadows. Their fear is not due to shame about who they are or what they believe. Far from it. They are often distressed to think that choosing to be filmed in the dark or from behind, or with their voices distorted, suggests they harbour some secret guilt, when they feel guilty of nothing. Nevertheless it is quite common for people who have broken no law, and who are seeking to share their experience in order that proper debate can take place, to feel they must remain anonymous. They fear the unwelcome, unexpected guest, the sudden threatening knock on the door: not from any secret police but from the tabloid press of a free country.

So it was with Susan and Jane. They told me how in March 1990 their local Council had placed an advertisement in the local paper seeking foster homes for children in care. Jane had answered this advertisement. There are some 38 000 children in care in Britain and not enough homes to go to. So councils take active steps to recruit them. Jane offered care of a very specific kind: short-term fostering in an emergency for children under five. So, for example, if grandparents fall ill and a mother is called away, such foster parents are already registered with the Council to help out. Such provision reflects the best values of a caring community. But Susan and Jane had applied three times to the Council and been turned down three times. Their ineligibility to be registered as carers hinged on the fact that they are lesbians.

I think there is little doubt that the best home in which a child can grow up is normally that of its own father and mother. I believed that then and I believe it now. Armed with this conviction, I strode into this story to be abruptly pulled up short by certain hard facts. There aren't enough such heterosexual families willing to adopt children in care. There aren't enough registered even to foster. Less than ideal situations prevail. But – as I'd already learned from the stories of donor insemination babies, and late pregnancies, and surrogacy – agencies set out to provide children with as near an ideal as possible. The phrase in law constantly quoted to me was – 'serving the best interests of the child'.

Now just such an agency had gone to work assessing Jane and Susan's eligibility – the Social Services Department of their particular Council. Over and over they had been questioned, their home scrutinized, Jane's children interviewed. And not one but eight different social workers had at different times given them a going-over.

None had any reservations in recommending them as foster carers. So far so good.

Jane had been sufficiently motivated to persist in her application, but was growing weary. 'I just wanted to offer a service to the Social Services for children who needed a bit of looking after. A short-term home. And at every point we've been pushed back.' Susan chimes in:

'We're just a normal family with normal values. Fairly open-minded about people, be it race, religion or anything like that. So we would give an open view. But, to be honest, a five-year-old or under-five is only interested in whether they get food, shelter and a loving family. The rest isn't important.'

Susan is wrong. They are not a normal family in that they are not heterosexual. But nor do they make a fuss about how they are. They are not politically active in the gay community, nor are they high-profile about their sexuality.

It was the Council sub-committee that persistently turned them down. The Council's policy is based, firstly, on the ideal of ordinary family life as right and natural for children. Secondly, they believe it matters to have a male-female relationship, because otherwise the child may be sexually confused. Thirdly, the Council considers what it calls the 'stigma' attached to homosexuality, which they believe could leave children open to teasing or bullying. All this they explained to me. They also explained that their new policy was to judge each case on its merits.

Jane and Susan's case had been found full of merit, yet the Council had disregarded the advice of its own officers. Why? Councils are politically elected and answerable directly to the public. The Chairman of the Council's Social Services Committee spelled it out:

'We are members of the public. We represent members of the public so we are going to some extent to take into account how people feel about these issues. If we disregard public opinion altogether, then I think we would be failing in our duty. So in that sense we have to move rather slowly and cautiously.'

The 'best interests of the child' suddenly weren't such a priority after all.

There is an ironic coda to this decision. At the time, changes to adoption law were being considered by the government minister responsible. He, if anyone, would surely be striving to balance the best interests of the child, the expressions of public opinion and his own sense of moral imperatives. He set out his case:

'I've made it clear to the local authorities that I think they should all in every case make the most strenuous possible efforts to find a married couple to adopt each child for whom they are responsible. If they cannot find a married couple then they are lawfully entitled to find a single person to adopt that child, and I would guess the vast majority of single people selected for adoption will be heterosexual.'

He then went on to discuss his own view of family life:

'I think most children actually need relationships with a mother and father. I think that is the best preparation for their adult lives. I think that gives them the security, but it also gives them a feeling that they're able to share in an experience shared by the vast majority of their contemporaries.'

The Minister expounding such traditional family values was none other than Tim Yeo MP. Five months later, the unmarried Julia Stent gave birth to his daughter.

Sometimes, and just occasionally, things were better managed in the past. Today Judith Weeks and Pat Romans would probably not have been assessed at all, let alone registered as foster parents. Over the twenty-eight years they've been together, they have adopted one daughter, Kate, and fostered over fifty children, including one seriously disabled girl, Louise, who has been with them nineteen years. They are clearly exceptional and remarkable people. They changed my mind for me. Any ruling, however much 'in the best interests of the child', that would prevent such a couple fostering and adopting would be flawed. The world can ill-afford to let such kindness and natural mothering instinct go to waste. Judith and Pat give us all pause for thought.

They are in their fifties now, active Quakers, one a teacher, one a social worker. They are amply shaped, cosily cardiganned. They defy the grotesque parody of lesbians as always shaven-headed, leather-clad dykes. It was Judith's job as a social worker that made her familiar with adoption procedures. She adopted as a single woman without any particular reference to Pat:

'I think we have to put it in its historical context. Sexuality wasn't such an issue in those days, and wasn't talked about so much. Certainly I don't think we ever saw it as a bar. But we ourselves did think very carefully as to whether we were doing the right thing for the children. We had to address some of those issues. Male role models, for instance. We took that seriously. We made certain from early on the girls had good relationships with men. They had a granddad who was nearby. And we made sure they went off to stay with heterosexual friends. Because we were conscious of that, they probably did so a little bit earlier than children might normally. I think Katie was three when she first packed her suitcase and went off for the weekend.

'We decided to be completely open about our relationship, so there weren't any secrets around. We made sure that people at their school knew, so that they wouldn't be stigmatized. And if anyone said anything to Katie about our relationship, she'd just say, "Well, yes, they are lesbians – but it's not a big issue." I think Kate has always said she lives with Mummy and Mummy's friend. And of course many children anyway live in homes that haven't both a mum and dad. There was a funny occasion when it was Katie's sixth birthday party. I was sitting with the children round the table and Pat was pouring out some drinks. One little girl leaned across the table and whispered to Katie, "Is that your servant?" She was trying to work out how Pat fitted in. We thought that was fascinating.'

Their lifestyle is as comfortably cosy as the rambling cottage where they live. Not people drawn to flamboyance, they've managed to make others aware of their situation in such a way that everyone has taken the fact in their stride. Judith again:

'I do feel very strongly that if people stop being open about their sexuality the children are going to be living in a situation where at best they suspect there's a secret they don't know about, and that can be damaging, or at worst they can be drawn into the secret and told that when they go outside the home they mustn't talk about it. I couldn't bring children up like that because honesty and straightforward living are absolutely essential to help children become integrated individuals.'

Such openness often had an amusing and beguiling consequence. Pat tells me how 'Katie was always very keen to explain to people the sleeping arrangements, where we both slept: this is so and so's room. Talk about "coming out" with a vengeance!'

They sit either side of the fire, comfortable womanly figures, like the loving aunts one trusted as a child. I trust them now – with their forthrightness and their lack of self-regard, as though fostering some fifty children came about quite casually. Of course it didn't. And they have both been quite exact about how they created for their daughter Katie several extended families:

'We belong to a network of lesbian friends who meet up twice a year. Katie's always been very welcome at those weekends. And of course we're Quakers, and that area of our life is really important. Through Quakers Katie has done all sorts of youth activities; weekends away. It's quite a dimension of her life.

'I think we would be denying a truth if we said that our girls had never wanted a father, because obviously they have. Children in any situation look outside and imagine they see an ideal world, and want what's there. But no one's life is 100 per cent complete. There are always losses of one sort or another. I think the whole of life is made of compromising. You lose one thing but you gain another. Our girls have lost having a father but they have gained other rich experiences they probably wouldn't have had in a more conventional family. In fact our two long-term children have grown up to do very well indeed and Katie, our eighteen-year-old, is very busy proving that you can be brought up by lesbians and be heterosexual. She's thoroughly enjoying that – and of course it's good for us.'

This remark is made with evident pleasure. I feel brutish for bringing up all the reasons people use today to argue against the idea of lesbians and gays adopting or fostering: that homosexuals might abuse children; that such children will be seen as odd; will grow up with their sexual options distorted.

Pat and Judith are saddened by what is happening now, by what they see as a narrowing of tolerance since they were young:

'It's to do with the political climate. The traditional family is supposed to be a mother and father and 2.2 children. As society is moving further and further away from that model, there is a struggle to keep it all intact. We have made a few backward steps of late and this, I think, is one of them. As to the idea of abuse – statistically, of course, 97 per cent of abused children are abused by heterosexual men; statistically, gay men are much less likely than heterosexual to abuse children. Yet we let the myth that gay men abuse children go unchallenged!'

They are also saddened by an unanticipated consequence of government policy, that if the first choice for adopting and fostering is heterosexual couples, and homosexuals are only used, as the Minister phrased it to me 'as a last resort', then those children who are hardest to place – the most difficult, either in terms of behavioural problems or physical disability – end up with socially disadvantaged parents. Pat wants to put on record her disapproval of such prioritizing:

'If you think it through to its logical end, it doesn't make any sense at all. It's a topsy turvy kind of placement that takes people you consider to be in some way second-rate, who just about squeeze through in terms of qualification – and you put with them the most difficult and needy children, who require the most skills. That is a dishonest way of going about the whole problem.'

As I leave this family home – tea and scones have been provided and, yes, there were roses round the door – I am silenced by what I have seen and heard. Pat and Judith have been making the case for lesbian adoption. But they aren't just remarkable lesbians, they are remarkable people, beyond the sexual categories of judgemental bureaucracies. Of all the stories I have encountered, theirs most indicates the policy of not rushing to a generalized moral conclusion but evaluating each case on its merits. And over fifty children would probably agree with me.

Death of a Child

In the parish church of Ashbourne in Derbyshire is a monument recording the death of a child. Penelope Boothby was nine years old and the apple of her parents' eyes. She was known, records tell, as an intelligent little girl, conversationally adept, the joy of the household, and admired beyond its confines for her grace and charm. Joshua Reynolds, it's claimed, painted her portrait. And even after death the mighty paid her tribute: her neo-classical effigy is the work of Thomas Banks, one of Britain's leading eighteenth-century sculptors.

If none of Banks' mightier monuments survive, the sleeping form of Penelope Boothby bears witness to his sensibilities in providing the grieving parents with a tender focus for their grief. The figure lies on her side, her head cushioned in an abundantly soft pillow, her hand clasped towards her chin in repose rather than prayer. Round her head she wears a coiled scarf, as was the custom; the multiple folds of her dress reach to her ankles and, in revealing the limbs beneath, convey the softness of its fabric. A broad ribbon cinches her waist and falls in profusion beside her. The difference in texture from the dress itself – even the sense of it being a different colour – transcends the marble. It is a living image of the child.

Here are no religious emblems, crosses, candles or angels. She, her parents must have thought, is angel enough. But it is the inscription that crowns the heartbreak of the tomb:

She was in form and intellect
Most exquisite.
The unfortunate parents ventured
Their all on this frail bark
And the wreck was total.

The death of a child is the greatest of all tragedies. In a culture not given to belief in a life after death, where in some celestial reunion we all might fall into the arms of those we love, children are our immortality. Their destiny is to outlive us, and in so doing mark our place in the long chain of being. It is a consolation, as we move towards our own ends, to see new life spring up around us. As we drift into the lean and slippered pantaloon, it may be some comfort to watch the youthful vigour of those who carry our genes, and reflect – in the turn of a head, the cadence of a voice – how we once were. Such a legacy may do something to ameliorate the terrors of oblivion, or to reconcile us to our own inevitable end.

Thomas Emerson wrote in his journal: 'Our fear of death is like our fear that summer will be short, but when we have had our swing of pleasure, our fill of fruit and our swelter of heat, we say we have had our day.' But what of those who have had no 'swing of pleasure' or 'fill of fruit'? How do parents deal with the impending death of a child?

Roy Grainger couldn't face it when the news was first broken to him that his four-year-old daughter Helen had a malignant brain tumour. He tells it baldly: 'I asked, "That doesn't mean she's going to die?" They said, "Yes it does." That was it.'

People's memory of how bad news is broken to them is often distorted by the shock. Some don't remember at all; others get the details wrong; some can't grasp the significance of what is being said. For this reason doctors trained in grief counselling are often advised to make a tape recording of exactly what they are saying as they break bad news. The idea is that the patient or relative then takes the tape away and plays it over in less pressured moments. Only at that point do they take in the true weight of what is being spelled out.

Roy may not remember how the conversation with Helen's doctor proceeded, but both he and his wife remember what happened to him when he got home:

'I just cracked for three days. Couldn't face anybody. Couldn't look at Helen. Couldn't do anything. And I cried all three days. Someone said later that what I was doing was mourning Helen while she was alive. I actually mourned her death while she was alive. So I know how I'll face it: I'll face it very badly.'

Linda, Helen's mother, dealt with her grief in a different way: 'When they told us, I simply got on with it and played with her. You've got to be open-minded. I think we differ, Roy and I. I believe in God and I do pray a lot and it does help.'

In November 1989 Helen Grainger had an operation at the Royal Liverpool Children's Hospital (RLCH). She was also given radiotherapy. It was then that her parents were told her brain tumour was malignant. A second opinion in London confirmed it. Roy and Linda simply refused to accept what they saw as a death sentence. There is now a 50 per cent chance of recovery from childhood cancers across the board but, of all cancers, brain tumours remain stubbornly hard to treat; if, after the first bout of treatment, the cancer persists then chances of success in future are greatly reduced. At this point parents face a terrible dilemma. Should they simply go along with the expert advice of their medical consultants, trying all the conventional therapies on offer? Should they go in search of an alternative treatment that just might work? Or should they withdraw intrusive and painful treatment and help their child die peacefully? And who should have the last word – the parents, the doctors or the child?

I met the Grainger family in the summer of 1992. Helen was the youngest of three children. The family lived in the leafy suburbs of Cosby in Merseyside. Their home was ample and comfortable, the obvious fruit of Roy's energy and forcefulness as independently self-employed. But there was about its broad spaces and cushioned comfort a suspended air, a sense of things being incomplete, or rather inert, as if those who lived there had ceased to care about their surroundings and had other things on their minds. As indeed they had.

Roy had channelled the vigour and drive that fuelled his work into a campaign to save Helen's life. He had resolved to leave no stone unturned, no opportunity unexplored. The three days of weeping had revealed to him that he could not face the prospect of Helen's death. Instead he became preoccupied with her cure:

'What we're doing is waiting for the miracle that everyone's waiting for – the cure for cancer. We just feel that if we can keep Helen alive, we're going to find that ultimate answer. Hopefully we will be around long enough.'

Helen was at that time in the care of Dr Heather McDowell at RLCH. I asked how she responded to a parent's urgent question, 'What can you do to save our child?'

'I tell them that we work nationally and internationally with other cancer specialists. That we know what's going on around the world because we go to conferences, we speak to colleagues around the world quite often. The treatment that's available in this or any other oncology children's department in Great Britain is the best you can have in the world. So what we offer would be a good base line to start.'

Unhappily, the hospital treatments couldn't stop Helen's brain tumour from growing. When the doctors explained as much, Roy took things into his own hands: 'I had already seen programmes on alternative treatments and other things that could possibly cure cancer, and I said, "Right, if ever conventional medicine turns its back on me, I will then seek cures from other spheres".'

Other spheres meant Mexico. Linda, Roy and Helen set off for the Hoxey Clinic in Mexico, which offers an alternative therapy not recognized by orthodox medicine. No one, it seems, has been able to involve the Hoxey Clinic on the international network of which Dr McDowell speaks:

'We have written to them on several occasions asking what treatment they give and what they have published in reputable journals so that the rest of the medical profession can actually share this wonderful treatment. And we have met with no replies.'

Mexico disappointed not only the doctors but the Graingers too. Even the Hoxey Clinic declared that Helen's tumour was too far advanced to cure. But Roy still wouldn't accept defeat. Their next move was to America.

'I rang around. I spent eight hours a day on the phone. I pleaded and begged doctors in America to listen to us. Eventually I got in touch with a doctor in San Francisco. That ultimately led to a ten-hour brain operation in San Francisco that saved Helen's life.

The venture cost tens of thousands of pounds, which Roy, ever diligent on his daughter's behalf, raised through local Round Table and other appeals. The people of North-West England are warm-hearted and generous. The parents of Laura Davies – the little girl who went to Pittsburgh for a multi-organ transplant – also raised thousands of pounds, over in Eccles, a mere 30 or so miles away. Roy gave up work in order to redouble his efforts.

The treatment in America was in November 1990. By summer 1992, when I met her, Helen was still alive but extremely frail. The brain tumour remained and she had occasional fits. Her mental development was retarded and she attended a special school to help her slow progress, but she was still able to enjoy going there. At RLCH she was receiving as much treatment as her delicate condition allowed.

I asked Dr McDowell how she responded to parents seizing the initiative, spending money on alternative therapies in the face of her own expert advice:

'At the end of the day all parents have to be very clear in their mind that they have done the most for their children. They are going to have to live with that decision for the rest of their lives, when their child dies. So I cannot say, "Don't go. It's a rip-off." But what I would say to parents who cannot afford this treatment is that they should in no way feel that they have been inferior parents because of it.'

Roy, a man of absolutes and of passion, feels he had no option:

'How could I live with myself for the rest of my life? If we'd not gone to America, she'd have had only four months to live. If after that four months we'd buried her, I'd be left wondering whether if I'd gone to America we might have succeeded. No. We took a gamble at a certain time and we were proved right. We saved her life. She's still alive today, eighteen months later.'

Roy's life had now been consumed by one burning purpose. His eloquent protestations about his daughter swept the conversation along, only to be suddenly swamped by a gust of grief bringing him to the brink of tears as he battled with his fear of losing her.

'We want to keep Helen alive. Helen is ours and we will decide. We are aggressively looking for a cure. We are in tune with the doctors. We don't conflict with them. If anything we push the doctors to the extremes of finding new treatments for Helen, rather than them pushing us.'

Where, in the midst of all this distress and this searching, is Helen herself? I ask him what she thinks of it all.

'Helen is young. She doesn't understand totally. She knows she's sick. She knows she's got a brain tumour. But she doesn't know the seriousness of the situation. She accepts all the treatments. She knows, once they're over with, she ends up back to normal; she ends up playing.'

Helen is a pretty child with curling blonde hair and pale eyes. Always she is in pretty clothes that accentuate her doll-like beauty. Her illness – or perhaps our being there – makes her diffident. She is small for her age and quiet-spoken. But she plays responsively with her mother and father, who clearly set aside much time for such precious moments. I ask Roy and Linda whether Helen knows about death. They don't think so, but they seem to avoid speaking of it to her. Linda – a practising Catholic – has simply explained that when you die you go to heaven. On one occasion Helen had this exchange with Roy:

'She said, "When I die I'm going to heaven."

'What makes you think you're going to die?'

She said, "Well, my grandmother died."

And I said, "Well, we all die sometime. We all go to heaven sometime."

And she said, "Yes," and accepted it as such. She didn't seem to relate it to her illness.'

According to Dr McDowell, Helen's remarks might have been more loaded than her parents wanted to believe.

'Children are very perceptive. They know what's going on. You can't hide much from them, even the seven- and eight-year-olds. They may actually come up with some very pertinent questions. But some parents are adamant that we do not address the subject of death. So we wouldn't. We would wait for the child's questions. Then we say the parents can answer as they like, but the staff on our unit will answer as truthfully as possible.'

Roy's hopes of a miracle cure arriving in time to save his daughter were disappointed. According to Dr McDowell:

'Generally speaking, most of what parents discover when they go in search of cures is research that is very, very premature, either in laboratory work or even preliminary studies with adults. Then you have to ask the question: is it the child's right to have the last few days or weeks of life in comfort, rather than undergoing totally experimental treatment which may make them terribly ill, or may actually kill them? You have to weigh that up.'

These are the issues being weighed whenever newspaper headlines oversimplify such stories in lurid terms: 'Hospital Refuses Treatment for Dying Child'. Despite financial pressures, at the moment treatment will still be made available for a child if medical consultants and parents agree it is worth it for the child's sake. The balance of considerations put parents on the rack, torn between the love that wants to hang on at all costs and the caring impulse to make a child's final days peaceful.

Helen died on 1 November 1992.

Hers was indeed a frail bark and the wreck was total.

Death is not simply a medical event: it is not even primarily a medical event. It doesn't belong to the doctors. But there is a danger that, because doctors and nurses help negotiate the route by which we arrive at our death, we look to them to endow it with significance, to strive to delay the moment, to chart and measure it, and finally to certify it as having happened.

But death is our own. It belongs to us and to those we love. In many ways, we need to reclaim our right to death as we want it to be. The temptation is to surrender our final days into someone else's keeping – while retaining some atavistic hope, against all the evidence, that it will not happen, at least not yet.

Louise Lotz, facing the death of her seven-year-old son Victor, struggled with choices similar to those faced by Roy and Linda Grainger but came to an altogether different resolution. Victor was diagnosed as having leukaemia in March 1989 when he was three. At that point Louise knew there was a 50 per cent chance of recovery, so Victor went into hospital for a four-week course of chemotherapy with follow-up treatment by radiotherapy. At that point things seemed to be going well, and the mood was one of quiet hopefulness.

Treatment continued for some two years. But eight months after it was completed, at Christmas 1991, Victor relapsed. The leukaemia was back and at that point the medical prognosis was worse than the first time round. Now there were three options: a bone marrow transplant, more heavy chemotherapy, or simply no further treatment at all. All along, Louise, who is a single parent, had talked with Victor about his condition, paying particular regard to what he had to say:

'I think he knows a lot. He's taking it in. It's quite clear he's taking it in. I think he understands about leukaemia. And at that point he didn't want either the chemotherapy or the transplant. He'd been through so much, and it hadn't helped. He just didn't want more. He didn't want anything more to do with needles, or any of that. He couldn't face it again.'

Loving him as she did, Louise allowed Victor's opinion as much weight as her own. Together they asked to have no further treatment.

'He's the person that has the leukaemia after all. It's Victor that it's happening to. I think it's Victor who's important, not me, or the doctors, or the world, or society. It's really what we can offer Victor and what he wants.'

Victor's views, those of a seven-year-old, highlight the issue of informed consent. Every adult has the right under the Patients' Charter to give or withhold his or her informed consent to proposed treatment. But what about children? At what stage can a child comprehend information well enough to make a valid choice?

Dr Heather McDowell thinks it's not a matter of age, but of maturity:

'You must be satisfied in your own mind, and so must the parents, that the child actually knows what they are doing. Below the age of consent, you'd have to think very hard if a child wanted to refuse consent.'

But in the late 1980s a law came into effect that could tilt the whole equation of choice between parents, doctors and children. The Children Act requires that a child's voice must be heard in all decisions that affect it, and nothing could affect a child more than having a potentially fatal illness. So how much weight was Louise prepared to give Victor's views?

'I think if the consultant had said, "There's an 80 per cent chance of him responding to treatment, he'll have a very good quality of life, and the treatment won't be very unpleasant" – if Victor had dug his heels in and said "No", then I'd certainly be wondering what was going on.'

But that was not the case. Victor's chances of recovery were low. His doctors respected his and Louise's decision to refuse further treatment. It was at that point I met them both. It is hard to describe the sense of serenity that prevailed in their home. It was as though they had reclaimed for themselves something that was precious, taken back into the family the right to live without any pressure of tests and treatments, their days governed by charts, visits, injections. Without all the medical paraphernalia, they were concentrating on what mattered for them – living Victor's last months together as they wanted them to be.

Like any other home with two boys (Victor had an elder brother, Peter, aged nine), it was bright with coloured toys, untidy, friendly and easy-going. Louise spoke gently and with dignity; certainly without self-pity or depression. I asked her what had swayed Victor's decision:

'I felt he knew something more than I knew. He had such a clarity about himself, he had a calmness, a sense of peace. I felt his decision came from somewhere I wanted to respect. Ultimately we all came to the same conclusion. There was great harmony about it.'

So it was not a medical decision at all really?

'Not really, no. I think there's more to Victor than a bunch of cells going wrong. I think there's a whole person, and perhaps the cancer's part of him, just like any other part of him, and that needs to be accepted and respected.'

How then does she plan to make the most of Victor's life?

'By focusing on the day that we're in, the moment that we're in. Just responding to that. Not seeing too much of the past, too much of the future. Saying, "Here's this minute – what can we do with it? How shall we make it happy?"'

And how is Victor handling it?

'I think he handles it remarkably well, and I think if he can cope, then surely we have a duty to. I think he's quite radiant, in a way. He knows what's happening, and he's with it, he stays with it.'

But does Victor understand about death?

'There are a number of questions children ask about death. They need to know that the person goes under the ground, but that we don't believe that's all of the person. We believe there's a part that lives on. I spoke to him about a candle, giving a little light, and that we all have that light inside us that goes on for ever. Only the shell gets put under the ground.

'I'm a Christian, and I think Victor is, too. And there are churches who pray for Victor. And there are people who aren't even formally Christians who pray in their own way, or meditate on Victor's situation. I feel quite sustained and I'm pleased about that.'

And herself?

'Oh yes, I pray. Absolutely. Certainly. I've formed a discipline of praying in a certain way. That helps me a lot.'

There is a stillness about the place even as Victor clashes his bricks and Louise clatters the coffee cups. I sense that the others in the television crew feel as I do, lumpen intruders into some private mystery. We avoid eye contact, thoughtful and moved as we proceed with the filming.

Victor is tall for his age, slender, with a natural grace. He is beautiful, with a wide open face but a sense of privacy about himself that is oddly mature. But then he and his mother are on a strange journey together. Death has come to their door, and they have not allowed him to throw their lives into panic. They have let death enter their home, but not defeat them. I had a sense of the sacred, being in their presence.

Victor died in October 1992, a month after the *Heart of the Matter* programme was transmitted. A year later, on the anniversary of his death, we talked to Louise again. She had taken Victor first to a hospital, then to the Springhill Centre near Aylesbury, an alternative hospice catering for all sorts of people in need. There they lived together in a small house of their own. Victor's death had come unexpectedly when he was home for a weekend.

'He'd been ill in the night. Not dreadfully ill. He'd had vomiting and diarrhoea. He was talking. He was quite lucid and quite strong because he was very thirsty and he actually got up and got a drink off the windowsill. He did talk about what he called "going upstairs", which was his metaphor for death, like "going through the cupboard", "shutting up the shop". He didn't want to upset me, I think. So I thought, "This child's sick. We'll have to stay another day." I didn't really think he was going to die any minute. I went downstairs to fetch a phone number to cancel an appointment – and when I came up he was dead. I felt just a sense of calm – and well, he's done it, and well done. And he was fine.'

We each deal with personal tragedies in terms of our own personalities. It is not always immediately helpful for society or its prevailing ethic to tell us how we should behave and make us feel guilty for not doing so. For example, the prevailing ethic in the medical world says that you should tell the dying directly about their condition. That may in some abstract sense be better psychologically than deceiving or lying to loved ones, or involving oneself in a web of deception and delusion about unavoidable realities. But for some people it is just not possible.

Roy and Linda Grainger could no more have made the choice Louise Lotz made than Louise could have chosen their way. The point of programmes such as *Heart of the Matter* is not to judge or prescribe, but to show the variety of human response to moral dilemmas that arise in people's lives. It is an arena in which viewers can speculate about how they themselves might behave in such circumstances, and be given confidence in their own judgements. In the course of such programmes, exceptional stories come to light that give a new perspective and possibly a new insight into a problem. No story, in my experience, has been more extraordinary than that of Maurice and Wendy Adams. They chose to give birth to a son who was already dying.

Maurice and Wendy are committed Christians. I put this statement at the head of their story because it is clearly the most important fact about them, and the sustaining principle that underpinned their behaviour at every point, behaviour that brought them into a degree of conflict with medical authority.

In 1989, when Wendy was in the twentieth week of her third pregnancy, she went along for a routine scan, taking her two other children, Victoria and Sam, with her:

'The woman doing the scan took a long time over it. She told me it was a boy, and then said she'd like to see me again the following week. I began to wonder, because I had the children with me, whether she didn't feel free to say anything that might alarm me.'

Two weeks later the consultant told them their baby had a heart defect so serious that he would die within a day or two of birth. He offered an abortion, or continuing the pregnancy to birth with full medical support. They chose the second option:

'We feel that abortion's wrong anyway. But we had to think about it in our own situation. Not just Maurice and Wendy or the baby. But what about Sam and Victoria, our children, and our friends and neighbours? You're talking about losing a life out of society, not just losing a life out of a womb.'

Neither of them rushed this decision. They took time to consider the circumstances set before them with much sensitivity by their consultant. But something he said made a great difference to Wendy:

'He said that the child would probably live for two days, maybe even five days. And I wanted to know him for those days. I wanted to hold him and actually have the child. It was a strange feeling to anticipate the loss. But, as a Christian, I felt certain God would give me strength. I also knew God was a God who healed, so that was a possibility for me. Overall, I felt utterly convinced that God would give us the strength and the peace to face the death of the child.'

The first thing they did was to give their son a name: Joshua.

'Otherwise you start calling the baby "it", and we felt if we're going to have this child as part of our family, we need to know him. So the children knew that Joshua was with us in the womb and would soon be with us in life, but not for very long. Compared to previous pregnancies, the child in my womb became more of a child than a blob. I saw him very quickly as a child with a personality, realizing we'd only got a few days. The pregnancy was special.'

Maurice and Wendy sit side by side talking to me, on the bright sofa in their bright front room. They are so identified with each other that they pick up each other's sentences, complete each other's thoughts. Maurice interrupts:

'Many people in this world feel that death and life are two completely separate departments. For the Christian it's all one department. Death is only a matter of stopping breathing, it's only a physical matter. So we could go with security to the children, without worry, without instilling in them an element of guilt and fear – or of saying, "Oh dear, woe is me. What has life done to us to deserve this?" – and say, "This is the natural progression of life. It happens in farmyards, it happens in jungles." At whatever level, we could talk to the children about it. "It happens with pets, it happens with animals, it happens with granddad and grandmum and it happens to children." Death is an extension of life and as Christians we bring our children up to know that death is an extension of life and life is an extension of death. And if you ask our children "What do you think has happened?", they'll say "Oh, we've got a brother Joshua. He just happens to be living with Jesus rather than with us." I would prefer to instil that kind of hope and faith in children rather than the fear that death is something strange to run away from, because we can't always run away from it.'

As well as telling their children, Maurice and Wendy told a close circle of friends and family. Wendy remembers:

'Our support from friends and family was far greater, remarkably supportive, and that helped us cope. But there wasn't anything special. If a child lives with us for a long time or a short time, they demand the same love and respect. So the bedroom was prepared. The cot was prepared.

'Towards the end of the pregnancy, we felt it was only fair to extend the numbers of those we told, because everyone was saying, "Oh, it's coming soon. How are you feeling?" We had to tell people so they could be prepared for the grief. Some of them were surprised that I seemed so happy and confident.'

There had, of course, been tears shed. How could there not be? But, looking back, Wendy tries to put into words how she felt: 'I didn't feel unhappy. I felt totally at peace – carried by peace. I had cried out to God with tears – and I put that sense of peace down to prayer and to trust in God.'

Arrangements had been made to induce Joshua, to avoid clashing with Christmas, but in fact Wendy went into labour two weeks early and had a perfectly normal delivery. Maurice was with her.

'At the end of the day a dad's spirit linking with a son's spirit makes no difference what the son's like... So there was normal bonding between dad and son, and mum and son. We thought, "Great, we've got a son." That was as far as we could think because the moment was the moment. I couldn't have thoughts of the next day or the next week. I just had enough strength for that moment.'

In the hours that followed, Maurice was to summon up further reserves of strength to deal with the crisis precipitated by Joshua's birth. Because the baby had arrived early, the team and consultant fully briefed to deliver him were not on duty. The new team, reading Joshua's notes, were no doubt surprised to find themselves dealing with something special. Maurice and Wendy speak with unqualified praise of the attention they received at that time. They knew that, once born, Joshua would be given another scan immediately to assess his condition more accurately. It is what happened next that threw them into confusion and remains an indistinct memory. As Maurice recalls it:

'I can't quite remember how they said it, but they came back with a smile and encouragement and said something like, "Well, it's not as bad news as we thought." That's when my mind started ticking: what do they mean?'

As they began to explain, did hopes soar?

'No, not really. Confusion set in.'

And for Wendy?

'I thought what they said was that they might now possibly be able to offer us this series of operations through the child's life, all of which were high-risk operations. I felt bewildered, because that wasn't what we were expecting to hear. They did say the child might actually survive up to seven days now without intervention. So part of me felt relieved – he's arrived safely, and the two days I'd set my heart on may now be seven. Every moment seemed precious.'

However, it quickly became clear that the medical team had a different focus from that of the parents.

'Basically the paediatric consultant saw the problem as being with the child, and he wanted us to make a decision about the baby. They wanted us to have Joshua put on life-support tubes and to run all the tests to decide if an operation could go ahead. Joshua would have been taken away from us – in the local hospital, then to the hospital where the heart operations are done. It would all have been taken out of our hands. We wanted to make a decision about the family but we were put under pressure to make a big decision immediately. We felt it was a decision not just about Joshua's heart, and any medical intervention. It was also about the family.'

Wendy wanted to give thoughtful consideration to these new options in her own place:

'I wanted to be in the peace and security of home, and talk it over together in peace. They had said that maybe Joshua could live a few more days. So I felt, I've got a bit of time. Please let me just have that little bit of time to decide.'

At this point things got distinctly sticky, with Maurice and Wendy keen to leave but sensing that the medical team wanted them to stay.

'The consultants wouldn't let us go out of the room, literally out of the room where we gave birth. There was an implied sense of you stay here, we'll go out and you talk it through. We will come back and want to hear your decision. There was a sense that if we didn't go for the option they offered, they'd be very dissatisifed with us. It was at that point I said to Wendy, "Get dressed." She was in her nightie. We actually literally put the shoes on our feet. We were saying, "Yes, we'd love to make a decision; we want to work with you but we don't want to make the decision here." We felt it was becoming more of a battle than a partnership. They were saying, "Do you know what you're doing...? Do you know that operations nowadays are very skilful?" And we did know all that. But it was a broader issue. It wasn't just a medical decision. It was difficult to get out of that room and we didn't go on the best of terms.'

It was a great relief for them to be back home. Joshua was feeding normally. The only sign of his illness was that his fingers and toes were a little blue. Close friends came round; there were prayers and discussion. Photographs were taken of Joshua in Wendy's arms, Joshua in Maurice's arms, Joshua with his brother and sister. They look like ordinary family snaps from any typical album. Nothing of their pain and sadness has left a trace on the glossy surface. But Joshua is there, a most certain member of the family; focus of their love, and already focus of their grief.

Next day brought another shock.

'The doctor called and we knew then we were under enormous pressure because she mentioned that the consultant at the hospital was talking about making Joshua a ward of court. The GP handled it very well. She said the same thing as the consultant – "You may be withdrawing the potential of further life for your child, and if you don't decide for the operation we may have to take legal action to give the child what we feel is best for it."'

It is interesting to note, given the debate about abortion, that the medical profession who would unquestioningly have aborted Wendy's baby at twenty weeks was, a mere twenty or so weeks later, threatening legal action to provide elaborate surgical intervention in a high-risk operation on a child with a seriously faulty heart.

Maurice was mortified that they could even consider making Joshua a ward of court. In the powerful emotions of the moment, he now admits, he was perhaps not entirely fair to the medical team.

'I thought, here's a chance for them to learn something more about paediatric heart surgery, and I don't want my child to be a guinea pig. I felt they weren't thinking of the best interests of my son, but of the best for society and the furtherance of medical skills. That's probably not a fair assessment in retrospect.'

Wendy had a further fear: 'I wondered whether perhaps they'd assessed us wrongly and thought we were religious fanatics who pinned every hope on a healing, which wasn't the case.'

Nonetheless, the crisis over the treatment of Joshua lay right across the fault line of ethical debate about who is responsible for a sick child. Unlike Victor Lotz or Helen Grainger, Joshua was too small to give his view. That left the decision entirely to his doctors and parents. Professor Ian Kennedy is an expert on medical law and ethics:

'Parents have duties towards their children. They don't have rights over them as if they were a piece of property. A child exists in its own right. Therefore, although parents are of course the prime movers – the people who are the most concerned, the people who have to care for the child, grieve for the child – at the same time society has certain rules within which they must live, certain principles to which they must pay respect. So we are anxious to set limits to what parents may or may not do.'

John Harris is Professor of Applied Philosophy at Manchester University:

'It's a reasonable presumption that parents have the child's best interests at heart. But that is a presumption which may be defeated by evidence. And where the evidence is to the contrary, then I believe the parents have no special role at all. Their role as decision-makers for the child is dependent on the assumption being true that they have the best interests of the child at heart.'

At the moment medical ethics tend to define 'the child's best interests' as more than vegetative survival. Much discussion focuses on the quality of life. If consciousness is absent, to what extent can life be said to persist? These are finally subjective matters, even though society and its thinkers seek to arrive at a consensus.

Joshua had been born on Sunday, and taken home on Sunday evening. The GP's visit on Monday morning ended in an agreement that Maurice and Wendy would see the consultant at the specialist hospital the very next day. An appointment was made. In the event, Joshua died before they could keep that appointment; at about 9.30 a.m. on the third day of his life.

'I think the evening of the Monday night he'd stopped feeding. So I felt concerned. He wanted to be with me. He was only happy if he was lying next to me, quite at peace next to me in bed. I suggested that Maurice slept in the other room, because he would definitely have to carry the brunt of facing people and having to think through big issues the next day. But then I woke him in the night. I had this growing sense that Joshua was dying. We prayed again for him. We all woke the next morning. Joshua was still alive, quite at peace, and passive. His breathing had become more difficult. Maurice took the children to school. We treated it as a normal day. Maurice came back and I remember being tearful and saying, "I think he's going." And he just died in our arms. It was a very precious moment. I don't think I've ever experienced grief like it.'

For Maurice, too, it was a profound moment:

'For a dad to see his son born, then to see a son die... To hold someone through death, particularly your son, this is a moment no man could ever write, no musician could ever compose. This is in the hands of a Maker, a Creator, who has the control of life and death and we were at total peace. It's quite amazing to have grief and sadness at the same time as peace and tranquillity.'

As we talked we were all aware that Wendy was again pregnant. By the time the programme went out, Maurice and Wendy had a newborn son: Jacob. But did Maurice ever allow himself to wonder whether Joshua, given all the hi-tech operations, might have come through and still be with them?

'I don't think in that way at all. I feel totally at peace about the decision we made. Joshua's body might have been in one piece, but I honestly wonder about his emotions. He would have been institutionalized. He'd be more in hospital than at home. He would have to go back for more and more operations up to at least eight years old. If you know anyone with chronic long-term illness, it wears them down so.'

What does he now make of how the doctors' motives and perspective differed from his own?

'Life is not just a beating heart and breathing lungs. That just happens to be the physical life. But life has a spiritual dimension as well as a physical dimension. The doctors' view was, "We have the technology, we have the skills, it's very high-risk but we could do something to make his heart a little bit better." Their motive would be to do the best for Joshua as an individual. I had no skills to mend his heart, but I have skills, as a father, to mend his family...'

The parameters of our religious or philosophical view of life govern everything each of us does. Maurice and Wendy acted within their view of the Christian family presided over by parents, with children very much cherished and seen as primarily the parents' concern. They made choices, allowable within law and commanding the respect of those close to them and all those who heard their story.

Sex in the Classroom

There is a painting by Lord Leighton called *The Captive Andromache*. It is vast, some 200 x 400 cm, the huge canvas taking up an entire wall of the Manchester City Art Gallery. I did not see it there until I was in my forties and then I gasped at its gigantic size. For I had known it all my life, but only as a modest print filling the entire wall above the mantelpiece in the back room of my parents' semi. I grew up familiar with a particular detail. In the lower right-hand corner a man holds a toddler in his arms, and the child is pulling at its father's nose. From the age of two my father would, as a treat, lift me up to the picture far above, and draw my attention to this family intimacy. Whereupon, and with much laughter, I would pull his nose too. Thus I learned behaviour, copied with family encouragement, from the world I saw around me. How else are we to know what to do?

I have long since ceased pulling noses as a mark of affection. But I did, when I began to kiss boys, learn a thing or two from Rhett Butler and Scarlett O'Hara. In the buttoned-up climate of desperate respectability that was the lot of the lower middle classes, it was made clear to me that the existence of sex was not to be acknowledged. So its equipment, mine included, was to be kept well out of sight. As a mere child I stood shivering on a Blackpool beach while a towel with a cord threaded through it was tied round my neck lest forbidden parts of my naked body be glimpsed by the aging deckchair brigade ranged around. By the age of ten I had developed a rapt interest in Classical sculpture. It was the only way.

Learning to grow into a sexual being was seriously hampered by the attitude of grown-ups who slammed doors in my face when I was tempted to step through them and threw sand in my eyes as I was about to take liberating walks along the shore. Cinema they could not touch, and I acquired attitudes and techniques from watching the stars of the 1940s playing out their passions. Theirs was the style and behaviour I aspired to in those awkward teenage years. Well, you had to start somewhere!

I hope things have got better for young people since then – less guilt, fewer inhibitions, more pleasure. I have brought up two children who have found their own paths through the sexual minefield without conspicuous damage to themselves or others. Perhaps it's easier than adults think.

Heart of the Matter has delved into the sexual behaviour of the young on more than one occasion and in more than one country. The pill has made it more permissive. AIDS has made it more treacherous. Our programmes have uncovered the way in which today's adult world instructs, informs, misinforms, controls, ignores and neglects the sexual emergence of its young people. In working on these programmes, I have come to realize that the English are particularly and peculiarly shy of sex. In no other country do parents so thoroughly depend on teachers to spell out the details of sexual encounters. Having done so, those parents then complain if those teachers are being too explicit, too 'dirty'. There is much talk of the 'innocence' of childhood and the need to preserve it from the sullied adult world of sex. There are calls for a return to family values, and for sexual matters to be set in such a context. Above all, sexual intercourse remains illegal for girls under sixteen, and homosexual intercourse before the age of twenty-one. The realities of biology and contemporary behaviour are otherwise. That is where the dilemmas lie.

Have you noticed that people are still having sex?
All the pronouncements had absolutely no effect:
Parents and counsellors constantly scorned them.
But people are still having sex and nothing seems to stop them.

The words are those of the rap lyric we used to accompany *Heart of the Matter*'s exploration of teenage sex in New York. In the early nineties it had become what one teacher called a 'life and death issue'. The issue, of course, was AIDS, and New York was being a good deal more up-front about it than Britain. It needed to be. By 1990 over a million people in America were HIV positive, and the highest incidence among teenagers was in New York.

In 1990 the incoming Chancellor of New York's Board of Education, Joseph Fernandez, had launched an HIV/AIDS education programme in the high schools. It took the bold step of making condoms available to any pupil who asked. Boldest of all, parents were given no say and teachers were not obliged to inform them if their child had asked and been supplied. 'We are acting quite aggressively,' Jill Blair, Board of Education Special Assistant, told me. 'We're prepared to modify our programme on the results of evaluations, but we're not prepared to compromise or risk the lives of young people.' I assumed the first half of that remark was intended to appease parents. The second half expressed their real attitude. Parents certainly did need appeasing. The opening phase of the Board of Education plan went ahead in November 1991. By January 1992 it had run into trouble.

I go to the Montefiore Medical Center in the Bronx to meet Dr Karen Hein, one of America's top experts on HIV and the driving force behind New York's adolescent AIDS programme. She is a brisk and bright medic, clear-skinned and with a mouth so full of teeth that all the time she speaks she appears to be smiling. She smiles a lot anyway, which makes you feel pleased to be in her company. She is also fiercely intelligent and confident in the transparent logic of what she is doing. What she hasn't reckoned with is the implacable logic of those who oppose her. Their case – if teenagers don't have sex they don't get AIDS – is, as a statement, unanswerable. Karen Hein hangs her case on that 'if'. It wasn't until the launch of her AIDS programme that she caught wind of the opposition there would be to it:

'At the official presentation to the Board of Education, I showed my first slide about the epidemic in New York. One of the Board members, who's since become involved in opposing it, said to me, "Isn't it amazing how the experts can lie with numbers!" I was horrified. Then he asked why was I chosen, as opposed to somebody with the opposite point of view. I said, "Opposite point of view? I'm an expert in adolescent health. I've done research for twenty years. I'm here to present the facts to you. There is no opposite view to the fact that I care about these teenagers." That was the beginning of my awareness that there was going to be a polarization.'

The facts Dr Hein was making known had until then remained undetected. One of the axioms about sex is that people lie about it. But doctors don't lie about HIV. Dr Hein again:

'In this one hospital in the Bronx we have sixty-five young people with HIV between the ages of thirteen and twenty-one. Sixty-two of them are or were in New York City public schools. [In America 'public school' means state school.] Most of those young people have not disclosed they have the virus, in some cases to their own families let alone to schoolmates. We know the extent of it. The general public don't. It's a large invisible part of the epidemic right now and we don't want to wait another decade until everybody knows a teenager with AIDS before we take this action.'

To charges that making condoms available in schools encourages young people to be promiscuous, Dr Hein has a ready, well-researched, answer:

'Comparative studies between five Western industrialized nations [one of them was Wales!] and the USA revealed that the age of first intercourse remains more or less the same, but in places where there was access to services (including contraceptive advice) the rates of sexually transmitted diseases and unintended pregnancies were much lower. So information and knowledge leads to responsible sex, not more sex.'

The protest, however, came from those who wanted the message to teenagers to be 'no sex at all'. These objectors strongly questioned the assumptions made about young people's behaviour in the television commercials about AIDS then being transmitted. In each mini-episode a boy and girl, sexually attracted to each other, are drawn through drink or drugs to have casual sex. The voice-over sets alarm bells ringing:

'This is where they party, where Denise met Michael. They

danced, they joked, they did a little crack and then a pill; then she took the wrong step that ended everything. Only she doesn't know it yet. Drugs make you forget and if you forget how risky sex can be, you could catch the AIDS virus and not know it for years.'

Dr Karen Hein maintains such a scenario reflects the reality of life in New York public schools. What I find when I stand at a school gate asking around, entirely supports that view. It's estimated that 50 per cent of New York teenagers are sexually active. 'Is that right?' I ask. 'Maybe more,' I'm told, 'and the majority are having sex without protection.' This programme will not be seen in America so the young people are very outspoken. Perhaps American teenagers are like that anyway. The boys agree the situation favours them: 'Your father's proud if you get to have sex with five girls in one year. They'll give you a reward. "That's my boy; he's a man! I'll take you out to dinner. I'll get you your own car."' I recall on the instant that people lie about sex, but I get the general drift of their inflated remarks – 'It's a bit harder for girls. No father's going to say, "Oh go ahead, give my baby girl condoms so she can go out and have sex".' They all agreed that parents didn't know what was going on. Typically: 'My mother thinks I'm starting to have sex now. I've just turned twenty years old. I lost my virginity when I was fifteen.' Statistics concerning a subject about which people lie must be intrinsically suspect. But by way of comparison, a survey of 1000 British women who responded to a questionnaire in the magazine *Nineteen* in 1994 found the average age at which they lost their virginity was fifteen and a half: nearly 25 per cent had sex by the age of fifteen, 10 per cent by fourteen.

The Staten Island Ferry is reckoned by the New-York-for-$10-a-day type of guide books to be excellent tourist value. For a few cents you embark from Lower Manhattan, where the twin towers of the Trade Center strike a chill shadow in the streets below. You move out into open water, skirting the Statue of Liberty standing gaunt and beleaguered on its own island; then the ferry draws into the quieter waterfront and more suburban landscape of Staten Island. It's fine and impressive doing it once. I had to do it three times. The problem was the weather. Early morning fog swathed everything in metal-grey deadness. It is a frugal or hastily-made television programme that leaves its presenter to explain, 'If there wasn't any fog, you'd be seeing the New York skyline.' That was not our way. So, discovering on our first trip that the camera could make nothing of the murk around us, we returned later in the day to come and go until the shots, the lights, the weather were just right. As we went back and forth across the water, the Statue of Liberty looked ever more grimly unwelcome and stoic. The ferry, however, acquired a sudden festivity with the arrival of a jazz band who came and went with it, as we were doing. They played and collected money all the way. By then we needed a little light relief for we had spent the morning with William and Nancy Alfonso and their daughters Venus and Yvette, and they had given us plenty to think about.

William Alfonso's story is heroic in its way. Born in the Bronx into a large, poor Hispanic family, he'd been living out on the streets from the age of eleven, taking drugs, doing everything and anything; having sex himself from the age of twelve. 'I've been out there. I see'd it.' Somewhere along the trajectory of this catastrophic life, something stopped him and changed him. Certainly he was intelligent and streetwise enough to have seen what disasters lay ahead. But many perceive as much and still don't or can't escape. William Alfonso had, by an effort of will, taken hold of his own destiny and wrought it into something worthwhile. He was now a modest pillar of society, a family man with a wife, two daughters, owner of a corner house in a suburb of green lawns and well-behaved neighbours. He was also a dedicated Christian, worshipping at the spacious evangelical Gateway Cathedral, and seeking to practise Christian virtue in every aspect of his life. 'We're simple folks; we are simple, simple people. We didn't wake up one morning wanting to sue the Board of Education and its Chancellor, Fernandez, but, by God, someone has to do it. Someone has to stop him.'

William Alfonso is neat, with dark, Hispanic looks. Now in his late thirties, he has the balance and lightness on his feet of someone who was recently good at sport. His black, wavy hair is slicked back against his head, his black eyes are clear and challenging; as he speaks his hands gesture vigorously to emphasize the force of his convictions. His wife Nancy sits docilely by his side, her rosebud mouth and over-plucked eyebrows giving her a placid, doll-like air. This is a family that thinks as one, and that one is William Alfonso, a man convinced his constitutional rights are threatened.

The First Amendment of the American Constitution declares that no law shall prohibit 'the free exercise of religion'. William Alfonso considers chastity before marriage to be one of the tenets of his religion and he perceives the availability of condoms in schools as a direct challenge to it. 'By bombarding my children with sex education and condoms they are taking away our rights to bring up our daughters as we have chosen.' That very week condoms have been available at Curtis High, the school his daughters attend. He is incensed:

'Statistics say that 50 per cent of kids are having sex. So they focus on and bombard the kids with sex, sex, sex, condoms, condoms, condoms. How about the 50 per cent of kids not having sex? What's being done for them? What's being taught for them to stay exactly the way they are?'

And the way they are, in the case of Venus and Yvette, is drop-dead gorgeous. It is William's blessing to have fathered two Hispanic beauties, young women achingly conscious of their own emerging voluptuousness. It can hardly have escaped her overwrought father that his eighteen-year-old is more than living up to the name he gave her. Venus has dark curls cascading down one side of her classic features and spilling onto her shoulders, a gypsy's heavy eyebrows, a languorous smile on pouting lips add to her exotic beauty. Yvette is younger, puppyish and plump. But luminous dark eyes light up her face. She, too, will soon turn heads.

The two girls share a room girlishly decked with pretty dolls, fluffy animals, coy china figures. The feeling is delicate and feminine, still childlike, no garish teenage pop posters, no indications of throbbing hero worship. The only incongruity is a bottle of scent labelled 'Poison'. Venus? Poison? These are the heavy clues you find scattered through a Eugene O'Neill play. Perhaps the Alfonsos still have to take their long day's journey...

'We teach our daughters to stay virgins until marriage and they're to have sex only in marriage with that one guy. That's God's plan for their life. They know and respect that they'll be blessed by God. God will bring the right young man into their life. But let me tell you this, too. There is no guarantee. I'm not naive enough to say that definitely, without a doubt, my girls will wait till they get married to have sex. But my wife and I know we have done our job to teach them what was God's will in their life when it came to sex.'

There is no guarantee, but there is – literally – the key: the Alfonsos' equivalent of the chastity belt, but worn round the neck where it passes for jewellery:

'I went out and had two gold keys made. And on one side of the key we had engraved "God", and on the other side engraved "Dad". I said to them I would like you to accept this, as a reminder every day that you have it round your neck that you made a covenant with God and with Dad to stay pure and clean. And the only time that you will use this key is on your wedding day, because your husband will be the only man you will offer yourself to.'

The girls were told they did not have to accept the keys. Unsurprisingly both daughters were wearing them for our interview, and their views were meekly in accord with their father's. One said 'I don't like the school to influence me. The school's there to teach me maths and science and English. Not to start teaching me how to have sex.' Should they teach *Romeo and Juliet*, I wondered, or only as a warning?

In truth, Venus and Yvette were delightful young Americans, enjoying a close, happy family, not yet ready to look beyond or be critical of the emotional armlock their father had on them. In Venus I even detected an insouciance of manner that made her already her own woman:

'With my friends, if you do it, you do it. If you don't, you don't. They don't think any less of you. A lot of my friends are virgins, there's a few that aren't. They don't think any less of you, and I don't think any less of them. I don't agree with what they do, but they're still my friends.'

This seemed so eminently sensible, I suspected Venus might

already be capable of discarding the shaming key just whenever she chose.

William Alfonso has come a long way – from poverty and crime in the Bronx to taking New York's Board of Education to court. His Christianity is the mainstay of his life, and his grip on his daughters is a blend of pride, panic and tenderness. But does it give him the right to a similar grip on the lives of all the other teenagers of New York, who their teachers hope will grow in maturity as they learn to make informed choices – about sex and everything else – for themselves?

Dr Hein is adamant he has no such right:

'Some teenagers will choose abstinence and many won't. Encouraging abstinence, encouraging the delay of the age of first intercourse – these are all fine but we can't leave it at that. We must make accessible to young people the services needed by those who choose to have intercourse. We can't have an AIDS package that doesn't consider the teenage population.'

Two years later, in 1994, sex education was running into trouble in Britain. Again, teachers were under fire for delivering advice and lessons that were too explicit for the traditionalists. In some cases it was claimed they used sexual slang that, many felt, was more appropriate to the building site than the classroom. What's more, so the accusations went, while expounding in abundant detail on a whole range of sexual activities – oral sex, homosexual sex – teachers seemed to avoid, almost as a matter of principle, any use of the vocabulary of judgement or morality.

In March 1994, a teacher at a Leeds primary school was denounced in the press for what had been reported on the lessons she was giving to children not yet eleven. It transpired that a nurse, Mrs Brady, employed by the Leeds Community and Mental Health Trust and the Royal College of Nursing, had been invited to Highfield Primary to provide sex education suitable for ten- and eleven-year-olds. One of the pupils had asked about Mars Bar parties and Mrs Brady's answer had been relayed to parents, some of whom complained to the press. In the days that followed, governors and parents backed Mrs Brady, politicians backed off, and the press story died.

More stuff to unsettle the sexually anxious came from the Government's own Ministry of Health. Alarmed by the fact that Britain has the highest rate of unwanted teenage pregnancies in Europe, the Department had commissioned a sex guide for young people, *Your Pocket Guide to Sex* by Nick Fisher, intended for publication early in 1994. It was colourful, direct and explicit. It did not say that sex was a precious gift to be reserved for the sanctity of the marriage bed, and that anything other than straightforward intercourse was taboo. It did not say these things for two reasons. Firstly, the vast majority of people in this country no longer believe them to be true. Secondly, those who do believe them to be true commonly have allegiance to a church or faith whose beliefs they keenly pass on to their children within the intimacy of family life. It is unlikely that children of such parents would be unaware of such values. Their exposure to other values – freer, more permissive, but values nonetheless – constitutes part of their moral education and is ultimately the test of their moral commitment. Resisting temptation, after all, requires greater moral virtue than hiding oneself away from it.

The book caused a storm. Its author called it explicit, the Health Minister called it smutty, and the tabloids had a field day. The book was officially withdrawn and Penguin picked up the publication rights. It was against this background that *Heart of the Matter* set out to ask whether the high rate of teenage pregnancies was the result of too much sex education or too little.

Catherine Dryden is one of Bradford's statistics: a laughing, pretty girl, easy enough to be with and to like but hard to pin down, to bring into focus. Her baby Alice, at the time only a few months old, had been born when Catherine was fifteen and still at school. Catherine had been on the pill at the age of fourteen and when Alice had been conceived. For both circumstances she has a simple explanation. First the pill: 'I had very bad periods and I was becoming anaemic so they thought if they put me on the pill it might sort my periods out.' And the pregnancy? 'The pill didn't work because I was ill, but the doctors don't tell you that when you get it. But if you're not well, it doesn't work.' Catherine smiled as she gave me these guileless explanations. But something made me uneasy. She was effortlessly deflecting any blame on to the doctors, yet at the same time she wasn't furious that such a supposed lapse on their part had so drastically changed her life. Perhaps, I thought, she might be shy of talking to an interviewer? I pressed on. Slowly she disclosed how it was that she and her friends had drifted into having sex:

'I don't think there was a virgin in our form, girls of thirteen and fourteen. It was usually with older boys that you met at a night-club or a pub. That was the social life of most of the girls. We weren't interested in the boys at school because they were all immature. They had not grown up properly yet.'

Would there be sex at the first meeting? 'Well, I wouldn't personally, but a few of my friends would.'

Into this matter-of-fact conversation Catherine introduces a new and altogether more fanciful notion – love:

'I hadn't really thought about sex until it actually happened. I thought it was horrible, couldn't even contemplate the idea of me doing it. My ideas of love came from films and things – sailing into the sunset, that sort of thing. But I know now it isn't like that. You think you're in love and he's the right person and we're gonna be together forever, sort of thing. It's like living in a dream world and it happens, and you think, "Oh God, what have I done?"'

'And was it romantic?' I ask.

'Not very. No, now I come to think of it, it wasn't. It was like you're not supposed to drink before you're eighteen years old. The thrill of being caught added to the excitement. At first it wasn't something you'd brag about, but then it got to be a bit of a joke. You'd brag about how many different positions you could do it in. And we'd laugh, but we didn't really take each other seriously. We thought, "She's lying, she wouldn't do that." But later on we found that we would do it and we weren't quite as innocent as we made out.'

The relationship with Alice's father had ended before her birth. 'It started out as a bit of fun and then it got too serious. We both got bored so that's why we split up.' I find it hard to reconcile being serious with being bored.

'Well, he was getting very jealous of me going out myself or out with my friends from school and I got jealous of him when he started flirting with other girls in the pub, so we realized we were being too committed, so we decided to finish it.'

In her amiable, unaffected way, Catherine is probably typical of many young women embarking on sex: inspired by frothy romantic images culled from the mass media, encouraged by the teasing and boasting of friends, then dashed by the fumbling reality and the quick knowledge that you're not going to 'live happily ever after', or even 'live happily' at all. Catherine was seven months' pregnant when the doctor diagnosed her condition. The family rallied round:

'I think Mum had a fair idea I was having sex. But my mum and dad were divorced. I don't think my dad had any clue. I told my dad's girlfriend at the time. She took me to the chemist. It was positive. She actually told him in the supermarket. He came home and just gave me a hug.'

As her father, Jim, tells it:

'I just said, "Have you got something to tell me?" And she just started to cry. We threw our arms around each other and both started to cry. I just wanted to hold her and love her and tell her everything was going to be fine.'

Until that moment, Jim did not have a clue about Catherine's sex life.

'The range of emotions when she told me – shock, surprise, anger, guilt. I suddenly realized my daughter was a woman capable of having a baby. Anger probably towards the boy. Guilt because I wasn't there. I sat and thought about it for a long time. If I had been there, and me and my ex-wife had been together, maybe it wouldn't have happened.'

Jim has now given up his job to care for his daughter and his granddaughter – an odd twist to the nuclear family. Both are on state benefits and likely to remain so, for Catherine plans to continue her education: 'The college I'm going to has a crèche, so Alice will be taken care of.' Her views on being a burden on the state are as opaque as her other opinions:

'I wish I wasn't. If I could do it any other way I would. But I need the money to look after Alice. They're just trying to put the blame for the mess on somebody and it seems to have fallen on teenage mothers and single parents. I think that's unfair because it's not all our fault.'

Catherine remains resolutely unwilling to take responsibility for what's happened to her. So who might be to blame? Jim maintains that he and his wife spoke openly of sex to Catherine. She has no recollection of it. What she does recall is how little or late was what she learned at school:

'We watched a video about the menstrual cycle, about three years after everybody had started their periods. All the girls in my form started between ten and twelve. The video was way too late. If they want to cut down on the amount of teenage pregnancies, I think they should introduce it at junior school. I think the younger they are the better.'

Catherine's is a story to horrify those who would control young people's sexuality. There is now a groundswell of feeling in some circles that there should be limits on the sex education being given in schools. But there are two reasons why governments must involve themselves in sex education: unwanted babies and AIDS. The most practical and immediate protection against both is offered by the use of condoms and this is what many schools are teaching.

Lesley Boon, head teacher at Wyke Manor School, Bradford, walks a tightrope, balancing between on the one hand informing young people adequately and on the other inadvertently prompting a scandal such as engulfed the Leeds primary.

Over in the school library I come upon a scene that would give traditionalists a heart attack. Wyke Manor has embarked on an initiative of peer group teaching and such a lesson was in full swing. Round a table littered with packets of condoms and small squares of thin plastic – I was myself to be educated in their use in the course of the lesson – a group of boys and girls aged thirteen and fourteen were settling down to hear what eighteen-year-old Lynne Dutton had to tell them. She was a no-nonsense, straight-talking lass and there was no sniggering or whispering, blushing or nudging. Indeed, the mood could only be described as positively wholesome as Lynne, with an adept flick of a packet, deftly released a condom and unflinchingly demonstrated how to place it on an upright plastic penis:

'When I started doing these groups I thought it was a bit more fun to use carrots, different vegetables. Me and my mum used to go to the supermarket and pick the biggest out. But she got slightly embarrassed with my dad there. Then I went on holiday and left them in my locker. They went mouldy and smelly. Now I use the condom-demonstrator.'

The carrot story was for me. Now she addresses her pupils:

'So, which one should we have – a black one, a coloured one, pina colada or a minty one?' There are boys and girls from the Asian community in her group, all there with their parents' approval. Lynne issues important warnings:

'Look for the kite mark. That is important. I know that places in Bradford sell condoms, three for 50p, that do not have the kite mark. They may say they're electronically tested, but the fact is they're rubbish. They will not protect you. So I would not bother spending your money on something like that. Put a bit more towards buying something like this.'

The pupils take a lively interest. What about pub dispensers, machines? Lynne has the answers. 'Also make sure the packet has a date on. Be careful you use them before the date, because if not they go a bit awful.' The demonstration proceeds. 'This is a condom for girls to have in their handbags. Go careful if you have long, sharp nails ... or it'll snag and all your sperm can get out.'

Finally we get round to the small square sheets of thin plastic, and even I lean forward attentively. Will I ever learn all there is to know about sex? I wonder. It's getting a bit late, but today, sitting beside unblushing thirteen- and fourteen-year-olds, I learn something new:

'It's for when you're having oral sex. The fluids that you get, like vaginal fluid, if the woman has HIV and the man, say, has an ulcer or a sore in his mouth, he may get some of the fluid in his cut and he may get HIV. It's a million to one chance, but this plastic is to make sex fun and safe as well.'

By way of emphasizing the fun, Catherine introduces a game. Three cards are set out on the table naming categories: Safer, Unsafe, and Safe Sex. A pack of cards is then dealt, and each player in turn has to decide into which category the activity described on the card falls. Wanking, toe-sucking, anal intercourse, fingering, all feature before I sneak away from the class and go outside, where I stare blankly at the sky for a while, marvelling at how much things have changed.

Word of this kind of teaching has leaked out and alarmed people like Valerie Riches of a lobby group called Family and Youth Concern. She wants to encourage the teaching of the traditional ideal of one partner for life, no sex before marriage, and sees current sex education as encouraging promiscuity. She would certainly make common cause with William Alfonso over in New York:

'The methodology of teaching these days in practically every subject is learn and do. They go out and discover, which is fine in an academic subject. But saying this is how you have sexual intercourse, this is how you prevent girls getting babies – don't be surprised if they go out and practise it!'

She's right there. The idea is that young people will not have babies until they want them, and not get AIDS at all. I wonder what is so alarming about that. Whatever the answer, the Government, in pursuit of family values, has taken steps to limit AIDS awareness lessons. From August 1994 new sex education guidelines came into operation which moved AIDS awareness from the science curriculum, where it was compulsory, and put it within the optional personal and social education curriculum. This gives parents the right to withdraw their children from such classes. At the same time, the new ruling inhibits teachers from giving individual contraceptive advice to young people – a move directly opposite to the approach adopted in New York.

All these developments came too late for Julie Reynolds, who I met frying sausages at a barbecue with friends, celebrating her degree results from Bradford University. Julie fell in love:

'I suppose once you get into a relationship it's very, very easy just to be on the pill. There's a false sense of security that goes with a relationship. You think you know this person – you're in love so you tend to forget that AIDS stuff, or it just gets put to the back of your mind. It's not relevant because this is two people who are in love, that care about each other, and who are not doing anything wrong.'

The affair was too good to last. After three months it finished. A week later Julie fell ill:

'I had swelling glands in my armpits, my neck and my groin. I had a rash and I had diarrhoea. They tested me for glandular fever and came back and said it wasn't glandular fever, just a glandular type virus. Three months later I was watching on TV when a woman described the symptoms I'd had. She'd gone to the doctor for tests and it wasn't glandular fever, it was AIDS. At that point I knew. I went for tests and it was confirmed.'

Julie was well and optimistic when we met. She is a buoyant, bubbly girl with plenty of friends. She'd done AIDS projects at college. But what she hadn't been taught was how to deal with interpersonal relationships as they develop on the way to sex:

'I think quite a lot of young women and men are pressured into sex much more than they actually want to do it: you must be given the skills to be able to say to yourself, "Now this isn't actually what I want." I did in fact wait a long time. I'd known him a substantial amount of time before I slept with him. But all my friends had slept with people. It's the peer group as well as what I felt society was expecting of me. What matters is having the skills to negotiate what you want or don't want, having the assertiveness to say, "No, I'm only going to sleep with you if you wear a condom."'

Julie had lacked the confidence to first know and then assert her own wishes. So had Catherine. Yet we live in supposedly liberated times with every encouragement to schoolgirls to be as assertive as men – to carve out careers as lawyers, pilots, engineers, soldiers. Why, in the intimacy of turbulent emotions and entwined bodies, do they lack, at that crucial moment, the ability to control their situation? The thrust of sex education – carrots and square plastic sheets notwithstanding – must be to endow young women with that final freedom, to be themselves. It failed Catherine – who has a baby. It failed Julie – who has AIDS. It also failed Nadya – who was raped.

The city of Liverpool was a celebrated and prosperous port through the decades when the British Empire was in its heyday. Along the quays its warehouses were stacked with produce from around the world. Tea-clippers choked the Mersey. Seamen of all nations – Chinese, Portuguese, Lascars – flocked into its doss houses and crowded dwellings; Irish families and gypsies were drawn to its labour markets. It was to Liverpool that Hareton Earnshaw travelled in the early pages of *Wuthering Heights* and plucked from the streets the strange orphan child he took home and nurtured as his own and who grew up into Heathcliff. Liverpool, perceived from the Brontës' home on the Yorkshire moors, was a thriving, exotic place where the world mingled and took its chances.

Liverpool fell on hard times but the legacy of its great days still lingered. It led to the musical explosion of the 1960s when, for a time, the Mersey Beat set the pace for what went on elsewhere. It spawned musicians and poets, playwrights and players. Liverpool became the city of youth culture. Throughout it all, the people have retained their unique spirit – open and friendly, direct to the point of cheekiness but stopping short of Yorkshire bluntness. Liverpool is always a pleasure to be in. Its people talk to each other, to strangers, to you. They are jovial and jokey, with a raw, edgy wit that helps them cope with the odd scraps of destiny that come their way. Alan Bleasdale's television series *Boys from the Blackstuff* captures both their cynicism in the face of a brutal world and their capacity to ridicule it and even enjoy their lot. It is a state of mind that infects that part of England round about.

Nadya comes from that part of England. She lives in a wide, airy house, set in a tangle of garden, where people come and go, local friends drop in, friends from abroad come to stay. She is open, talkative and gregarious. At the age of eighteen she was also naive. Chris, her mother, a woman with a degree from London University and a career in teaching, had sought to shift the climate of her own upbringing:

'I was quite protected. The parameters were quite clear. From a girls' convent grammar school to sudden contact with men at university was quite a shock, but those built-in parameters kept us safe to a certain extent. Nowadays there's a lot more freedom and a lot more contact between boys and girls, and I think that's been a big improvement.'

Here was a mother of three daughters, aware in her own life of the inner anxieties and inhibitions created by old-fashioned family controls, eager to promote openness and happiness among her children, yet offering unobtrusive care and protection when she felt it was needed.

In June 1992 Nadya left school with sufficient A-levels to go to university and study languages. She was not only good at them but enjoyed the exhilaration and challenge of conversing in German with German friends. She was also keen to know Spanish and was studying Arabic. With her fluency, confidence and enthusiasm, it's possible to imagine top language jobs in Brussels or the UN lying in wait. But first she would take a year out, and when she decided to go to London for a while, Chris, the discreet mother, checked out the job that had been offered to her, and arranged accommodation with a friend she knew. Nadya was never the lost, bewildered teenager adrift in an alien land:

'I never actually felt alone in London. I was living with my mum's friend so I saw her as a bit of a mother figure. And I was in quite a close working environment with older people whom I really had a relationship with, so I just got on with it.'

One night in March 1993, six months after arriving in London, Nadya and a group of friends went to a small club not far from Piccadilly. There were others in the party whom she didn't know: 'Some blokes from Sandhurst, friends of a friend, a big crowd just wanting to have a great time. I was out to have a really good dance.' The club was typical of thousands of small-scale joints catering quickly and easily for transient crowds. It was little more than a box-shaped room with a dance floor in the middle, seats all round a bar, toilets, bouncers on the door: the minimum. It was crowded that night so everyone was packed close. Nadya and her friends got stuck into the dancing, people were smiling, stranger nodding to stranger. Nadya felt safe and happy.

I hazard a guess that Nadya dancing is probably a lovely sight. She has a tall, willowy build and, being of exceptional slimness, moves with a lithe grace that cannot fail to catch the eye. Clumsiness does not know her. Her features have the long, narrow line of a Botticelli woman – straight nose, green eyes and a full lower lip. Above and around her, a haze of auburn hair is the first thing you notice; its abundance standing round her shoulders, as crowning a glory as any cliché deserves. It is not surprising she was noticed.

Being noticed is a risk women run, and even court. It is an opening salvo in our engagement with the world, and Nadya was in London to engage with the world. So when a man – dark, good-looking – started watching her from the edge of the dance floor, she felt his eyes upon her and knew they were not disapproving. There is a satisfaction to be had in such a happening: the sensation is mined by a host of pop songs, it kicks off a thousand commercials. It stands at the very brink of an encounter. And Nadya looked back.

'He was quite good-looking, and I was quite flattered that this bloke was staring at me. I walked past him to go back to my seat, and he said, "I've been trying to catch your eye all night." I didn't think anything of it. I walked past him again and he was drinking. I think I asked what he was drinking, and he said, "Oh, have a sip," and we sat down together.'

Nadya had had a few drinks. Her natural openness flowered under his attention. 'We just sat there and talked. Then we actually snogged as well.' A shadow of uneasiness crept into Nadya's mind, but only about her friends: 'I was a bit dubious whether I should let my friends see me with him, because they might have said, "Haven't you come out with enough friends?", but they hadn't noticed.' So they went on talking and kissing. However, when the stranger suggested they go outside, Nadya didn't follow but went back to her friends.

Soon she was on the dance floor again, and trying to drag the stranger in among her friends. 'I don't like isolating myself. I like being with a lot of people and all having fun together.' But the stranger didn't dance. He bided his time. When Nadya finished dancing she was hot and exhilarated, but mainly hot. Again he suggested they go outside. 'I literally 100 per cent thought let's go out for a bit of fresh air; I didn't think he meant anything else. I may have been naive to think that.' Naive but not yet into any situation she didn't want or couldn't handle. What happened outside shifted the discreet balance that had so far characterized the encounter. He led her to the side of the building, where there were fewer people:

'We had a kiss; you know, he's a good-looking bloke. Then the next minute he's pushing my shoulders down and I saw his penis in front of me. I didn't want to but you feel threatened. I found I was giving him a blow job. If you'd had a bit to drink, it doesn't seem so bad at the time. It's over in a flash. Over.'

It's at this point that Nadya's experience coincided with that of Julie, and how many others?

'I hadn't had real long relationships or sexual relationships with a bloke. So you think, "Well, maybe this is what you're meant to do, maybe this is what you're expected to know. Maybe men can do what they want with women. Maybe they can make you do what you don't want to do." You don't actually feel as though you can say no.'

It is possible to imagine that at this point the stranger felt their encounter had Nadya's full agreement. In the midst of such ongoing intimacy it is unlikely that it occurred to him to wonder just how pleased his partner was to be doing as he indicated. And in the absence of any spoken words, what sign was Nadya giving him of her distaste for what was happening? After all, when two people are making love, until one of them gives some signal – verbal or otherwise – that can clearly be read and understood by the other, there is an implicit sanction to their mutually exploratory erotic experience. That is how sexual maturity expresses itself. But sexual maturity involves learning nuances of sexual management that the crudities of many films, the sexual posturings of pop stars, totally disregard. No fault of theirs: they aren't meant to be sex manuals. Yet where is one to learn to negotiate the hazards of sex except from the world around? Hadn't Catherine mentioned films and lyrics? Did I not fall for the style of Rhett Butler and Scarlett O'Hara? In the discussion following the *Heart of the Matter* that told Nadya's story, Germaine Greer called sex a blood sport. But Nadya didn't know that at the time. That evening she went on to make matters worse.

'We went back into the club and he asked for my phone number and address. I didn't actually think, "I hope he rings up", but the easiest way is to give it to him and then hopefully he'll leave you alone.' Regrettably, a willingly given phone number does not signal 'leave me alone'.

'We were standing on the side of the dance floor, and he suddenly grabbed my wrist and pulled me into the toilets – the men's toilets. He pulled me into a cubicle and shut the door. Then he turned me so I had my back to him and pulled my back down. My head hit the floor. I was completely disorientated. He was tugging at my shorts and the tights underneath. I was struggling to get myself up. I was completely and utterly defenceless. Then it just felt as though he was sticking a knife into me. I don't think I've ever experienced anything so painful in my entire life. It literally felt as though he was cutting me apart.

'I didn't scream. I didn't cry for help. It's amazing how helpless you can feel, among thousands of people – and nobody can help you and you can't help yourself. If you do scream you're frightened he'll do something to harm you even more.'

Nadya pulled up her shorts. He did up his trousers, and said merely, 'I'll go out first. You follow later.'

It was one of the boys she'd gone to the club with who took her to the police station. The police were sympathetic and took her to a clinic where she was examined, samples were taken, and she was finally allowed to have a bath. 'They were really good to me.' The ordeal that, rumour has it, raped women can undergo in such circumstances, did not begin then. It was to come much later. She helped with a photofit picture, a man was arrested. He denied the crime, but

Index